CRITICISM, PERFORMANCE, AND THE PASSIONS IN THE EIGHTEENTH CENTURY

Great art is about emotion. In the eighteenth century, and especially for the English stage, critics developed a sensitivity to both the passions of a performance and what they called the transitions between those passions. It was these pivotal transitions, scripted by authors and executed by actors, that could make King Lear beautiful, Hamlet terrifying, Archer hilarious, and Zara electrifying. James Harriman-Smith recovers a lost way of appreciating theatre as a set of transitions that produce simultaneously iconic and dynamic spectacles; fascinating moments when anything seems possible. Offering fresh readings and interpretations of Shakespearean and eighteenth-century tragedy, historical acting theory, and early character criticism, this volume demonstrates how a concern with transition binds drama to everything, from lyric poetry and Newtonian science to fine art and sceptical enquiry into the nature of the Self.

JAMES HARRIMAN-SMITH is a lecturer at Newcastle University. He is a trustee of the British Society for Eighteenth-Century Studies and a former trustee of the British Shakespeare Association. His articles have appeared in *Theatre Journal*, *RECTR*, *Journal for Eighteenth-Century Studies*, *Studies in Romanticism*, and *Etudes françaises*.

CRITICISM, PERFORMANCE, AND THE PASSIONS IN THE EIGHTEENTH CENTURY

The Art of Transition

JAMES HARRIMAN-SMITH

Newcastle University

CAMBRIDGE
UNIVERSITY PRESS

CAMBRIDGE
UNIVERSITY PRESS

University Printing House, Cambridge CB2 8BS, United Kingdom

One Liberty Plaza, 20th Floor, New York, NY 10006, USA

477 Williamstown Road, Port Melbourne, VIC 3207, Australia

314–321, 3rd Floor, Plot 3, Splendor Forum, Jasola District Centre, New Delhi – 110025, India

79 Anson Road, #06–04/06, Singapore 079906

Cambridge University Press is part of the University of Cambridge.

It furthers the University's mission by disseminating knowledge in the pursuit of education, learning, and research at the highest international levels of excellence.

www.cambridge.org
Information on this title: www.cambridge.org/9781108840590
DOI: 10.1017/9781108890847

© James Harriman-Smith 2021

First published 2021

A catalogue record for this publication is available from the British Library.

ISBN 978-1-108-83549-7 Hardback

To my mother

Contents

Illustrations

Acknowledgements

This book began as a PhD thesis at the University of Cambridge. I could not have asked for a better supervisor for that project than Fred Parker, nor for a better team of examiners than Christopher Tilmouth and Tiffany Stern. I would not have got this far without the benefit of all their excellent advice, encouragement, and research.

To my friends, colleagues, and students at Newcastle University, I also owe a great deal. Whether for giving me feedback on draft chapters and book proposals or for discussing scepticism, the history of madness, musical aesthetics, eighteenth-century pronunciation practice, the perils of actioning, and much else besides over coffee, in corridors, and between lectures, I am particularly grateful to Michael Rossington, Anne Whitehead, James Procter, Rebecca Woods, Matthew Grenby, Jennifer Richards, Jo Hicks, Emma Whipday, Adam Mearns, Zoe Cooper, Martin Dubois, Ros Haslett, Joseph Hone, Jake Jewusiak, Ella Mershon, Fionnghuala Sweeney, and Ella Dzelzainis.

I am just as grateful to all those friends and colleagues elsewhere in the world who read my work or listened to my ideas for this book. David Wiles and Jed Wentz helped me think about performance practice in new ways; Blair Hoxby taught me a different approach to the passions; Paul Monod and Emma Salgård Cunha made me re-evaluate John Dennis and the religious sublime; and Katherine Hambridge, Clare Bucknell, Matthew Ward, Lucie Vivian, Renée Vulto, Sean Ferguson, and Kathryn Hill, with all their intelligence and kindness, have brightened many of the toughest parts of the writing process.

Bethany Thomas, Linda Bree, Sarah Lambert, Natasha Burton, Katie Idle, Tanya Izzard, Raghavi Govindane, Catherine Dunn, my two anonymous peer reviewers, and everyone else at or associated with Cambridge University Press will always have my thanks for the work they have done in making my manuscript into a book. Without the librarians and archivists at the British Library, Cambridge University

Library, Robinson Library, Folger Shakespeare Library, and National Library of Scotland, there would never have been a manuscript in the first place.

Finally, I gratefully acknowledge here the influence of Roger Harcourt, who taught me why English literature was important, and the curiosity, enthusiasm, and love of my wife, Anne-Charlotte Husson, who has been at my side from this project's start to its ending.

Note on Style

This book follows the *MHRA Style Guide* (third edition). Note, however, that I have maintained, as far as possible, my sources' idiosyncratic use of punctuation, capitalisation, and italicisation in order to support my argument for the significance of these features as traces of transition. For a similar reason I have also quoted eighteenth-century critics' own quotations of other texts: such citation practices are, I suggest, useful evidence for the kind of critical attention once given to the dynamic and iconic qualities of art.

Introduction
Iconic and Dynamic

What is transition? Transition names a process of change between objects whose properties define that transition: emotions, chords, gradients, colours, genders.[1] It also names the moment, long or brief, in which such transformation occurs. To identify a transition is thus to acknowledge both the dynamic quality of a process of change and the iconic quality of a rich and recognisable moment. Further, the identification of transition appears to grant meaning: this came from that or that must lead to this; here was the moment when everything was possible or there was the point of no return. As a tool for the making of meaning, criticism has relied upon transition's simultaneous invocation of the iconic and the dynamic. This reliance is particularly visible in eighteenth-century writing about the theatre but is by no means limited to it.

* * *

Hamlet sees his father's ghost, Zara questions the foundations of her faith, King Lear curses Goneril, Alicia goes mad, Macbeth sees an air-drawn dagger, and Jaffeir threatens to murder his wife. Known as 'points', 'hits', or 'turns', these moments were among the most criticised and celebrated of the eighteenth-century stage.[2] One performer's rendition of a point would be set against that of their rivals and predecessors in that role. A writer's ability to create such striking moments was a key part of their appeal to audiences more interested in the pathos of a tragedy than its plot. It is the contention of this book that all such points, hits, and turns were often and may again be considered as expressions of what I call the art of transition. I give this name to both the writer's capacity to connect powerful emotive subjects into a compelling sequence and the performer's ability to give physical expression to that sequence through the presentation of sequential passions. Consider those points I just evoked, where we may find, as eighteenth-century audiences and readers were pleased to find, Hamlet's sudden transition from scornful commentary on the state of Denmark to the terror of 'Angels and ministers of grace defend us!', the frustrated anger that bursts through Zara's avowal of her love for Osman, the melting conclusion of Lear's imprecation against his 'thankless child', Alicia's flights of hatred and despair, the restless combat between ambition and fear in Macbeth, and Jaffeir's confused vacillation between rage and love. From scorn to terror, from love to anger, from fury to self-pity, from hatred to despair, from ambition to fear, from rage to love, each of these points may be understood as moments of transition.

We can distinguish different kinds of transition in these moments: there is the physical transition between performed passions, occurring in a flash or drawn out over several seconds; there is equally the conceptual transition between one idea and another within a text. We might call the former 'embodied' transition and ascribe it to the actor; we might call the latter 'literary' and ascribe it to the author. To do this too strictly, however, is to diminish the potential of transition as a critical concept and to repeat a move that occurred at the turn of the nineteenth century, when critics like Charles Lamb and William Hazlitt argued that no performance, with its physical transitions, could fully capture the intellectual significance of the sequences of thought and feeling written by the playwright. Instead of accepting such a hard division between the transitions of the actor's body and those conceived in the author's mind, this book recovers a more complex critical standpoint. Such a standpoint recognises that a performer might sometimes add new ideas to their script (for better or worse), and such a standpoint also reflects the belief that an author may sometimes write with such power or clarity that their words bring about a physical response in the actor, reader, or audience member. While the differences between performance and script remain important, what matters first is the very fact of transition itself. Take Hamlet's encounter with the ghost on the battlements of Elsinore: this point is a moment of embodied transition, as the actor's body tenses into terror; this point is also a violent shift of subject, from statecraft to the supernatural – yet it is the way all these changes are enfolded into the instant that make it one of the most famous passages both in the eighteenth-century theatre and in the period's editions of Shakespeare's works. A sensitivity to this point as a point of transition, both on the page and on the stage, allows us to see how it is not just famously iconic but changing and dynamic also. When we sense this, the movement inherent in the moment, we share in an eighteenth-century appreciation of dramatic art.

The successful practice of the art of transition creates a hit. This hit depends upon transition's ability to imbue the iconic moment with dynamic potential, opening a range of little-understood pasts and possible futures. This is a key insight of eighteenth-century writing about drama, especially tragedy, and this book – itself mainly focused on tragic drama – both identifies how such an insight was made and examines how a sensitivity to transition can inform our own critical practices today. I draw my evidence from letters to, between, and about actors; manuals purporting to teach the art of public speaking; paintings of famous performers; promptbook markings that accentuate sequential patterns; periodical reviews and retrospectives; the notes and the punctuation of playscripts; and many other objects that fall within what James Boswell once called 'literary productions relative to the art of acting'.[3] By examining how these sources make use of the art of transition, I demonstrate the validity of transition as a fundamental concept for three things: first, for the analysis of the composition, criticism, and performance of eighteenth-century drama; second, for the reintegration of that drama into a multidisciplinary and multimodal environment; and third, for the tracing of an evolution in attitudes towards theatrical affect that runs from Shakespeare's *King Lear* to the essays of Lamb and Hazlitt.

Transition, Attitude, and Tone

Jaffeir threatens to murder his wife Belvidera in the final scene of the fourth act of Thomas Otway's *Venice Preserv'd* (1682). In his *Dramatic Censor* (1770), the critic Francis Gentleman offers his commentary on this famous point: his writing will serve here to ground the concerns of my work, from the importance of transition in writing about drama to the wider context within which this concept operates, both in the eighteenth century and now. As was typical for hits, points, and turns, Gentleman made use of Jaffeir's threats as an arena for comparing two prominent figures in the London patent theatres: David Garrick, the actor-manager of Drury Lane, and Spranger Barry, the leading male actor of Covent Garden.[4] Otway's play was a staple of the repertoire at this time, and it tells the story of a failed attempt to overthrow the Venetian senate. Jaffeir's friend Pierre is a part of this conspiracy, while his wife is the daughter of a senator. Treated poorly by his father-in-law, Jaffeir accepts Pierre's invitation to join the ranks of the conspirators and places Belvidera in their custody, along with a dagger to kill her with if he betrays their loyalty. After one of the conspirators assaults Belvidera, she confronts her husband and forces him to reveal the plot to her father and the other senators in return for the merciful treatment of Pierre and his associates. But the senate breaks its word and condemns them to death. This brings us to the end of Act IV, when Belvidera tells her husband that all his co-conspirators have been arrested.

Gentleman compares the performances of Barry and Garrick through each of the turns of the drama. Up to this moment, they have been neck and neck: Barry 'could not be surpassed' in Jaffeir's speeches to his father-in-law in the first act, but 'we must give Mr. GARRICK considerable preference' for his version of the point 'where Belvidera is delivered to the conspirators'.[5] Now, however, when Susannah Cibber's Belvidera tells Garrick's Jaffeir 'of the torments which are preparing for his friends', the manager of Drury Lane decisively proves his superiority to his rival:

> Mr. GARRICK steps forward and beggars description, by an amazing variety of transitions, tones and picturesque attitudes; the distracted confusion which flames in his countenance, and the gleams of love which shed momentary softness on the stern glow of rage, exhibit more complicated beauties than any other piece of theatrical execution we have seen.[6]

Gentleman's praise for his friend and benefactor is hardly without bias, yet it contains in miniature two approaches to the definition of transition that will structure my discussion here. First, it places transition alongside 'tone' and 'attitude' as theatrical techniques employed by Garrick for the production of a spectacle that 'beggars description', and it is through comparison to writing about the other, better-known, technical aspects of performance that the peculiarities of transition become clear to us now. Second, Gentleman enumerates the feelings of 'confusion', 'love', and 'rage' that the actor's techniques express in this point and thus indicates how transition – along with tone and attitude – intersects with eighteenth-century understandings of emotional and mental states. Something of the nature of that intersection is evident here in Gentleman's praise of the scene's 'complicated beauties' and his use of metaphors of fire to capture the unfolding dynamic of the passions of the point, as scripted by Otway and exhibited by Garrick.

To start with the trio of transitions, tones, and attitudes, a wealth of research in the fields of both theatre history and what Abigail Williams calls 'the history of sociable reading' allows us to define the techniques described by the latter two terms with ease.[7] In Tiffany Stern's overview of acting practice, she notes that attitudes were a crucial part of Garrick's style, being moments when the performer paused and held a pose, thus 'indicating (and encouraging) reflection about the part performed'.[8] As Stern goes on to argue, such a technique produced either 'applaudable *tableaux*, or high-class claptraps'.[9] The hostile review in Theophilus Cibber's *Two Dissertations on the Theatres* (1756) of Garrick's perform-ance as Romeo provides a counterpoint to Gentleman's praise of this performer's 'picturesque attitudes' in *Venice Preserv'd*.

> He is now going to the Tomb [. . .] Yet on the opening of the Scene, — the Actor [. . .] advances about 3 or 4 Steps,—then jumps, and starts into an Attitude of Surprize:—At what?—why, at the Sight of a Monument he went to look for:—And there he stands, till a Clap from the Audience relieves him of his Post.[10]

Cibber's dash-ridden prose offers a parodic re-enactment of what he considers to be the ability of attitudes to disrupt the smooth unfold-ing of a performance in favour of audience gratification. Yet whether praised or criticised, such poses were a well-established part of per-formance in the period. Barton Booth, who acted a generation before Garrick, is held up by Cibber as an example to follow, since his 'attitudes were all picturesque' and gained their grace from this actor's study of classical sculpture and history paintings.[11] This practice, first trialled by Booth in a performance of Joseph Addison's *Cato* (1713), had itself been modelled on the Italian castrato Nicolò Grimaldi's use of iconic poses in opera.[12]

In the noisy, fully lit, and undisciplined theatres of the eighteenth century, the execution of attitudes played an important role in engaging the eyes of the audience in the face of a host of other distractions. Tone had a similar purpose, compelling audience atten-tion even from those unable to make out what was happening on the stage. As such, Glen McGillivray argues, tone was a crucial 'part of the rhetorical [. . .] armoury of the eighteenth-century actor'.[13] Yet an actor's tone of voice could, like the execution of attitudes, be both criticised and praised according to its variety and decorum. As Thomas Sheridan put it in 1762, 'A just delivery consists in a distinct articula-tion of words, pronounced in proper tones, suitably varied to the sense, and the emotions of the mind', and there are many examples of the judging of actors' voices according to these criteria.[14] Richard Cumberland, at a distance of sixty years, recalled the 'deep full tone' of James Quin and Susannah Cibber's 'high-pitched but sweet' recita-tion of verse,[15] while Thomas Davies, again at some historical distance, praised Booth's 'strong, yet harmonious pipe', which could reach 'the highest note of exclamatory rage' without hurting the music of its tone.[16]

But what of the first term in Gentleman's trio? With his 'harmonious pipe' and 'attitudes [. . .] all picturesque', it should be no surprise that Booth was also held up as a paragon of transition, with Cibber praising the way in which, whenever this man assumed one attitude or another, he 'fell into them with so easy a transition, that these masterpieces of his art seemed but the effect of nature'.[17] As with all descriptions of historical practice, we should ask ourselves whether Booth ever actually did this (as Bertram Joseph has argued) or whether Cibber is simply using an actor who died in the 1730s to criticise Garrick's dominance of the theatre in the 1750s.[18] However, given my focus on how theatre criticism functioned in the eighteenth century, the settling of such a question is of less importance to me than the way in which Cibber here presents transition as something that occurs *between* attitudes.

Unlike the techniques of tone or attitude, both of which are keyed to the expression of something, especially an emotion, transition seems concerned with the arrangement of these subjects into sequence. It is, in Cibber's account, the process by which Booth assumed an attitude appropriate to the material being performed. Yet the very nature of transition, as something at once essential but necessarily liminal, has made it resistant to definition, either by scholars of the long eighteenth century (who rarely discuss the term at any length)[19] or even by those writing in the period itself.[20] In 1800, Charles Newton admitted that he did not 'recollect the Mention of this Grace of Oratory in any Author' when he came to explain 'Transition' in the introduction to his *Studies in the Science of Public Speaking*.[21] Yet, like Gentleman and Cibber, he also recognised its significance, arguing that 'good [. . .] Readers or Speakers' are those who 'nicely discriminate and strongly mark every TRANSITION'.[22] Newton offers a definition of the term in the context of public performance as 'the passing on to an entirely new Subject, Sentiment, or Passion', which he later condenses to 'the passing of one Passion or Sentiment to another'.[23] Strikingly, Newton's effort at defining transition bears comparison to Samuel Johnson's more general explanation of the word in 1756 as a 'passage in writing or conversation from one subject to another' (itself copied from the *Dictionnaire de l'Académie française*).[24] Using these definitions, it appears that when Gentleman praised the 'amazing variety of transitions, tones and picturesque attitudes' employed by Garrick in his performance of Jaffeir, he praised three distinct but interconnected things. Garrick's voice was adapted to the character's rage at one moment and to his love at another. Garrick's body occasionally came to adopt a variety of held attitudes specific to such emotions too. And Garrick's transitions functioned as a passage between distinct tones and attitudes, joining them together to form a compelling spectacle.

There is, however, another way of understanding transition. Gentleman's placing of the word alongside tone and attitude suggest that it serves as more than the passage between different expressions of emotions and has instead the status of an object of appreciation in its own right. Consider, for example, John Hill's comments in 1755 on Garrick's performance as Archer in a production of George Farquhar's *Beaux' Stratagem* (1707), where he claims that 'Till this performer play'd this part, we never knew what beauties it was capable of, in the sudden transitions from passion to passion'.[25] The actor's 'sudden transitions' (or perhaps Farquhar's scripting of them) are positioned here as one of the 'beauties' of the comedy. When writing about Garrick's Lear, Gentleman makes a similar comment, arguing that 'the transitions of Lear are beautiful'.[26] In both these phrases, transition is less something that occurs between bits of a play and more one of the defining features of the drama itself. Transition here refers more to a moment of transformation or metamorphosis or, to use one of Johnson's other definitions of the word, a 'change'. A tension in how transitions might be apprehended now emerges. On one hand, it is seen as a dynamic passage between two things, and we find Jaffeir's expression of his love so striking because Garrick transitions into it from rage; on the other, transition is itself the iconic object of our admiration, a moment of transformation or change that amazes us.

A description of what might constitute true excellence in acting written a few years before Garrick's debut by Aaron Hill (no relation to John) captures this tension. Hill praised the performer who 'stops short, upon *pensive* PAUSES and makes *Transitions* (as the Meanings *vary*) into *Jealousy, Scorn, Fury, Penitence, Revenge, or Tenderness!*'[27] Like Newton's description of transition as a 'passing' and Johnson's of a 'passage [...] from one subject to another', Hill's wish for an actor who 'makes *Transitions* [...] into' new embodiments of emotion captures what we might call the dynamic quality of transition, operating to connect distinct subjects. At the same time, however, Hill's placement of transitions 'upon *pensive* PAUSES' both makes an important distinction between transition and pause and, crucially, intimates the iconic quality of such moments too: after all, the hypothetical actor 'stops short' at such places. A little later in the same text, Hill repeats the same tension when he describes 'the very *Instant* of the *changing Passion*' to be found in a point: this is a paradox brought about by transition, a technique which both operates as a dynamic passage between '*changing*' passions and makes these changes into iconic 'instants' of metamorphosis.

Tone, attitude, and transition are thus all significant techniques for the performance of a text, but it is Gentleman's third term that creates a productive tension between the iconic and the dynamic qualities of spectacle and, with its double logic, helps exhibit what he calls the 'complicated beauties' of the moment. 'Exhibit' is Gentleman's term and reminds us that, while we may distinguish between the literary transitions written out by Otway and those embodied by Garrick, we should also recognise how closely intertwined the two phenomena are: the 'complicated beauties' of this moment are produced by both actor and author, since both figures seem to have used the power of transition to shape emotion into art. This becomes especially clear when we consider the intersection of Gentleman's first tricolon of techniques (transition, attitude, tone) with his second tricolon's elocutionist emphasis on emotional states (rage, love, confusion) and read Gentleman's commentary alongside Otway's script and other artefacts of Garrick's performance.

The Language of Fire

Gentleman located Garrick's rendition of Jaffeir's feelings in the actor's famously mobile face when he described how confusion 'flames in his countenance'.[28] Otway's text also places these unstable emotions here by having Belvidera describe how her irate husband's 'lips shake' and how his visage becomes 'disordered' as she tells him of Pierre's fate.[29] From this exchange on, it is easy to trace Gentleman's 'rage', 'love', and 'confusion' through the remaining lines of the scene: Jaffeir calls his wife 'Traitress' and confusedly tells her 'thou hast done this; | Thanks to thy tears and false persuading love' (IV. 495–96), but seconds after saying the word 'love', he succumbs to that tender feeling, inviting his beloved to 'Creep even into my heart, and there lie safe' (IV. 499). This sequence is one of several within this point, for Jaffeir's rage will soon replace his love once more. Again, there are textual triggers for this: Jaffeir calls his heart his wife's 'Citadel' and then exclaims '— ha! —' at the mention of this word, which recalls the Venetian prison where his friends are incarcerated and returns him to his rage, the dashes marking the transition (IV. 500). Newly aflame, he tells Belvidera to 'stand off' and finally draws out the dagger he has been fumbling throughout the scene (IV. 500–02). As his anger builds, Belvidera's pleas for clemency fail to have any effect, until she throws herself to her knees and cries 'Oh, mercy!' (IV. 516). These words bring about another transition for the actors to embody. Jaffeir follows his wife's cry by continuing the pentameter with a weakly phrased prohibition – 'Nay, no struggling' – but Belvidera completes the line with a much stronger, enjambed imperative – 'Now then kill me | While thus I hang about thy cruel neck' (IV. 516–17). Unable to do so, Jaffeir's resolution breaks: proclaiming that 'by immortal Love, | I cannot longer bear a thought to harm thee' (IV. 522–23), he throws the dagger from him, embraces his wife, and closes the act with the wish that Belvidera speak to her father and 'conquer him, as thou has conquered me' (IV. 537).

By presenting Otway's writing in terms of the emotional states named by Gentleman, I find myself repeating a distinctly eighteenth-century practice of thinking about drama as a sequence of passions. If a theatregoer had been particularly inspired by Garrick's rendition of Jaffeir's feelings (or Cibber's of Belvidera's), they might, for instance, have bought a copy of the recently published *Art of Speaking* so as to learn from its author, James Burgh, how to give similar performances at home.[30] After a fifty-page essay dispensing advice on the most appropriate tones and attitudes to adopt when representing everything from affectation of piety ('canting' tone and hands 'clasped together') to desire (suppliant tone and 'bending the body forward'), Burgh provides over eighty lessons to his reader.[31] Each lesson – one of which is reproduced in Chapter 1 – consists of a short text accompanied by marginal annotation and in-line typographic symbols. Modern performers, employing Bill Gaskill and Max Stafford-Clark's technique of 'actioning', might work through such examples today by employing transitive verbs to describe what their characters are attempting to do to someone alongside their lines, writing out such things as 'I greet', 'I question', 'I threaten', 'I reassure', and so forth.[32] Burgh, however, writes in the margin what emotion should be present at each point in a speech. He does not *action* scripts, but rather *impassions* them, reminding the performer to switch between the exhibition of 'remorse' and 'despair' when executing Claudius's attempts to pray in *Hamlet*[33] or to move between 'vexation' and 'spiteful joy' in a dialogue between Shylock and Tubal made famous after a performance of it by Garrick's mentor, Charles Macklin.[34] Each of Burgh's examples is published under a header naming the key passions contained within, and, although Burgh does not include the confrontation between Jaffeir and Belvidera in his book, it would not look out of place with Gentleman's enumeration of 'confusion', 'rage', and 'love' as its title.

Blair Hoxby makes use of *The Art of Speaking* to support his argument that approaches to tragic drama between the start of the sixteenth and the end of the eighteenth century placed pathos (rather than plot) at their centre. Specifically, Burgh helps to indicate the extent to which passions, not actions, were the 'dramatic units of crucial significance in early modern tragedy'.[35] In addition to his 'impassioned' examples, Burgh also exemplifies this in his introductory essay, where he ties specific tones and attitudes to individual feelings. That tragic plays were about passions and that, accordingly, their performance was too is also clearly part of many of the examples already given here. Gentleman spends many more words discussing Garrick's performance of Jaffeir's love and rage and comparing this actor's capacity for emotion to Barry's than he does reminding his reader of the specifics of Otway's plot. In Aaron Hill's articles on acting, he imagines a performer capable of considering how 'the *Meanings* vary', but only as a way of guiding their transitions into the most appropriate passions. As for Newton, his definition of transition as 'the passing on to an entirely new Subject, Sentiment, or Passion' not only supports Hoxby's claim to the validity of passion as the object of performance but also – thanks to his inclusion of the terms 'subject' and 'sentiment' – indicates how, at the dawn of the nineteenth century, the specific emphasis on passion's primacy had now declined. Indeed, it is essential to recognise that Hoxby's case for the crucial dramatic significance accorded to the passions should be understood in terms of the evolving and uncertain definition of passion throughout the early modern period, ranging from the basic etymological sense of a powerful feeling that is suffered (from the Latin *passio*, and ultimately the Greek πάσχειν, itself at the root of *pathos*) to the elaborate categorisations of the philosophers and the priorities of elocutionists like Sheridan or John Walker.[36] Different understandings of what constituted passion had, as Joseph Roach has shown, significant ramifications across the eighteenth century for the study of acting as the dramatic expression of a character's feeling. Specific to my argument here, such definitions and redefinitions of the passions allow us to sharpen our understanding of how the emotional climaxes of dramatic, especially tragic, points might be considered as products of the art of transition.

René Descartes would recognise Jaffeir's love for Belvidera as a 'primitive passion'. In his *Passions de l'âme* (1649), he named wonder, hatred, desire, joy, sadness, and love as a specific set of passions, which – like the primary colours in painting – could, through their combination, produce the full spectrum of human feeling.[37] For Descartes, Jaffeir's love, along with any other passion, would be caused, maintained, and strengthened by some movement of the spirits.[38] Descartes's spirits, inspired by the animal spirits of Galen, act upon the soul when their movements agitate the pineal gland in which the soul resides. The movement of these spirits is also responsible for the distinctive bodily expression of each passion: from a Cartesian point of view, Jaffeir's lip trembles because his animal spirits are shaking it as part of the rage he is experiencing. Such a mechanistic, even hydraulic, understanding of the passions serves to standardise human feeling into a set of operations that produce highly legible traces. Descartes's writings thus proved extremely influential among not just those analysing human behaviour but those seeking to reproduce or represent it also.[39] Translated into English in 1650 and much reprinted and discussed thereafter, the influence of Descartes's ideas is visible in Otway's writing: that Jaffeir's 'disordered' face is a sign of rage and Belvidera's 'panting breasts, and trembling limbs' a universal marker of fear means that the physical description of these characters serves to infuse spectacle with emotion for a time when passions were the paramount part of dramatic literature. As well as in the author's implicit stage directions, we can also trace Descartes's influence in advice given in the eighteenth century to those who wished to know more about the performance of such writing. Burgh's description of the exact tones and attitudes necessary for the expression of a specific emotional state owes, for example, a debt to Cartesian schematisation of emotion. Earlier in the period, Charles Gildon, in a volume purportedly written by the actor Thomas Betterton, urged aspiring performers to imitate 'History-Pieces' when assuming a pose or attitude and so also encouraged a Cartesian approach.[40] This was because one highly influential maker of such 'History-Pieces' was the painter Charles Le Brun, whose *Méthode pour apprendre à dessiner les passions* (1698) owed its standardisation of the appearance of the passions to the theories of Descartes and swiftly became an important transdisciplinary vector for the philosopher's ideas.[41]

Nowhere, however, is the intertwining of a Cartesian understanding of the passions, as mediated by Le Brun, and the historical appreciation of theatre practice more apparent than in certain paintings that depict eighteenth-century actors performing the celebrated points of their time. Johan Zoffany painted Cibber and Garrick as Belvidera and Jaffeir in 1763. As Shearer West has made clear, this image is no record of performance, but rather an interpretation of performance based on a shared critical framework for the representation of emotion.[42] On Garrick's visage, as painted by Zoffany, the eyebrows contract, a clear symptom of the agony of Jaffeir's soul, while Cibber's upraised face and opened eyes speak to the tender feelings she experiences.[43] Whether Garrick or Cibber ever adopted this precise attitude, or even whether this picture shaped either their subsequent performances or Gentleman's own memory of the scene, is impossible to determine. What can be said, however, is that this point was significant enough to warrant immortalisation in oils and that Zoffany's composition itself performs a representation of the passions, drawing on Cartesian traditions shared between discourses of painting and acting in order to produce an iconic attitude.

Yet the details of this painting, reproduced on the cover of this book, represent more than an iconic attitude.[44] Like the theatrical point they remediate, they also incorporate the tensions of transition and thus the dynamic potential that such tensions grant. Garrick's brow may be contracted, but the rest of his mobile face has few of the marks of rage; his hand holds the dagger aloft, but its point dips and the strength seems to drain from his wrist; Jaffeir may be standing over Belvidera, but the twist of his body and the distribution of his weight has as much fear and confusion in it as anger. Descartes and Le Brun can help us recognise the extent to which this painting, like other interpretations of this moment, is a portrayal of the passions of love and rage, but the iconic clarity of such a Cartesian approach has its limits: its mechanistic understanding of the way that the animal spirits generate passions has trouble accounting for the complex existence of those passions in time, and thus for the connective role of transition in a point. To return to Gentleman's account of Garrick's performance, he does not simply name the passions of love and rage that are expressed in this scene: he also writes of the 'confusion' that the actor must animate, an indeterminate emotional state that the discrete approaches of Descartes cannot adequately encompass. Such 'confusion' is one of a few distinctly non-Cartesian terms in Gentleman's writing. The language of fire employed by him is another, used in an effort to capture the dynamic unfolding of human feeling through the turn: the 'stern glow' Garrick gives to Jaffeir's rage is broken by 'gleams of love', while 'distracted confusion [. . .] flames in his countenance'. Fire provides Gentleman with a metaphor capable of capturing the dynamic transitional qualities of the scene, allowing him to depart from a basic Cartesian schematisation of the moment. Zoffany's painting does something similar by using a variety of sources of light as visual metaphors for the complex existence of passions in time: the guttering lamp he places in the foreground burns like Jaffeir's fitful anger, while the moon shines over the Grand Canal with the same calm and cooling light that seems to emanate from the skin of Belvidera.

It was the arc of light left by a burning coal as it flew through the air that inspired Isaac Newton's reflections on the reception of impressions in time, and it is such later theorisations, more able to account for the unfolding of feeling, that allow us to explore the concept of transition further.[45] With his example of the burning coal, Newton refuted Descartes and argued that we do not register impressions mechanically in an instant but rather continue to experience their effect for some time, as, in this case, ethereal particles continue to oscillate within the optic nerve following the impact of photonic particles upon it. As Roach argues, 'it was a short step from [Newton's] motor and sensory vibrations to the emotions', a step made easier by the already well-established use of acoustical analogies to describe the physiology of the passions in time.[46] Such analogies appear in acting manuals: Aaron Hill considered the passions to be 'what the keys are in a harpsichord' and John Hill, over a decade later, described actor and audience as 'perfectly concordant' strings.[47] John Hill's metaphor in particular may owe something to David Hume's description of the human mind in the second book of his *Treatise on Human Nature* (1739), which nicely encapsulates the paradigm shift from the Cartesian 'hydraulic or pneumatic push of animal spirits' to 'the acoustical metaphor of vibration' associated with David Hartley:[48]

> Now if we consider the human mind, we shall find, that with regard to the passions, 'tis not of the nature of a wind-instrument of music, which in running over all the notes immediately loses sound after the breath ceases; but rather resembles a string-instrument, where after each stroke the vibrations still retain some sound, which gradually and insensibly decays.[49]

Such a description of the human mind helps to explain what Gentleman's invocation of a 'variety' of transitions, tones, and attitudes, not to mention his metaphors of fire, endeavours to express. The passions embodied by Garrick were not, in his view, simple frozen icons (and only become such in the hostile view of someone like Theophilus Cibber), but rather 'complicated beauties', unfolding in time, whose complexity depended on the tripartite union of transition, tone, and attitude to manifest. While the latter two terms here lend themselves to discrete, direct representation of an object, transition does not: it is simultaneously an object to be appreciated and a passage between emotional states. As such, transition is a concept that forces us to consider the expression of the passions (the prime subjects of tragic drama) as a sequence, and so chimes with an increasing eighteenth-century awareness of the existence of these passions as part of a sophisticated apparatus of sensibility, what Daniel Webb described in 1769 as the 'chain' that 'runs thro' our feelings'.[50]

The preceding summary of Cartesian, Humean, and Hartleian approaches to the passions provides an eighteenth-century context for understanding Gentleman's and others' appreciation of the transitions of Garrick's Jaffeir as a powerful combination of iconic and dynamic qualities. To grasp the full power of this combination, however, it is necessary to examine the relationship between transition and the making of meaning. No author is a better guide to this than Hume, whose *Treatise*, besides its much-quoted description of our mind as a string instrument, also makes extensive use of the concept of transition in order to explain those apparent connections between our perceptions that make things meaningful to us.

Beggaring Description

Hume presents the human mind as the product of successive perceptions. These perceptions are of two kinds: 'Impressions' are those perceptions which 'enter with most force and violence' and include 'all our sensations, passions and emotions'; 'ideas', by contrast, 'are the faint images of these in thinking and reasoning' (*Treatise*, p. 1). 'Transition' is one of a small number of words Hume uses to describe what occurs between perceptions. Hume thus examines 'transition of passion' (as a transition between impressions) but also transitions between two ideas and between an idea and an impression. Regardless of the kinds of perception in question, however, the key feature of almost all the transitions discussed in the *Treatise* is the ease with which they occur.

Hume explains these cases of 'easy transition' in several ways. As far as impressions are concerned, there is clearly 'an attraction or association' among them, 'though [. . .] only by resemblance' (p. 283). One of Hume's examples for such association of impressions would not look out of place in an eighteenth-century acting manual: when illustrating the way certain passions resemble others, he explains how this facilitates a progress by which 'Grief and disappointment give rise to anger, anger to envy, envy to malice, and malice to grief again, till the whole circle be completed' (p. 283). As for ideas, 'The rule, by which they proceed, is to pass from one object to what is resembling, contiguous to, or produced by it' (p. 283). Thus 'When one idea is present to the imagination, any other, united by these relations, naturally follows it, and enters with more facility by means of that introduction' (p. 283). Perhaps Hume's most famous observation of an easy transition, however, concerns the relationships between impressions and ideas. At the beginning of a section discussing sense impressions and memory in relation to knowledge and probability, Hume observes that

'All our arguments concerning causes and effects consist both of an impression of the memory or senses, and of the idea of that existence, which produces the object of the impression, or is produced by it' (p. 84). When, for example, you or I sense heat, we each have the idea that it is caused by the fire we stand beside (p. 87). Hume subjects such an inference to sceptical analysis by asking how we come to make the transition from heat to its supposed source in a fire and how we come to believe that anything is caused by something else. Ultimately, he shows that our inference is nothing more than a habitual, customary transition, built, for instance, upon our repeated experience of having always felt heat in the presence of fire. This results in what Hume calls the 'most violent' of all the 'paradoxes' of his *Treatise*:

> The necessary connexion betwixt causes and effects is the foundation of our inference from one to the other. The foundation of our inference is the transition arising from the accustomed union. These are, therefore, the same. (p. 155)

We might seem to infer that fire necessarily causes heat, but what we are actually doing is performing a transition we have made so many times that it is now habitual. We can never thus truly know whether the fire caused the heat or not: instead, we have simply made the transition meaningful.

Hume shares with Gentleman, Hill, and many others examined in this book an interest in observing and evaluating transition. Yet it should be clear from the above summary that Hume's transitions are, in some respects, very different from those taken up in accounts of performance. Whereas the transitions of Jaffeir are spectacular and arresting, those that Hume is interested in are often easy, unremarkable, and habitual. Yet, as Sarah Kareem has argued, Hume's achievement in the *Treatise* was to make the gaps between our perceptions and the role of transition in our interpretation of them highly visible. This allowed Hume, and others, like Adam Smith, 'to render the taken for granted world briefly available as an object of wonder'.[51] In other words, it allowed Hume and Smith to treat our everyday perceptions of the world, and the habitual, scarcely perceptible transitions between them, as something that was as wondrous as the exceptional, spectacular transitions between Jaffeir's love and anger performed upon the stage. When we feel heat, we might now think that it comes from some other source than the flame because we are conscious of the contingency of the connection between our two perceptions; when Jaffeir grows angry, we are struck by the extraordinary way that Otway's script and Garrick's body move to this passion from a state of loving tenderness. Smith and Hume themselves use the language of the stage to make this point, with the latter claiming the 'mind is a kind of theatre' (p. 252) and the former evoking the machinery of the opera house when trying to explain that 'species of Wonder, which arises from an unusual succession of things'.[52]

Kareem's work on Hume and Smith shows how their sceptical study of perceptions and the transitions between them creates an opportunity for wonder. The description of theatrical transitions undertaken by Gentleman, Hill, and others does something similar, as they hold up the transitions of stage and page for appreciation. Yet, as Kareem herself points out, the 'critique of induction's defamiliarizing effect' – the sceptical attention to perceptions and transitions between them – 'is inevitably temporary'.[53] Smith writes of being 'insensibly drawn' to treating Newtonian principles 'as if they were the real chains which Nature makes use of'[54] and Hume of 'our natural propension' to believe in the identity and simplicity of an object (p. 253). Something similar happens in writing about theatrical transition: sometimes the appreciation of an iconic and dynamic instant of change gives way to an effort to explain that instant and make it the subject of a new discourse, often in terms of the author's or performer's knowledge of human nature. Thomas Davies, for instance, praised Garrick's performance of *King Lear* for the way in which the actor 'had pursued the progress of agonizing feelings to madness in its several stages',[55] and William Richardson held that Shakespeare's plays contained specimens from which one could extract 'the laws that regulate the intellectual system' of every human being.[56] These are very different approaches to those espoused by Gentleman and Hill, not least because – by taking the spectacle of transition as a starting point – they inevitably look beyond that spectacle in an effort to find an answer to the very questions it provoked. To borrow once again from Kareem, it would be truer to say that an attention to transition creates meaning by providing an opportunity for two kinds of wonder: a wonder at the spectacle of the stage transition, with the attention fixed on its combination of iconic and dynamic qualities, and a wonder about that spectacle, with our critical attention instead driven by those same iconic and dynamic qualities to provide some kind of explanation for the moment they create.

Gentleman recorded that Garrick's Jaffeir 'beggars description, by an amazing variety of transitions, tones and picturesque attitudes'. In so doing and regardless of the historical accuracy of his account, he exemplified the critical standpoint that I recover in these pages: one which considered transition as a fundamental part of successful drama, both in the actor's physical transformations and in the author's scripting of sequential passions. Unlike the much-examined judgements of 'tone' and 'attitude' in a performance, writing about transition forces us to recognise a productive tension in drama between the iconic display of a passion and its dynamic potential. Aaron Hill captured such a tension when he wrote of 'the very *Instant* of the *changing Passion*' that an actor should strive to produce for audiences more interested in pathos than plot. Hill's, Gentleman's, and others' writings about tragedy in particular all reflect developments in the period's understanding of mental and emotional states, a development which, from Descartes to Hartley and Hume, provides a foundation for a critical focus on the peculiar status of transition for an artform that works in both time and space.[57]

That critical focus is far from monolithic across the eighteenth century. For Gentleman, Garrick's performance 'beggars description', but, for others, this actor's and his script's transitions *beg for* description and explanation. Somewhat like the easy transitions that Hume unpicked to re-invest our everyday experience as something (briefly) capable of arresting our attention, the spectacular transitions of the stage gave to audiences both an object to appreciate and one to explain, one to wonder at and one to wonder about. In trying to answer the questions of why Jaffeir's love returns and prevents him from killing Belvidera or how exactly Lear goes mad, critics like Richardson take transition as a starting point for a new discourse, and so risk minimising that powerful combination of dynamic change and iconic instant that had captured the attention of so many of their contemporaries for so long.

* * *

Hamlet seeing the ghost, Zara questioning her faith, Lear cursing his daughter, Alicia losing her mind, Macbeth reaching for the dagger, and Jaffeir threatening his wife: all these points were once and may again be read as expressions of the art of transition; to do so, as I have argued, is to see them anew as instants of changing passion, of simultaneous stops and transformations, and as potent combinations of the iconic and the dynamic. Each of these examples appears in the pages that follow.

Chapter 1 examines the elaboration and growth of a set of critical priorities, transition prime among them, crystallised by Aaron Hill in the 1730s. Offering what he claimed to be a purified version of pantomime's techniques for arresting attention, Hill wrote of how an actor could become a 'true FAUSTUS' for the theatres through transition, creating iconic and dynamic moments of suspension during which they could shift mind and body from one passion to another. Hill's emphases continue into the time of Garrick, whose 'pensively preparatory attitudes', particularly those of his Hamlet, were praised as intellectual achievements and blamed as pantomimical claptraps.[58] They also provoked innovative attempts to notate them. Ultimately, pauses and the transitions that occurred upon them became moments when an actor could be described as asserting their artistic autonomy. Critics, identifying such pauses, revealed new rhythms and nuances in dramatic speech while also imposing and tightening focus to the point that their accounts sometimes amount to the treatment of the dramatic as the lyric. The realisation of Hill's dreams – a theatre where sophisticated emotion replaced slapstick motion as the key source of spectacle – soon risked becoming a Faustian pact, for an insight into the transitions and passions of a play seemed to demand as much private attention to the page as public engagement with the stage.

No play of the eighteenth century better reflects the theoretical developments sketched in Chapter 1 than Aaron Hill's *Zara* (1735), his translation of Voltaire's *Zaïre* (1732). Chapter 2 traces the fortunes of this play, from its first performance under Hill's direction outside the patent theatres to Garrick's reworking of it at Drury Lane. I show that *Zara*'s scepticism of established religion and her father's deathbed proselytising are used by Hill to produce what his friend John Dennis called an 'enthusiastic' passion, and I suggest that Voltaire's work may have appealed to Hill for its handling of religious material – material that, in Dennis's view, was supposedly capable of producing the most extreme sequences of sublime emotions. Yet as well as a work rich in enthusiastic passion, Hill's *Zara* is also an exposition of what this man would describe as 'dramatic passions'. These 'dramatic passions' are not just the product of particularly powerful ideas but ideas in their own right: characters speak of what they and those around them feel, and the line between the idea that inspires the passion and the passion itself, so firm in Dennis, weakens. Hill's dramatic passions are thus present as instruction and entertainment. Love is the supreme example of this, an idea and an emotion capable of including all others, and one which Hill's English – through the nominalisation of French adjectives and verbs or through the use of typography – took care to highlight. Those who read, saw, or performed *Zara* could witness the outward marks of many passions and trace on stage and on the page their performance through transition to the very instant. Such opportunities made the play perfect for what Hill called an '*Experiment*' on taste and acting in England in the 1730s. When Garrick came to revive this experiment twenty years later, Hill's dramatic passions become the property of Garrick himself, as he re-writes sections of the play to favour his character of Lusignan, cutting lines whose effect can be achieved by fluid physical transition and making the actor-manager the centre of attention.

Descriptions of Garrick performing points made compelling through sequences of extreme passion are not confined to his acting of plays, and Chapter 3 considers his performance of odes in order to demonstrate both how eighteenth-century attention to transition crossed twenty-first-century modal boundaries and how the recovery of this approach might help us understand anew a form of public poetry that brought together star performers and musical accompaniment. Focusing jointly on two works of 1769, Garrick's delivery of his *Ode to Shakespeare* and Daniel Webb's *Observations on the Correspondences between Poetry and Music*, I show how transition, as a technique for emphasising the passions through contrast and comparison, aligns the dramatic and lyric modes. This is especially true of the Shakespeare ode, which positions the Elizabethan playwright as both Britain's national dramatist and Britain's national poet, a figure who is simultaneously lyric and dramatic through his mastery of the passions. Indeed, Garrick, who incorporated references to his own performances of Macbeth, Hamlet, and Lear into his ode, also might be seen to make the same claim for himself as the pre-eminent interpreter of Shakespeare.

King Lear, the subject of Chapter 4, was considered by Thomas Davies to outrank Hamlet as Garrick's most significant part. I argue here that the scale of Garrick's achievement in *King Lear* depends on the extent to which this play (following Nahum Tate's and Garrick's alterations of Shakespeare's text) offered a remarkable sequence of contrasting emotions for performance. A key source for the extreme emotional variation inherent in each of the play's points is madness. The representation of all the nuances of Lear's insanity required a mastery of the art of transition, yet Garrick's practice of such an art was not without its challenges. While both hostile and laudatory commentators on his performances explored the aesthetic, sociological, and psychological questions of how to perform a king's madness, performance editions and promptbook markings reveal Garrick's own efforts to perfect his rendition of the part's transitions through the use of everything from innovative make-up to minute textual editing. Garrick's edits included the reduction of Tate's romantic subplot, yet he never, despite his many claims to be restoring Shakespeare's Lear, excised it entirely. As the second part of this chapter shows, the Tate-Garrick versions of Edgar's pretend madness performed an essential function, serving as a source of what Lord Kames called 'seasonable respite', a kind of structural transition designed to moderate and so maintain spectators' emotional engagement in the tragedy.[59] Such moderation is alien to Shakespeare's play of 1608, and, while the eighteenth-century Lear can tell us much about the uses of transition to create a celebrated performance in Georgian London, it thus also serves as a critical standpoint for re-evaluating the structures of Jacobean tragedy.

Chapter 5 charts the uses of transition in literary criticism of drama and builds upon my use of Hume's approach to transition in this introduction. First, I demonstrate the existence of an attention to transition as a key element in some prominent literary critical writing of the later eighteenth century. Second, I argue that, within such writing, the understanding of transition evolves from that explored in my earlier chapters. Borrowing a term that Elizabeth Montagu, William Richardson, and their contemporaries make frequent use of, one might describe this evolution as a shift from dramatic transition to 'dramatic character', motivated by what Hume and Smith identified as a quintessentially human urge to connect and explain sequential perceptions. Montagu does this as she argues for the moral impact of Shakespeare's incessantly enthralling dramatic characters, and Richardson makes the same move when he claims that Shakespeare's dramatic characters are such perfect imitations of life that their passions and transitions might serve as the subjects of philosophical enquiry into human nature. In the third section of this chapter, I use Maurice Morgann's *Essay on the Dramatic Character of Falstaff* (1777) to illuminate the tensions inherent in such a critical standpoint, as efforts to explain moments of spectacular dramatic transition in terms of character risk minimising the spectacle that invited such explanation in the first place. This chapter is thus above all interested in the shift from pathos to pathology, from the critical appreciation of Constance's pathetic articulation of her grief in *King John* to the philosophical diagnosis of maternal affection that motivates it.[60]

The pathologisation of pathos through the explanation of striking transitions between the passions anticipates certain Romantic attitudes to drama, which denigrate the performance of a character in favour of the study of that figure's psychological constitution. With reference to Charles Lamb's writing about Garrick, I thus sketch, by way of conclusion, the decline of the art of transition as something that was both embodied and conceptual after 1800. This decline has had a long-lasting effect, one which this book endeavours to counter by providing an exemplary sensitivity to the meaning of those movements inherent in a transitional moment. The argument of each chapter does this by demonstrating what might be revealed about performance history, translated tragedy, lyric poetry, Shakespeare, and character criticism when these subjects are considered in terms of the art of transition.

CHAPTER I

Dramatic Transition

A Faustus for the Theatres

In the winter of 1723, the best-known transitions were those of the pantomime. Two versions of *Harlequin Doctor Faustus*, one at Lincoln's Inn Fields and one at Drury Lane, had 'met with such prodigious success' that 'there are scarce any in the Country, especially young People, who have had but a bare mention of it, that do not long as much for the Sight of the Doctor, as a French Head, or a new Suit of Cloaths'.[1] Those who did attend a performance at Drury Lane would see the doctor enter, studying his infernal contract 'with the greatest Inquietude' but – 'after several Pauses, and Shews of Anxiety' – eventually signing it 'with Blood drawn from his Finger by a Pin which he finds on the Ground' (p. 1):[2]

> Lightning and Thunder immediately succeed, and *Mephostophilus*, a Daemon, flies down upon a Dragon, which throws from its Mouth and Nostrils Flames of Fire. He alights, receives the Contract from the Doctor, and another Daemon arises, takes it from him, and sinks with it. The Doctor earnestly endeavours to get clear of the Fiend, but he soon stops his Flight, and by a caressing Behaviour quickly dissipates the gloomy Consternation that he painfully labour'd under; and now the Doctor, fill'd with unusual Gladness by every Action, shews his rising Joy. (pp. 1–2)

The anonymous author of this *Exact Description* here presents the spectacular opening dumb show of the pantomime (for few had speaking parts) as a series of transitions. Faustus moves from 'Inquietude' to terror to 'unusual Gladness' and 'rising Joy'. Those transitions structure a series of dynamically iconic moments that veer between the minutiae of a mimed pinprick to the descent of Mephistopheles upon a dragon. While such a sequence was particularly striking, other pantomimes also offered similar opportunities for transition. John Weaver's *The Loves of Mars and Venus* (1717) has, for example, Vulcan expressing '*his* Admiration, Jealousie;

Anger; *and* Despite' in a dance with the goddess of love, while she '*shews* Neglect; Coquetry; Contempt; *and* Disdain'.[3] Such traces of transition are significant because, as Darryl Domingo has argued, 'pantomime and poetics came to share a critical vocabulary' in the first half of the eighteenth century.[4] This chapter builds upon Domingo's observation to examine the 'shared vocabulary' of transition specifically, demonstrating how Aaron Hill attempted to purify this feature of the pantomime and so crystallised a set of aesthetic norms around transition whose influence can be traced throughout the 1700s. Yet for all Hill's efforts, the debt that his approach to drama owes to Harlequin can never be quite erased, and certain writers remained ready to find the lowbrow spectacle of pantomimic surprise in the artful transitions of a tragic actor.

The development of dramatic transition must begin with the recognition of the effectiveness of pantomime, and the Faustus entertainments of the early 1720s are the most striking examples of the form's appeal. John Thurmond's production, with its fire-breathing dragon, was so successful that it soon inspired a rival version of the same story from Lewis Theobald and John Rich at Lincoln's Inn Fields. This pantomime also yokes extremes of emotion: an infernal spirit tempts Faustus, played by Rich himself, into signing his contract by summoning the spirit of Helen of Troy, yet the doctor's love-struck gaze turns with a 'start' into surprise and disappointment when she and the demon both vanish (p. 25). Later, the doctor uses his new powers to play tricks on others: his servant 'with the utmost Shew of Pleasure' prepares to drink a glass of his master's wine, only 'to his unspeakable Terror and Surprize, the Bottle flies out of his Hand, and the Wine vanishes in a Flash of Fire'. His joy has become 'the greatest Dread and Perplexity', and the slapstick comedy of the moment turns on this transition (pp. 28–29).

Rich and Theobald's *The Necromancer, or Harlequin Doctor Faustus* surpassed Thurmond's entertainment to become one of the most frequently performed works of the eighteenth century, with over 300 recorded performances between 1723 and Rich's retirement thirty years later.[5] Like all pantomimes, the looseness of the form allowed for considerable variation between each staging, with the addition or subtraction of episodes to cater for new fashions or scenic capabilities.[6] Such popular and variable entertainments brought pantomime to the centre of English theatrical culture.[7] For the theatre aficionado Aaron Hill and many others, such success was not a welcome development. Hill wrote sarcastically, in the seventy-seventh issue of his *Plain Dealer* periodical, of having found a 'new, and unbroken *Mine, of Theatrical Treasure!*' in an obscure

German tome, which he is certain will work in 'the Contention of our
Rival Stages' as 'the never-to-be-forgotten, the Triumphant *FAUSTUS
HIMSELF* was of Happy *High German* Original!'[8] Having sketched out
a parodic plotline about a peasant raised '*among Beasts*', then tamed by
a 'Dwarf' to perform acrobatic impersonations of squirrels, cats, and apes,
Hill concludes with a dark vision of the future pantomimes such a tale
will spawn.

> By the second Week, after *Christmas*, we shall see a Dozen or two, of Bull-
> Dogs round the Tail of *Shepherd*, on *Drury-Lane-Stage*, without being able
> to *bite him*, while he *curvets* and *barks* with his *Back up*, and wheels safe, in
> *their Center*; — And Mr. *LUN*, at the other House, crawling up the Edge of
> one of his Scenes, and *sticking to the Roof, like a Spider* over the Heads of
> a *shouting Pit!* where he will *spin* himself into their good Graces, 'till their
> Necks are half broke, with the *Sublimity* of their Entertainment!'[9]

This image of Rich (as '*Mr. LUN*') turning himself into a spider and
breaking the necks of his fascinated audience is perhaps the strongest but
by no means the only attack made by Hill on pantomime. Having worked
briefly as a manager himself at Drury Lane (1709–10) and the Haymarket
(1710–11), Hill would have known how attractive a popular pantomime
must have been to the perpetually cash-strapped theatres, but his writings
testify to his belief that repeated staging of such entertainments came at
a high cultural price.[10] Numerous articles in *The Prompter*, a periodical Hill
produced with William Popple, take up this argument. A letter from
'Verax' in issue thirteen reported that the sender had saved a 'poor, lean,
ragged Phantom' by the name of '*Common Sense*' and heard her lament her
departure from a stage where 'Pantomime *introduced her constant
Attendants*, Absurdity, Noise, Nonsense, *and* Puppet-Show'.[11] On
13 December 1734, Hill wrote of a recent visit to the theatre as though he
were entering the wreck of English civilisation.

> METHOUGHT, I found myself amidst the *Ruins* of *Palmyra, in the Desart*; in
> a solemn, pompous VOID; with here and there, a *broken Column*, an
> unburied *Pediment*, or tottering *Arch*, in Prospect; to remind me, that,
> tho' over-run with *Weeds*, and nested-in, by *Insects*, This Empty Scene of
> Desolation, Horrid, as it now appear'd, had, *heretofore*, been grac'd with
> *Majesty*, and envied for its *Elegance*.[12]

This apocalyptic vision is all too easy to interpret. Hill had begun his article
with the observation that 'IN a Nation, which is declineing to its *Period* [. . .]
There, the STAGE, will be the first, to *feel*, and *manifest*, the Infection.'[13]
Pantomime (and Hill's other frequent target, Italian opera) were the

symptoms of a broader social and cultural malaise. In a letter to David Mallet in 1733, Hill spoke of how, given the recent programming choices of theatre managers, 'our *minds*, are like *sick* men's *stomachs*, too weak, to digest what is not minced and put into our *mouths*, by those, whose *taste* must prescribe for us'.[13]

The theatre had sold itself to the devil: making money from spectacular pantomimes at the expense of the nation's spirit. As Ned Ward put it in *The Dancing Devils* (1724), works like the Faustus entertainments were 'Fit only for the Approbation | Of Mortals in the lowest Station'.[14] Yet Hill was not without hope. He wrote to James Thompson on 5 September 1735 and wondered whether a certain way of acting and scriptwriting, one as full of surprises as a pantomime, might not reverse the decline of the English stage.

> I know, indeed too well, that nothing *moral* or *instructive*, is expected or desir'd, by the modish frequenters of a Theatre; But is it therefore, impossible, they should be *surpriz'd into* correction? —— The *passions* are the *springs* of the *heart*; and when powerfully struck out by the *writer*, and imprinted as strongly, by the *actor*, in their *representation*, can *force* their way over the *will*. (Hill, *Works*, II, p. 127)

The hope that Hill expresses here is by no means particular to him. Nearly forty years earlier, in the wake of Jeremy Collier's *A Short View of the Immorality and Profaneness of the English Stage* (1698), John Dennis and Charles Gildon, among many others, had argued that, through the performance of the passions, the stage could educate and improve the nation.[15] Yet Hill will be my focus in this chapter because, of all those writing about the stage in the first half of the eighteenth century and before, none provide so wide-ranging an example of thinking about the theatre. In his periodicals (both *The Plain Dealer* and *The Prompter*), his poetry, and his private letters, Hill considers almost every aspect of the theatre, from its current deplorable state to its potential for redemption and from the details of a particular performance to the specific techniques an actor would need to master in order to perform. Of course, as Christine Gerrard has shown, Hill's extraordinary career stretched far beyond the theatre too, and Brean Hammond has gone as far as calling this man 'the cultural glue that held the age together'.[16] By focusing only on Hill's writing about the theatre, I do not wish to deny his status as 'cultural glue'; rather, I consider Hill's remarkable breadth of interests as one of the reasons why his writing about acting was so comprehensive. Hill was alive to many, indeed most, of the intellectual movements of his day, and he found in the theatre an arena where lots of them met. It is striking, for instance, that while his periodical *The Prompter* began as a venue for general social commentary (able to offer prompts to 'every *Performer*, from the Peasant to the Prince, from the Milk-maid to her Majesty'), its coverage of attempted theatre reform in 1735 swiftly led the periodical to focus directly on the English stage as a microcosm of the nation.[17]

Hill's letter to Thompson, dreaming of a style of acting that would surprise an audience '*into* correction', which is to say, into morally correct behaviour, in fact recapitulated an idea that had already surfaced earlier that year in *The Prompter*, as part of the publication's new focus on theatrical matters. When writing publicly, however, Hill had made the striking choice to employ terms that betrayed his vision's debt to the very pantomimes attacked elsewhere in its run as the scourge of English cultural life.[18] In an issue that observed the poor quality of many contemporary actors (and the social good that was thereby lost), Hill sketched a culturally redemptive art of acting, which, through spectacular performance of the passions, would make the imagination into a new, and better, 'FAUSTUS for the *Theatres*'.[19] Hill reasoned that 'THE whole, that is needful in order to impress any Passion on the *Look*, is first, to CONCEIVE it, by a strong, and intent *Imagination*'. A performer then had only to '*recollect some Idea of* SORROW' and 'his EYE will, in a Moment, catch the *Dimness* of *Melancholy*: his Muscles will *relax* into *Languor*; and his whole Frame of Body sympathetically *unbend* itself, into a *Remiss*, and *inanimate*, *Lassitude*'. Thus transformed by the exercise of his mind, 'let him attempt to *speak* HAUGHTILY; and He will find it *impossible*. – Let the *Sense* of the Words be the rashest, and most violent, *ANGER*, yet, the *Tone* of his Voice shall *sound nothing but Tenderness*'. A transition into anger would instead require a new intellectual effort, '*conceiving some idea of Anger*' to 'inflame his Eye into Earnestness, and *new knit*, and *brace up* his *Fibres*, into an *Impatience*, adapted to Violence'. The spectacle thus produced, the assumption of sorrow and the transition from sorrow to anger, is as compelling as anything in the pantomime.

> All, recovering from the LANGUID, and carrying Marks of the *Impetuous*, and the *Terrible*, flash a *moving* PROPRIETY, from the *Actor*, to the *Audience*, that *communicating* immediately, the Sensation it *expresses*, chains and rivets, our *Attention*, to the *Passions we are mov'd by*. THUS, the happiest Qualification, which a *Player* shou'd desire to be Master of, is a *Plastic Imagination*. – This alone is a FAUSTUS for the *Theatres*: and conjures up *all Changes* in a Moment.[20]

The 'FAUSTUS' of this paragraph is no Harlequin, but rather the trained power of the actor's mind, which, as it acts, stirs the performer's passions into an emotional spectacle as capable of holding audience attention as any of Rich's or Thurmond's antics. Attention, Hill knew, was key: his letters record a belief that, in drama, '*attention* [...] ought, with all possible *art*, to be kept *fixed*, by the author' (II, p. 125), and it is such dangerously rapt absorption that his *Plain Dealer* article targets when it imagines Rich half-breaking theatregoers' necks as they try to follow his spidery movements. Once the audience's attention has been captured, then the theatre can, as Hill wrote to Thompson, attempt to surprise its clients into correction, letting the passions, or '*springs* of the *heart*', 'force their way over the *will*'.

Hill's writing combines references to the pantomime with language that makes performers and their publics seem like machines: their passions are '*springs* of the *heart*', and a performance 'chains and rivets' consciousness as actors' muscles '*relax*', their frames '*unbend*', and their minds '*new knit* and *brace up*' the nervous fibres of their bodies. Joseph Roach considers such language as evidence of Hill's debt to Cartesian physiology, especially its understanding of the body as a machine that operated 'under the mind's direction with high efficiency and in a predictable manner'.[21] Hill himself writes, for example, of the '*mechanic* [...] NECESSITY' that ensures your 'Voice shall *sound nothing but Tenderness*' when you '*recollect some Idea of* SORROW'.[22] In some respects, Hill's combination of Cartesian thought and pantomime practice is an easy one to make, since Harlequin's adventures also exploited both the machinery of the theatre and the Cartesian machinery of the performer's body. The Faustus entertainments make demands of trapdoors and of trapezoid muscles, of sliding flats and of swift reactions; although we now separate such mechanical and organic processes, such a distinction, as Roach argues elsewhere, was nowhere near so firm 300 years ago, before Romanticism and Darwin.[23]

It is the proximity between Cartesian understandings of the body and pantomime's practical reliance on the material affordances of Drury Lane and Covent Garden that helps to support Hill's dreams of a new Faustus for the theatre to recapture audience attention. John O'Brien introduces another key element when he describes such dreams as an effort to imagine 'how the power of *transformation* that had been thematized as an external force in the Faustus pantomimes of the 1720s could be internalized' (emphasis mine).[24] In the Faustus pantomimes alone, a salesman transforms into a woman, Harlequin morphs into a bear, and the dead return to

life. Other transformations, of humans into things and of one object into
another, were common, and they helped pantomimes exercise what one
reviewer called 'an enchanting fascination that monopolizes the mind to
the scene before it'.[25] Such moments of metamorphosis are behind Hill's
own explanation for why an actor's '*Plastic Imagination* [. . .] is a FAUSTUS
for the *Theatres*': because it 'conjures up *all Changes*, in a Moment'. Of
course, the changes that Hill has in mind are not the vulgar surprises of the
polymorphous Harlequin but those described earlier in his article, the
changes from one passion to another, the mental work required to cross
Cartesian categories and go from the 'passive Position of *Features*, and
Nerves' found in 'SORROW' to the active power of '*Anger*' convincingly.
Although the process is still a mechanical one, the agent here is the
imagination, which Hill calls '*Plastic*', in Samuel Johnson's sense of the
word as 'having the power to give form' – the power, in other words, to
reshape the body in the image of a passion.[26]

Quite how extensive that power is, though, only appears in the continuation of Hill's article.

> THUS, the happiest Qualification which a *Player* shou'd desire to be Master
> of, is a *Plastic Imagination*. – This alone is a FAUSTUS for the *Theatres*: and
> conjures up *all Changes*, in a Moment. – In one Part of a *Tragic Speech*, the
> conscious Distress of an Actor's Condition stamping *Humility* and
> *Dejection*, on his FANCY, strait, His *Look* receives the Impression, and
> communicates Affliction to his *Air*, and his *Utterance*. – Anon, in the
> same Speech, perhaps the Poet has thrown in a Ray or two, of HOPE: At
> This, the Actor's *Eye* shou'd suddenly *take Fire*: and invigorate with a *Glow*
> of *Liveliness*, both the *Action*, and the *Accent*: till, a *Third* and *Fourth* Variety
> appearing, He stops short, upon *pensive* PAUSES, and makes *Transitions*, (as
> the Meanings *vary*) into *Jealousy, Scorn, Fury, Penitence, Revenge* or
> *Tenderness!* All, *kindled* at the *Eye*, by the Ductility of a *Flexible Fancy*, and
> APPROPRIATING *Voice* and *Gesture*, to the very *Instant* of the *changing
> Passion*.[27]

As before, Hill describes a change of passion. This time, however, the
emphasis falls not so much upon the mechanical process by which the
performer goes about 'stamping *Humility* and *Dejection*, on his FANCY'
but rather on how such a process brings the author's script to life through
a sequence of theatrical metamorphoses. Indeed, no sooner has the actor
mastered one passion than Hill hypothesises that he may be required to
launch into another, shifting from '*Dejection*' to its polar opposite, 'HOPE'.
Accordingly, 'the Actor's *Eye* shou'd suddenly *take Fire*', with the speed of
this change bringing a '*Glow* of *Liveliness*'. This is not, however, the end of

the process, and the actor, Hill makes clear, will continue to perform his Cartesian conjuring, as 'a *Third* and *Fourth* Variety' appear and he, like Proteus, 'makes *Transitions*, (as the Meanings *vary*) into *Jealousy, Scorn, Fury, Penitence, Revenge* or *Tenderness!*'

When Faustus came to Drury Lane in the winter of 1722–23, he showed theatregoers the power of pantomime to create enthralling popular spectacles. Some of those in the audience, however, found the price of such performances to be too high. Aaron Hill – a man with interests in many parts of eighteenth-century society – saw in Harlequin's triumph nothing less than the debasement of English culture and said so, loudly and frequently, in his periodicals and letters. Yet Hill also saw an opportunity. The actor's imagination could supplant the tricks of the pantomime and become a new, but equally attractive, Faustus for the theatres. This was not as radical a move as it may now seem. In accordance with Cartesian physiognomy, the imagination of the actor would operate on the performer's body with the same mechanical precision as the stage technology that Harlequin's magic relied on. Such operations would transform the actor before the eyes of the audience: not from man to woman or dead to living (as in the work of Rich, Theobald, and Thurmond) but from jealous to scornful, furious to penitent, and enraged to tender. These emotional transformations, called transitions and occurring either 'suddenly' or in '*pensive* PAUSES', promised to redeem the English stage, supplanting the pantomime Faustus of 1723 with a sorcery of feeling, exercised by the actor's plastic imagination and capable of such affective magic as would reinvigorate tragic speech and surprise a stultified audience into correction.

The Very Instant of the Changing Passion

All, *kindled* at the *Eye*, by the Ductility of a *Flexible Fancy*, and APPROPRIATING *Voice* and *Gesture*, to the very *Instant* of the *changing Passion*.[28]

This sentence recapitulates the process of performance described in the rest of *Prompter 66*. Referring back to the actor's '*Transitions*', it reminds us how such physical transformation owes its genesis to the protean powers of the imagination, or '*Flexible Fancy*'. On top of this, however, Hill is also searching here for a way of understanding why this type of performance would fascinate. His formulation of what the actor is aiming for, the fit of his performance to 'the very *Instant* of the *changing Passion*', is his attempt to capture the peculiar tensions of a style of acting that relies on emotional transformation for stage effect. On one hand, the kind of performance Hill describes places great emphasis on the discrete and forceful rendition of a passion as it appears in 'the very *Instant*' (when hope replaces dejection or joy eclipses anger). On the other hand, however, the force of that iconic moment and its ability to engage an audience for any duration is predicated on the sense that no passion is simple or permanent but is instead dynamic: one emotional transformation will succeed another, each influences our understanding of those around it, and even a single passion is a complex and unstable entity. The passion, in Hill's words, is thus always '*changing*'. By writing of 'the very *Instant* of the *changing Passion*', Hill seeks to describe a multidimensional union of arresting moment and temporal flow, forceful impression, and vivid instability. This productive tension constitutes the motor of compelling spectacle, and so what actors and authors must aim for. To achieve these ends, the combination of the iconic and dynamic, they require not just the true Faustus of imagination but rigorous analysis of the ebb and flow of emotion within a text.

Hill himself was aware of this. As early as the third issue of *The Prompter*, he attacks Colley Cibber for his inability to render 'the rapid, ungovernable Impetuosity, of a *Hotspur*', the 'sanguinary, and disdainful, Subtleties' of Richard III, and even, at the other end of the spectrum, 'the dignified Inflexibility of a *Cato*'.[29] In short, Cibber is but one more proof that 'IT is a Prodigy to see an Actor, *General*, *Plastick*, and *unspecificate*': he, like so many others, cannot shape his mind and body to follow the emotional nuance of his role (unless, as Hill points out, Cibber was playing a fop).[30] Hill, in later issues of his periodical, gives examples of such nuances, displaying remarkable sensitivity to the text in order to do so. In issue 103, Hill offers a comparison of Tamerlane and Bajazet, with attention to how each part should be performed. Tamerlane, for example, contains as much 'Fire' as Bajazet, but 'That of *Tamerlane shines, inclos'd,* and *defended*'.[31] To prove his point, Hill offers several close readings.

> "*I* WARN *thee, to take* HEED. ————————I *am*
>   *a* MAN:
> "*And have the* Frailties, *common to* Man's Nature.
> "*The* fiery *Seeds of* WRATH *are in my* TEMPER:
> "*And may be* blown, *up so* FIERCE *a* BLAZE,
> "*As* Wisdom CANNOT RULE.

COU'D it have been *possible*, in plainer Words, to shew the *Struggles*, the *Restraints*, the active labour'd *Glowings*, of a *suppress'd Indignation*, painfully *withheld* by Recollection?[32]

Much of the work of Hill's analysis here is done in the body of the quotation, where small capitals, italics, and a dash make visible what he calls 'the active labour'd *Glowings*' of Tamerlane's mind. These markings are typical of Hill's quotation practice (and, in places, of his prose style too) and are worth considering in relation to recent work on the history of typographical markings. Dashes, in particular, have been analysed by Anne Toner as one of a group of what she calls 'ellipsis marks'.[33] Although she does not mention Hill in her study, his insertion of a dash at this point illustrates what Toner observes to be a crucial element of such a mark: that it 'in its essence yields to the performance of others'.[34] Hill's addition of a long dash to the original text of Nicholas Rowe's *Tamerlane* (1701) opens it up, revealing a place where the author's writing will yield to the actor's art. As Toner puts it elsewhere, such 'Ellipsis indicates to varying degrees, the submission of the text to external definition', and Hill's writing here carries out such a process on the behalf of the performer.[35] Of course, the dash is just one tool in Hill's arsenal of typographical techniques, whose usage aims to mark everything that a printed script elides but that the apprentice performer needs. What Toner's writing shows so well is that Hill's quotation practices are double-edged: on one hand, they illuminate the nuances that performance can give to written speech; on the other, they are – as a combination of capitals, italics, and dashes – more prescriptive than a single ellipsis mark, forcing the script into a carefully defined, submissive position.

Having thus worked over Tamerlane's speech, Hill goes on to point out the consequence of its newly visible pauses and emphases for the performer: 'shall an *Actor* be permitted to suppose, He *reaches This*, by smooth, untouching *Indolence*? the round, and easy *Oiliness*, of Utterance without *Mark*, or *Meaning*?'[36] In other words, the stage rendition of this passage must mark out the contours of its suppressed intense emotions with the same clarity as Hill's typographical innovation has done upon the page. Five further examples of Tamerlane's fire are then given before Hill clinches his argument with one final ingenious example.

HEAR him, when he *releases* the *Turk*, in Compliance with the Prayer of *Arpasia*.
  "Sultan,—*be* SAFE————reason RESUMES *her Empire*
  "*And I am,* COOL, AGAIN.
  AND, here, *I think*, we may *Sum up the Evidence.* ————Since *Reason* cou'd not RESUME, an Empire, which she has not LOST: nor cou'd *Tamerlane,*

with any propriety, have been said to *grow* COOL, AGAIN, unless He had been WARM in what forewent it.[37]

Hill's argument here demonstrates his attention not just to the particular moment of a passion but to the way such moments are part of a larger pattern of feeling. He argues for the intensity of Tamerlane's rage from the fact that it is retrospectively announced by Tamerlane himself. Such a textual clue amounts to a specific kind of implicit stage direction. However, rather than implicitly requiring a certain action, these directions are instead signals to the actor that they must have previously generated and exhibited a specific passion. Such directions can obviously appear in more than retrospective forms, and sometimes, as in Hill's first example, even turn on the name of the passion: Tamerlane experiences 'WRATH' even as he descants on it. The implicit signal for the actor to do the same is rendered explicit by Hill's commentary and typographical modification, both of which are proof of his sensitivity to this dimension of a playtext.

The theory and close textual analysis found scattered throughout *The Prompter* comes together in Hill's unfinished *Essay on Acting*. The work begins, for example, with an updated version of a method first published in *Prompter* 118.

> 1stly, THE imagination must conceive a *strong idea* of the passion.
>
> 2ndly, BUT that idea cannot *strongly* be conceived, without impressing its own form upon the muscles of the *face*.
>
> 3rdly, NOR *can* the look be muscularly stamp'd without communicating, instantly, the same impression, to the muscles of the *body*.
>
> 4thly, THE muscles of the body, (brac'd, or slack, as the idea was an active or a passive one) must, in their natural, and not to be avoided consequence, by impelling or retarding the flow of the animal spirits, transmit their own conceiv'd sensation, to the sound of the *voice*, and to the disposition of the *gesture*. (iv, p. 356)

The core of the *Essay*, however, is constituted by Hill's attempts to address two problems with this process. Lacking space in *Prompter* 118, he could only name them as '*two* formidable Difficulties' and leave them to his *Essay*.

> 1st. – How, (in Every *Part*) to KNOW the Passions, rightly; and *distinguish* them, from One another.
>
> 2dly, – By what Means (the Passion once *distinguish'd*) to assume its active *Image*, and impress it on the *Imagination*?[38]

It is above all the question of how to distinguish between the passions that runs through the entirety of Hill's treatise. The second difficulty, that of creating the iconic and dynamic combination of an 'active *Image*', is treated less directly, partly because the text is unfinished and partly because Hill maintains his faith in the infallibility of the Cartesian mechanisms for creating emotion: once a passion is distinguished and the imagination engaged, its uptake and expression is a matter of 'a *mere, and mechanic,* NECESSITY; without Perplexity, Study, or Difficulty'.[39]

Identifying the passions is the crucial first step. Making use of the greater space afforded to him in an essay, Hill starts by informing the reader that 'there are only ten dramatic passions', so-called because they 'can be distinguished by their outward marks, in action' (IV, p. 357). These ten passions – 'Joy, Grief, Fear, Anger, Pity, Scorn, Hatred, Jealousy, Wonder, and Love' – each constitutes the subject of one of the ten chapters of Hill's work.[40] They are also, of course, a structure for understanding all dramatic writing, not least because these passions are like Descartes's 'primary' passions: all other passions, according to Hill, are 'relative to, and but varied degrees' of them (IV, p. 357). This phrase is important, as it indicates to us that Hill does not see these ten 'dramatic passions' as stable mono-liths, but rather elements of a dynamic experience (the same kind of experience he called 'the very *Instant* of the *changing Passion*'). It is striking, for example, that Hill, in his first chapter on 'Joy', is careful to urge the actor to seek out not just the individual passion but those moments where 'the writer had intended any change of passions' (IV, p. 358). The actor should not seek out passions as a static background for a scene or speech, but rather focus on the process by which that emotion rises, evolves in the moment, and departs.

Consider the very first example of a passion in Hill's *Essay*. '*JOY*', we are told, 'is the passion, in the following transport of *Torrismond*'.

> "Oh heaven! she pities me.
> "And pity, still, fore-runs approaching love;
> "As light'ning does the thunder. – Tune your harps,
> "Ye angels! To that sound: And thou, my heart!
> "Make room – to entertain the flowing joy!
>
> (IV, pp. 358–59)

Hill's introduction to these verses is carefully phrased. This passage is a 'transport' that joy is 'in': but where exactly, though, is that joy? Does it arrive only at the end, when Torrismond himself pronounces the word? This would be confirmed by what appears to be Hill's own modification of the text: neither the exclamation marks nor the dashes here appear in any editions of John Dryden's *The Spanish Friar* (1681), and Hill's final line

carries both, making some implicit emotional direction explicit.[41] Yet the
earlier lines do not lack these markers either and must thus be understood
to denote how the individual passion of joy is far from uniform, containing
within it its own variations in expression, its ebbs and flows, culminating in
the final burst at the end of Torrismond's speech.

As this is Hill's first example, he does not explore such variation in detail,
contenting himself with observing that the actor must have 'discovered,
that the passion, in this place, is *Joy*' (IV, p. 359). Later in the *Essay*,
however, such nuances within a passion come under close consideration,
and it becomes clear that the work of distinguishing a passion's progress
requires considerable skill. In his analysis of anger, Hill declares the
existence of '*two modes*' for this passion, both of which he discerns in
a speech from Thomas Otway's *The Orphan* (1680), separated here by
a dash and an asterisk of Hill's own making.

> "— I say, my sister's wrong'd;
> "*Monima—my* sister: born, as high,
> "And noble, as *Castalio*. —Do her justice,
> "Or, by the gods! I'll lay a scene of blood,
> "Shall make this dwelling horrible, to nature.
> "I'll do't. * — Hark you, my Lord!
> "— — Your son – *Castalio* — —.
> "Take him to your closet, and, there, teach him man-
>   ners.   (IV, p. 372)

In a speech that is all 'furious, and intemperate *anger*', the lines prior to
Hill's asterisk must be spoken 'with a fierce, vindictive air, and voice high
rais'd, insulting, and impatient', while those after 'must, on the contrary,
be expressed, by affectation of a slow, smooth'd, inward rancour, by
a mutter'd ironical repression of voice' (IV, p. 373). The effect of such
variation is to create compelling spectacle, for 'when [. . .] the rage breaks
out, again', Hill continues, 'the representation becomes movingly varied,
and natural'. Such an effect is no cheap trick, although it is as powerful as
anything in a pantomime, for, in all this, as Hill concludes the chapter, 'the
voice seems to preserve a kind of musical modulation, even in madness'
(IV, p. 373).

Anger is far from the only passion whose nuances Hill explores. He
divides jealousy into the '*doubtfully* suspicious' and 'the violence of positive
belief' (IV, pp. 380–81), the latter of which is 'the utmost pitch, whereto
Jealousy (as Jealousy) can by nature extend itself [. . .] For the next step
beyond it, is *Anger*' (IV, p. 383). In the next chapter, Hill divides wonder
into '*Amazement*' and '*Astonishment*': the former entails an 'involuntary

rigour of intenseness' (IV, p. 384), while in the latter 'the recoil of the animal spirits [...] drive the blood upon the heart with such oppressive redundance, as [...] almost stagnates the vital progression' (IV, p. 385). All the gradations of jealousy are visible in Othello, while Hamlet's encounter with his father's ghost provides an excellent demonstration of amazement, which Hill finds himself breaking down, once more, into three separate movements: the 'starting spring', 'the shaken understanding', and 'the resolution of recover'd firmness' (IV, p. 386). The moment of the ghost's appearance is revealed, in Hill's *Essay*, as a moment where, at every instant, the passion changes subtly.

It is crucial, then, to distinguish here between the passion and its physical manifestation. As he works through his examples of each of the ten dramatic passions, Hill repeatedly proceeds from an archetype (joy is '*Pride possessed of Triumph*', anger '*Pride provok'd beyond Regard of Caution*') to a particular situation (IV, pp. 357 and 368). As this method is repeated, it becomes clear to the reader that Hill's analysis and textual markers serve to map out the course each speech imposes on the performer's passion. In some lines it should be intense, in others, less so; some phrases are to be hurried, while others are delivered with care. The performer is to summon the passion and then begin his speech, fitting it 'to the very *Instant* of the *changing Passion*' as the scene unfolds. Returning to Hill's first chapter, adherence to such a rhythm of preparation and execution is at the core of his advice to whoever acts in Torrismond's transports.

> When the actor has discovered, that the passion, in this place, is *Joy*, he must not, upon any account, attempt the utterance of one single word, 'till he has, first, compelled his fancy to conceive an idea of joy. And it would be his natural, tho' most difficult, way, to endeavour the effacement of all note, or image of himself, and forcibly bind down his fancy to suppose, that he is, really, *Torrismond–* (IV, p. 359)

In this paragraph, Hill offers an answer to the second of the difficulties he identified in *Prompter* 118: 'By what Means (the Passion once *distinguish'd*) to assume its active *Image*, and impress it on the *Imagination?*' To awaken the passion, the actor must annihilate the self and identify with the character completely: an effort that then prepares the imagination to take up the 'active *Image*' of the passion, capable of carrying him or her through the twists and turns of a speech. Yet no sooner has Hill offered this solution then he proposes an alternative. A successful performance of a passion may be achieved 'by annexing, at once, the *look* to the *idea*, in the very instant, while he is bracing his nerves into springiness' (IV, p. 362).[42]

This second method has its limits, however. When Hill presents it, he already warns the reader that it is to be used only by those whose fancy is yet 'to become ductile enough' and so remains 'defective' (IV, pp. 361–62). Later in the treatise, the idea that one could encourage the imagination by pre-emptively adopting the physical expression of an emotion is undermined by Hill's observation of the similarities between passions. There is, he notes, 'no other difference but the turn of an eye, in the expression of *hatred* and *pity*' (since both emotions involve a degree of condescension) (IV, p. 379), and fear shares with grief a 'languor, in look, and in muscles', differing only in 'a starting, apprehensive, and listning [*sic*] alarm' (IV, p. 366). One hardly need imagine how badly wrong a performance could go if scenes of hate replaced scenes of pity, and grief took over from fear. And if the actor is trying to ignite their imagination using physical expression, that expression must be unfailingly precise to avoid such dangerous category errors. The only guarantee of passion is thus the prior establishment of a '*strong idea*', an imaginative creation with the force to hold the actor to the demands of the moment.

Yet this raises a further issue. If the best actors are to have entered into their passion before speaking their lines, then they will do so either quickly or slowly, generating pauses of varying lengths, which have the potential to alter fundamentally the rhythm of a production. Hill writes of such pauses throughout his work. In his description of 'a *Plastic Imagination*' as 'a FAUSTUS for the *Theatres*', he describes how a skilled actor 'stops short, upon *pensive* PAUSES, and makes *Transitions*' into the appropriate passion (which then, as Hill's marked scripts show, has its own internal variations).[43] The use of '*pensive*' here to mean 'meditative' or 'full of thought' is apt, given the *Essay*'s presentation of this moment as that in which the performer's imagination takes fire and the transition is made.[44] Indeed, the term also serves to defend the actor, for it casts such pauses not as halting blanks but as moments of captivating emotional activity.

The impact and utility of such pauses are explored further in Hill's treatise. While he observes that such moments provide some physical respite, 'allowing frequent and repeated opportunities for a recovery of [the voice's] wasted strength, in easy and un-noted *Breathings*', he also argues for the spectacular potential of 'such beautiful and pensive pausing places' (IV, p. 368). Because the Cartesian mechanism Hill's actor relies on is the same as that supposedly at work in genuine passions, these moments will 'appear to an audience, but the strong and natural attitudes of thinking; and the inward agitations of a heart, that is, in truth, disturb'd, and shaken' (IV, p. 368). Unsurprisingly, a number of Hill's letters to actors and actresses thus urge them to make use of such pauses and, in doing so, provide us with further information about what Hill considered to be the most effective rhythms of performance.

Many of these letters were sent with marked scripts, where, one can imagine, Hill offered a handwritten version of the dashes, italics, capitals, and exclamation marks that he employed in his published work. On 8 October 1733, Hill sent, for example, 'the whole part of *Imoinda*' (from Thomas Southerne's 1695 adaptation of *Oroonoko*) to Elizabeth Holliday, telling her that he had 'mark'd, with a star, the properest places for pausing' (I, p. 140). Hill adds that 'the measure of time in a pause, should vary according to the sense', although 'it will, in general, be enough to rest, as long as might suffice, to pronounce such a word as *power*' (I, p. 140). Such a detail suggests a genealogical connection between the pauses described by Hill and modern stagecraft's use of the 'beat', which describes either (in Stanislavskian traditions) the smallest unit of action in a play or (more generally) a brief moment of time. Hill combines the two definitions, suggesting to Holliday that she can effect a change of passions in the time it takes to say the word '*power*'.[45] Hill's choice of measurement indicates the importance of these pauses: they offer the actor a chance to demonstrate their own power to set the tempo of the production and manipulate audience response to the emotional units of the text.

Holliday seems to have got the message. One week after his letter on pauses, Hill wrote again to congratulate her on her use of his markings (I, p. 151), which also included 'a few lines *thus*, under places where the voice is to be strong, high, and emphatical' (I, p. 140). Following on from this success, Hill then sent a marked-up version of the part of Torrismond to another actor, advising him to note the careful placement of pauses: 'First, for the sake of the sense; and next, for a *saving* to the *voice*' (I, p. 154). These are the same points about effect and economy made in the *Essay* and far from the only example of Hill's correspondence anticipating his theoretical writing (a sign, perhaps, of his desire to produce a practical method for professional performers). For instance, a marked script sent to the actor John Roberts turns, as the *Essay* often does,[46] to music, when it promises to show him how 'to quicken and inspirit the solemnity, where necessary, by musical variation, which will flow from a change, with the changing passions' (I, p. 169). At the same time, as with Holliday, Hill goes into far more detail in his letters than his *Essay* (in its unfinished state) ever does. A long letter, probably sent to James Quin (who came out of retirement to play Othello at Drury Lane in the autumn of 1734),[47] also provides a supplement to Hill's theoretical work, making a specific argument for the validity of extended pauses in many of the Moor's speeches.

> [Othello] says nothing, that is not *important*; therefore, *weight* should never be *absent*, in the *tone* that expresses it, no more than in the *look* that accompanies, or in the *action* that imprints it. A particular inference will follow this observation, with respect to *sentences*, where they have any thing strikingly peculiar, which should always be both preceded and closed, by a *pause* of considerable length; to awaken and prepare expectation, and the other to give time for reflection, that, so, the *image* may descend perfect, from the *ear* to the *understanding*. (I, p. 219)

The last sentence of this paragraph connects the experience of actor and spectator and defines the pause as a crucial element in the communication of the play's sentiments. In the first pause, the '*image*' moves from the mind of the actor to their body as they impress an idea upon their imagination and so transition into the appropriate passion and take up an attitude. In the second pause, as the actor closes off the passion, the '*image*' has the time to make the opposite journey in the spectator to that made in the actor, moving from the body to the mind, from the '*ear*' to the '*understanding*'. These are truly '*pensive*' pauses, moments of mediation and reflection that bring performer and public together in an appreciation of the text.

Such pauses thus serve to separate Hill's method from the unthinking spectacle of pantomime. As the actor prepares their passion, readying themselves to conjure with Faustian imagination, they demonstrate a level of intellectual discernment that is far removed from the acrobatics of popular entertainment. The actor must study their text in extreme detail, noting how 'the Meanings *vary*' and what passions are unfolding in a moment. The audience, eagerly awaiting the transformative release of emotion through all the variations of an individual line, may be no different from those at a pantomime, delighted by the metamorphosis of a salesman or the intricate dance of Harlequin. Yet, as the spectacle of the tragic passion ends, Hill hoped that something of the '*strong idea*' that drove it may have been passed to them. They now have an otherwise lost opportunity to learn, to exercise both '*ear*' and '*understanding*', and, who knows, maybe even – as Hill wrote to Thompson – 'be *surpriz'd into correction*'.

Thought-Inflated Pauses

In his acting treatise and periodical articles, as well as in his poetry, Aaron Hill elaborated an entire method of acting. Working from a Cartesian understanding of man as a machine driven by spirit, he put the imagination of the actor, the true Faustus for the theatres, at the heart of his work. A performer following Hill's method would have to use their imagination to approach a text with sensitivity, seeking to distinguish each of the passions of their role and, on a microscopic level, the unfolding of each emotion in the course of a speech, fitting their work 'to the very *Instant* of the *changing Passion*'. In such performances, transitional pauses, brief or long, played a key role: they gave the actor time to summon in the mind the appropriate passion, using the natural, '*mechanic* [. . .] NECESSITY' inherent in every human body, while also building a level of anticipation and interest in an otherwise jaded audience. Spectators could watch the emotion spread through the actor, transforming their body in a way not unrelated to the spectacular metamorphoses of the pantomime. These polymorphous '*pensive* PAUSES' and their transitions could vary in length and, for all their similarity to the tricks of Harlequin, differed in their status as a deeply intellectual process, preparing the actor to exhibit a detailed reading of the passions in their part, a reading Hill maps with dashes, exclamation marks, capitals, and italics. In the course of a performance, the spectator thus had the opportunity to receive, supercharged, the content of the play, to reflect upon it and, potentially, to be corrected by it too. Such an art, both captivating and cerebral, was designed to usurp the place of the lowbrow entertainment that Hill considered the ruin of the English stage, redeeming in the process the theatre as a positive influence over national culture and morals.

Hill's acting method, as I will show in this section, crystallised a set of ideas that, from 1740 onwards, came to dominate the celebration and censure of plays and players. The extent to which they were employed on the stage is, however, much harder to determine. Hill himself had little chance to put them into practice: he moved to Plaistow in 1738 and, hampered by a mix of financial and physical difficulties, found it increasingly difficult to attend the theatre in the last twelve years of his life.[48] However, he did continue to follow theatrical developments closely and apply his own thinking to evaluate new performers. One actor in particular impressed Hill enormously. After seeing this man perform Macbeth in 1744, Hill wrote an excited letter to Mallet, applying the terms of his *Essay*, to argue that this performer's 'peculiar talent lies in pensively preparatory attitudes; whereby, awakening expectation in the audience, he secures and holds fast their attention' (II, p. 35). Soon, Hill would be in touch with the performer himself, praising his *'thought-inflated* pauses' (II, p. 156), offering to annotate Othello for him (II, p. 266), and trying to persuade him to take the leading role in productions of Hill's own plays (II, p. 248). This man was David Garrick, who made his London debut in 1741 and swiftly rose to the heights of his profession, becoming actor-manager of Drury Lane in 1747, a position he would hold until his retirement from the stage in 1776, three years before his death at the age of sixty-one.

For almost the entirety of his career, Garrick was at the heart of British theatre. Much writing about and by this artist focuses on the same concerns that preoccupied Hill. These concerns amount to the question of how best to perform the passions of a play so as to capture the attention of a potentially unruly audience who, as Garrick himself wrote in one of his epilogues, often appeared as 'Crowds of City Folks! – so rude and pressing!' with their 'Horse-Laughs, so hideously distressing!'[49] For Hill, and for many others, it was Garrick's use of the pause – the moment of transition from one passion to another or from one nuance to its neighbour – that was his defining characteristic. Yet these pauses were controversial, and in the division of opinion over Garrick's pauses and attitudes we can discern the complex origins of dramatic transition as an attempt to render the attention-grabbing strategies of the pantomime respectable and morally useful. Those who censured the actor-manager's pauses considered them as pantomimic; those who praised them found them pensive. Through it all, however, the pause is clearly recorded as playing a crucial role in taming a theatre public who, throughout the period, were as liable to hurl fruit and abuse at the stage as they were to burst into applause.

The first night of Samuel Crisp's tragedy *Virginia* (1754) could have gone either way. Richard Cross, the Drury Lane prompter, recorded that 'Mr Carey had his fiddle broke by an apple playing the first Music.'[50] Yet Garrick, at least according to Arthur Murphy's biography of him, produced a performance that left those present enthralled. Its greatest moment was 'Garrick's manner of uttering two words'.

> *Claudius,* the iniquitous tool of the Decemvir, claims *Virginia,* as a slave born in his house. He pleads his cause before *Appius* on his tribunal. During that time, Garrick, representing Virginius, stood on the opposite side of the scene, next to the stage-door, with his arms folded across his breast, his eyes riveted to the ground, like a mute and lifeless statue. Being told at length that the tyrant is willing to hear him, he continued for some time in the same attitude, his countenance expressing a variety of passions, and the

spectators fixed in ardent gaze. By slow degrees he raised his head; he paused; he turned round in the slowest manner, till his eyes fixed on *Claudius*; he still remained silent, and after looking eagerly at the impostor, he uttered in a low tone of voice, that spoke the fullness of a broken heart, '*Thou traitor!*' The whole audience was electrified; they felt the impression, and a thunder of applause testified their delight.[51]

Murphy's account sketches the same pattern of pensive, transitional pause and stunning execution that Hill expounds in his writing. Garrick speaks only when he has achieved 'the fullness of a broken heart', and so fulfils Hill's dictum that the actor avoid the 'utterance of one single word, 'till he has, first, compelled his fancy to conceive an idea' of the passion of the scene. In addition to this, Murphy's comparison of Virginius to 'a mute and lifeless statue' that Garrick slowly animates owes a debt to the same Cartesian frameworks that Hill himself had employed. While this is not evidence for a direct connection between Murphy and Hill, it does indicate the extent to which both share a common critical vocabulary; one which, however, Murphy then departs from when he captures the effect of the animated Roman with a rather different kind of language. The 'spectators fixed in ardent gaze' are 'electrified'. Rather than the pneumatic action of animal spirits, emotional response now appears to be the result of galvanic forces. The paradigms for performing emotion were shifting.

Murphy's uneasy balancing of possessed statues and electrified audiences also appears in one of Garrick's few surviving comments on his own performance processes. Having been asked by Helferich Peter Sturz (then secretary to Christian VII of Denmark) to comment on the acting of the French actress La Clairon (Claire-Josèphe Léris), Garrick wrote him – as Roach has shown – a reply that mixed ancient and modern paradigms of performance. Acting and science are as intertwined here as they are in Hill, but this letter of 1769 places new emphasis on the actor's capacity for feeling.

> What shall I say to you my dear Friend about the *Clairon*? Your desection [*sic*] of her, is as accurate as if you had open'd her alive; she has every thing that Art and a good understanding, with great Natural Spirit can give her – But then I fear (and I only tell you my fears, and open my Soul to You) the Heart has none of those instantaneous feelings, that Life blood, that keen Sensibility, that bursts at once from Genius, and like Electrical fire shoots thro' the Veins, Marrow, Bones and all, of every Spectator. – Mad^m *Clairon* is so conscious and certain of what she can do, that she never (I believe) had the feelings of the instant come upon her unexpectedly. – but I pronounce that the greatest strokes of Genius, have been unknown to the Actor himself,

'till Circumstances, and the warmth of the Scene has sprung the Mine as it were, as much to his own Surprize, as that of the Audience.[52]

In Roach's analysis, Garrick places new emphasis on the actor's capacity for feeling in two ways: he promotes, first, the vitalist principle that 'Spirit no longer merely works on matter' (as in Descartes) but 'spirit emerges from a particular organization of matter', and, second, he implies that the sensibility of the performer operates 'on a physical plane below conscious thought'.[53] These two factors, the new attention to the vitalistic 'Life Blood' and the actor's unconscious springing of a mine, have no precedent in Hill. Yet, at the same time, Garrick's account of performance might also be said to share a number of larger traits with Hill's own writing: 'Surprize' is as crucial here as it is in Hill's visions of an audience 'surpriz'd into correction', and Garrick's awareness of the 'feelings of the instant' echoes Hill's own examination of the performer working 'to the very *Instant* of the *changing Passion*'.

Hill and Garrick thus draw on different but overlapping discourses about human emotion, and both still tend towards a similar conclusion of arresting emotional expression, of the kind described in Murphy's account of *Virginia*'s opening night. Crucial to the effect of that performance was Garrick's use of the pause, a technique not discussed in Garrick's letter to Sturz but much remarked upon by others, including Sturz's compatriot, Georg Christoph Lichtenberg, who, with the foreigner's eye for detail, recorded the mix of action and immobility in Garrick's rendition of Hamlet's encounter with the ghost of his father. Hill had also analysed this famous coup de théâtre in his *Essay*, breaking it down into three stages: the 'starting spring', 'the shaken understanding', and 'the resolution of recover'd firmness' (IV, p. 386). Lichtenberg's description provides an account of the first two of Hill's three stages, emphasising how they compel audience attention, freezing an otherwise restless audience 'as though they were painted on the walls of the theatre' ('als wären sie an die Wände des Schauplatzes gemalt') and causing a silence so complete that 'even from the farthest end of the playhouse one could hear a pin drop' ('man könnte am entferntesten Ende des Theaters eine Nadel fallen hören'). Thanks to Lichtenberg, one can argue that Garrick's rendition of this scene was so absorbing because of its ability to exploit, through a rhythmic pattern of action and pause, the nuances of emotion identified by Hill. The appearance of the ghost is the trigger for Garrick to 'start', one of a few technical terms for a sharp ('plötzlich') expression of emotion. In this case, the actor makes use of his entire body and costume to express his shock and fear: his hat falls to the ground; he staggers across the stage and needs the support of Horatio and Marcellus to stay upright. In this position or attitude a new pause opens up, during which the audience can see (and absorb) the Hillian impression of the idea upon him, even before he speaks, breaking another period of silence, this time at the 'end of a breath' and with a tremulous softness ('nicht mit dem Anfange, sondern mit dem Ende eines Odemzugs und bebender Stimme') that everyone present would strain to hear.[54] The precision of Lichtenberg's account offers a glimpse into the subtleties of Garrick's art while at the same time emphasising how every nuance serves to capture audience attention through a careful balance of transitions: from silent expectation to shock to a frozen terror.[55] By the time Garrick is ready to speak, his breathless voice fits perfectly with his shaken physical state. Hill would have recognised such techniques, although there is no evidence to indicate that his work was known to Lichtenberg, who only visited England and saw Garrick in the 1770s, long after Hill's death.

The similarities between Hill and Lichtenberg do, however, indicate the extent to which Hill's writing crystallised a set of critical priorities that would develop in the second half of the eighteenth century, drawing strength from new scientific paradigms (such as vitalism) and the specific talents of those who studied the theatre. Lichtenberg's detailed descriptions owe something, for example, to his medical training, but he was hardly the only educated theatregoer to echo Hill's thinking in a detailed account of Garrick's performance. In 1775, the music theorist Joshua Steele published his *Essay towards Establishing the Melody and Measure of Speech*. Among much else, the work contains Steele's attempt to record Hamlet's 'To be, or not to be' soliloquy, first, in 'the stile of a ranting actor' (Figure 1.1) and then, a few pages on, as performed by Garrick himself (Figure 1.2).[56] Steele's evaluation of each performance reveals the nuance with which a passion could be acted.

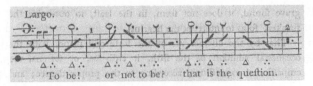

Figure 1.1 Steele's notation of the 'To be or not to be' soliloquy in the style of a 'ranting actor' (p. 40). By permission of the British Library (shelfmark RB.23.b.3187).

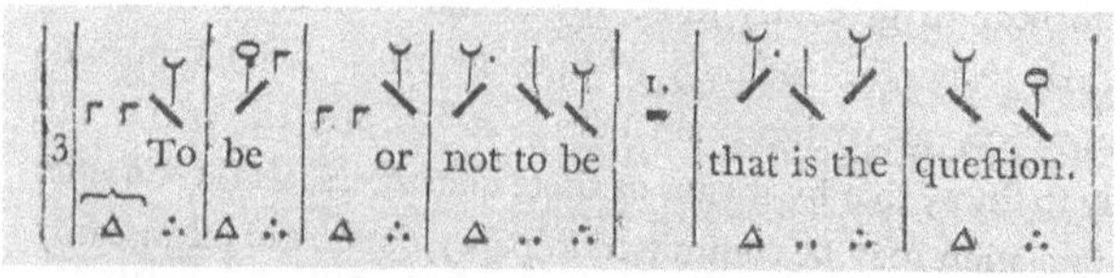

Figure 1.2 Steele's notation of Garrick's rendition of the 'To be or not to be'
soliloquy (p. 47). By permission of the British Library (shelfmark RB.23.b.3187).

Steele gives his first, ranting, version a pitch, as it also serves to demonstrate the potential for a bass accompaniment to heighten the effect of
speech. The angled bars beneath each crotchet and minim indicate
'Accent' (p. 24), with a curved bar used 'to shew that the sound hangs
longer on the first part of the slide than on the last, on account of the
vowels' (p. 38). In contrast to this, Garrick's rendition is without pitch or
tempo, although Steele continues to use his triangles and dots, which mark
'several degrees of emphasis of heavy ($\triangle$), light ($\therefore$), and lightest (..)' (p.
24). Peter Holland compares these two passages to demonstrate that
Garrick's version is 'about speed', since it reduces the length of almost
every syllable.[57] For Holland, this is, however, more than the 'bustle' that
characterised Garrick's animated acting style: rather, it shows 'a search for
the through-line of the speech, its architecture as important as its momentary effect'.[58] An important aspect of such a search, not examined by
Holland, is the use of pauses, revealed with precision in Steele's
transcriptions.

Both of Steele's versions begin with a two-beat pause. The next pause,
which falls between 'To be' and 'or not to be' is three beats long for
both Steele's ranter and Steele's Garrick, but, crucially, the Garrick
version differs in its placement of that pause. Rather than having an
entire bar of silence, Garrick is recorded as using anacrusis, cutting the
monosyllable 'be' short and displacing 'or' into the last beat of the third
bar. This echoes the metrical arrangement of the soliloquy's beginning.
Steele's other notation marks here indicate that Garrick's 'or' was
pronounced lightly, with a falling cadence, as opposed to the 'ranting
actor' version, which devotes a whole bar, a rising cadence, and a strong
emphasis on the first part of the syllable to it. To put this another way,
one might say that Steele's hypothetical ranter discovers a strong transition between 'To be' and 'or not to be'. Garrick, on the other hand, is
much more subtle, distinguishing the second half of Hamlet's balanced
phrasing with a series of falling cadences after a carefully placed pause.

While the ranter hammers home the antithetical construction of Hamlet's soliloquy, Garrick's off-beat silences and softer sounds oblige his audience to fall silent and pay close attention to the unfolding of Hamlet's passion. Such nuance made Garrick proof, in Steele's view, that 'There is a perfection in the pronunciation of the best speakers' (p. 48).

For Lichtenberg, Murphy, and Steele (not to mention Hill himself), the transitions of the '*pensive* PAUSES' represented an excellent opportunity for evaluating the excellence of Garrick's acting. Yet such pauses were also crucial to those wishing to denigrate Garrick. Thaddeus Fitzpatrick published a pamphlet in 1760, where he claimed to list twenty faults made by the actor in a single performance of *Hamlet*. In every item, Fitzpatrick's dashes mark a horribly misplaced pause.

   1 Oh that this too too solid—flesh would melt.

   2 Or that the everlasting had not *fixt*——
      His Canon 'gainst self-slaughter.

   3 As if increase of appetite had *grown* ———
      By what it fed on.

   4 I think it was to see——my mother's wedding.

   5 Their eyes purging——thick amber and plumb-tree gum.

   6 He would drown——the stage with tears.

   7   Or e're this,
      I should have fatted——all the region kites.
      With this slave's offal.

   8   That presently
      They have proclaimed———their malefactions.

   9   I'll have the players
      Play something like—the murther of my father.

  10   The play's the thing,
      Wherein I'll catch—the conscience of the king.

  11 Whether it is nobler in the mind, to *suffer*——
      The stings and arrows, &c.

  12 And makes us rather bear——— —those ills we have.

  13   Let not ever
      The soul of Nero enter——— —this firm bosom.

  14 When church-yards yawn, and hell itself breaths
      out———contagion to the world.

  15   O such a deed,
      As from the body of contraction plucks———

16 The very soul, and sweet religion *makes*———
   A rhapsody of words.
17   Proclaim no shame,
   When the *compulsive*—ardour gives the charge.
18   Mother, for love of grace,
   Lay not that flattering—unction to your soul.
19 It will but skin and film———the ulcerous place.
20 Why may not imagination trace———the noble
   Blood of Alexander, &c.[59]

As verbs are separated from their objects and adjectives from their substantives, Garrick appears as a performer incapable of the basic comprehension of a line. Indeed, a number of these examples demonstrate how a misplaced pause could alter the meaning and effect of a line completely. 'The play's the thing, | Wherein I'll catch—' is a particularly (and perhaps suspiciously) good example of this, as Garrick seems to diagnose his own tendency to work in catches or 'short intervals of action'.[60] The ninth item in Fitzpatrick's list, 'I'll have the players | Play something like—', has a similar satiric insinuation.

Fitzpatrick was far from the only critic of Garrick's pauses. Theophilus Cibber gives the actor's 'unnatural Pauses' a place in his own unflattering portrait of Garrick.

> Yet I may not therefore be blind to his studied Tricks, his Over-fondness for extravagant Attitudes, frequent affected Starts, convulsive Twitchings, Jerkings of the Body, sprawling of the Fingers, slapping the Breast and Pockets:———A Set of mechanical Motions in constant Use,—the Caricatures of Gesture, suggested by pert Vivacity,—his pantomimical Manner of acting, every Word in a Sentence; his unnatural Pauses in the Middle of a Sentence;—his forc'd Conceits,—his wilful Neglect of Harmony, even where the round Period of a well express'd noble Sentiment demands a graceful Cadence in the Delivery.[61]

Cibber's uncharitable prose exploits an uncomfortable association between the English Roscius and Harlequin. This association illuminates some of the consequences of Hill's own attempt to install the '*Plastic Imagination*' as 'a FAUSTUS for the *Theatres*'. Garrick, whose acting fulfilled and exceeded Hill's vision of a great performer, could (like parts of Hill's theories) seem to owe a dangerous debt to pantomime. The potentially compromising overlap occurred in the way both pantomime and Garrick aimed to capture audience attention and relied, to a greater or lesser extent, on iconic physical transformation to do so. The crucial distinction between the actor and the Harlequin was the former's intellectual capacity, his ability to analyse his script and express its every emotional nuance. Yet if Garrick (as both Fitzpatrick and Cibber claim) had no such discernment and scattered 'unnatural Pauses' throughout his act, then Garrick lost that which distinguished him from a lowbrow entertainer, becoming either a clown with his 'studied Tricks' or a mindless automaton, reliant on spiritless 'mechanical Motions'. Garrick was himself aware of such a danger and was careful to limit his engagement with pantomime. In a letter to his brother Peter in 1741, he confirmed the rumours that he had played Harlequin at the start of his career while minimising the importance of the experience.

> As to playing a Harlequin 'tis quite false – Yates last season was taken very ill & was not able to begin the Entertainment so I put on the Dress & did 2 or three Scenes for him, but Nobody knew it but him & Giffard: I know it has been Said I play'd Harlequin at Covent Garden, but it is quite false.[62]

Beginning and ending with denial, this passage only admits to its author's time in motley as a way of illustrating Garrick's own kindness. It might thus be taken as a miniature version of Garrick's career-long engagement with this form of entertainment. The great actor only used the powers of pantomime for social good, or, as O'Brien puts it, in the wake of Hill's theories and Garrick's labours as actor and manager, the works of Harlequin 'had been co-opted, their physicality and, just as important, their willingness to perform no purpose more important than their audience's sensual gratification, now accepted as itself a socially useful end'.[63]

Of course, Cibber would beg to differ, and it is the shadow of pantomime that allows the study of a performer's pauses to be more than an exercise of praise: an actor could triumph and fail before an audience attentive to the use of transformational silence. In his *Treatise on the Passions* (1747), Samuel Foote, himself an established actor, focused on the transitions Garrick made in his pauses to offer a balanced account of his near contemporary and theatrical rival. At first, the work takes issue with the star's portrayal of Macbeth, arguing that Garrick's shifts between emotions in this role are no more than a claptrap (a moment designed to elicit applause) which appeals to the lowest common denominator. Foote holds that it is because 'The Transition from one Passion to another, by the suddenness of the Contrast, throws a stronger Light on the Execution of the Actor' that those 'drawn in to applaud' are not the 'Judicious' but 'the Groundlings, who are caught more by the Harmony and Power of the Voice than Propriety'.[64] The ease with which applause is won devalues it.

Foote advises that the practice of spectacular transition, no more than a cheap 'Trick', should thus now be discontinued, for 'We all now know how the Shilling came under the Candlestick'.[65] Yet later in the same volume, even this critique of Garrick's acting eventually gives way to grudging praise of his ability to marshal emotion. In Lear's 'Recovery from Madness, and Recollection of *Cordelia*', 'The Passions of Joy, Tenderness, Grief and Shame are blended together in so masterly a Manner, that the Imitation would do Honour to the Pencil of a *Rubens*, or an *Angelo*'.[66]

Foote's artistic references here offer insight into a further ramification of eighteenth-century thinking about performance. If the actor is successful in demonstrating a nuanced understanding of the text, pausing and deploying transitions between the passions at moments that bring the character to life, then the actor is more than a servant to the dramatist: they are an artist, 'a *Rubens*, or an *Angelo*', personally responsible for the production of a work of art, albeit one that takes ephemeral form on the body rather than in a more lasting medium. Such an implication appears in other acting treatises of the mid eighteenth century. *The Actor*, written by John Hill (no relation to Aaron), began as a translation of Rémond de Sainte-Albine's 1747 work, *Le Comédien*, suitably modified to fit an English context.[67] In the course of the text, Hill reveals a complex attitude to the performer's critical and creative independence. Hill opened his work with the argument that 'good understanding' is 'necessary to the player' in order to distinguish 'the different steps thro'' which his author means to lead the passions and the imaginations of his audience; and by which he is to carry himself from opposite to opposite affections'.[68] The actor here is the servant of the author: by studying the text, he learns which emotions to trigger in himself in order to achieve the author's goal of engaging the 'passions and the imaginations' of those in the audience. Yet this relationship, we soon learn, is not as simple as it seems. In order to comprehend the author's intention, the actor must, as Hill recognises, also share some of the author's skills. Notably, the actor must be just as discerning as the author when it comes to the emotions he is to portray. In an unwieldy but not uncommon comparison of both poet and player to a painter, Hill ultimately comes to value both figures equally.

> As the painter often gives us a prospect of an extensive country in a very little piece, the poet sometimes in the compass of a few lines, gives his actor a multitude of different impressions: in this case the one as well as the other is to exert his skill in distinguishing to us, that things tho' placed near to one another in the small bounds of the representation, are not neighbours to

each other in the one case in the heart, or in the other in the prospect which is the subject of the picture. The player ought to have as strict an attention to these differences, and as nice a judgment in them, as the poet; he must no more than the painter, confound those things together between which nature has plac'd a vast distance, because they are to be seen in a small compass: But then he must very nicely conduct himself in those sudden transitions, thro' which he is to make one passion succeed to another; and that perhaps its contrary.[69]

The key phrase here is that 'The player ought to have as strict an attention to these differences, and as nice a judgment in them, as the poet.' Both poet and player must be good judges of emotion, able to deploy extremely different passions 'in a small compass' even when 'nature has plac'd' such passions at 'a vast distance'.

As well as connecting actor and author, Hill's description of 'sudden transition' reveals another aspect of this approach to drama. In this critic's view, the concatenation of two extremely different passions is the work of 'nature'. The performance of successive 'contrary' emotions can thus become both a powerful and a natural spectacle, something which distinguishes it from the supposedly unnatural entertainment of pantomime wizardry. Of course, this pairing of the natural and the spectacular was by no means easy. Yet the achievement of such a complex state – where the changes of the passion are pushed to their limit at every instant – created some of the most celebrated performances of the eighteenth century. One such performance, celebrated in John Hill's 1755 revised edition of *The Actor* and many other places, was Charles Macklin's rendition of Shylock.[70]

Theatre historians have long described Macklin's re-interpretation of Shakespeare's Jew as a powerful malevolent figure with respect to his predecessors' comic renderings of the part.[71] With a realistic costume and demeanour supposedly modelled on Jewish merchants observed in London, Macklin also made an unprecedented claim for anti-Semitic verisimilitude.[72] Such a claim did not, however, limit the spectacular effect of his performed passions. In his own writing, the actor recalled how his scenes were 'well listened to' and 'made [. . .] a silent yet forcible impression on [his] audience'.[73] One moment in particular reveals how that impression was created through a careful rendition of extreme and opposed emotion. According to Macklin, Shylock, in an exchange with Tubal, undergoes 'the contrasted passions of joy for the Merchant's losses, and grief for the elopement of Jessica'. As this veteran actor well knew, such a scene opened 'a fine field for the actor's powers'.[74] The details of the

190   L E S S O N S.

SPITEF.	Shyl. I *thank* thee, *good Tubal, good news,*
JOY.	*good news.* * *What* in *Genoa,* you fpoke with
* QUES.	them ?
NARRA-	Tub. Your daughter *fpent,* in Genoa, as I
TION.	heard, in *one night, twenty ducats.*
ANGU.	Shyl. Thou ftick'ft a *dagger* in me. I fhall
	never fee my *gold again. Twenty ducats* at a *fit-*
	ting! Twenty ducats! —— O father Abraham!
NARRA-	Tub. There came divers of Antonio's *credi-*
TION.	*tors* in my company to Venice, that fay, he *can-*
	not but break.
SPITEF.	Shyl. I'm *glad* of it. I'll *plague* him. I'll
JOY.	*torture* him. I'm *glad* of it.
NARRA-	Tub. One of them fhewed me a *ring,* he had
TION.	of your daughter for a *monkey.*
ANGU.	Shyl. *Out upon her!* Thou *tortureft* me, Tubal.
	It was my *ruby.* I had it of *Leah.* I would not
	have given it for as *many monkeys* as could ftand
	together upon the *Realto.*
NARR.	Tub. Antonio is *certainly undone.*
SPITEF.	Shyl. *Ay, ay,* there is *fome comfort* in that.
JOY.	‖ Go, Tubal, *fee* me an *officer;* befpeak him to be
‖ DIREC.	ready. * I will be *revenged* on Antonio. I will
* CRUEL	*wafh* my *hands,* to the *elbows,* in his *heart's blood.*
RESOL.	[Exit.]

Figure 1.3 James Burgh's presentation of the Shylock-Tubal dialogue (p. 190). Image provided by the National Library of Scotland. CC BY 4.0.

prospect so relished by Macklin were recorded in 1761 by James Burgh, who published an annotated version of this scene in his *Art of Speaking* as an exercise for the aspiring orator (Figure 1.3). Such a reader, not yet capable of a professional performer's fine discernment, could follow Burgh's own delineation of the scene's emotion.

Burgh's annotations, paired with a range of italics and ornaments, map out the passions of this passage. At its heart, there is the repeated contrast between Shylock's 'SPITEFUL JOY' and 'ANGUISH', yet this alternating pattern, even in the section shown here, contains variation.[75] Burgh's asterisks mark, first, a shift to a 'QUEST[ION]' and then a concluding burst of 'CRUEL RESOL[UTION]', reached through a moment of 'DIREC[TION]' set off with a double bar (‖). The heavy use of italics gives some sense of the emphasis required from the performer, with that emphasis (to judge from the use of exclamation marks) being rather more explosive in passages of anguish than in those that deal with joy or resolution.

Burgh was not the only admirer of this scene. The writer, actor, and occasional teacher of oratory Francis Gentleman recalled Macklin's performance of this moment in his periodical *The Dramatic Censor* (1770), recording that 'never were transitions from one passion to another better supported than in this scene: distraction, grief, and malevolence succeed and cross each other admirably'.[76] Four years later, Gentleman went on to publish an edition of *The Merchant of Venice* as part of his work on *Bell's Shakespeare*. This edition, like many of the other plays in the series, appeared with the claim of having been set from the promptbooks of Drury Lane and Covent Garden, and so offered the bookseller's clients the opportunity to buy a relic of performance for domestic consumption.[77] Gentleman's annotations and other paratexts are a key part of this offer. Perhaps with the *Censor*'s review of Macklin in mind, he comments that 'This conversation, or rather rhapsody, with Tubal, contains some of the finest transitions for an actor that were ever penned; which, as we may say, harrow up attention, when properly expressed',[78] and this is just one instance of many attempts by the editor to draw attention not just to the beauties of Shakespeare, as many others had done before him, but to the *theatrical* beauties of these plays.[79]

Indeed, the peculiar status of *Bell's Shakespeare* as a textual mimic of a visit to the theatre, complete with cast lists and long notes at the end of each act to serve as a surrogate for interval discussion, also means that this publication of the mid-1770s exemplifies many of the aesthetic priorities examined in this chapter.[80] Gentleman's 'Essay on Oratory', included in volume one of *Bell's Shakespeare*, uses the same vocabulary as Aaron Hill and Joshua Steele (to name only authors quoted in this chapter) to explain how 'READING and DECLAMATION consists of *emphasis, climax, modulation, pauses, breaks, transitions, tones, cadences,* and *gesture*' (1, p. 25). Elsewhere in this essay, Gentleman describes how certain moments are capable of engendering in the audience a 'sympathy of compulsion' (1, p. 22), an effect that Hill might recognise as a more sentimental version of the experience of a theatregoer '*surpriz'd into* correction'. As for the text of Shakespeare's plays, Gentleman's annotations are supplemented by numerous typographical markings, ranging from the insertion of dashes, exclamation marks, and question marks (all reminiscent of Hill's and others' discussed above) to the use of marginal inverted commas to indicate passages that should be cut from performance.

These suggested cuts have earned Gentleman the title of Shakespeare's first bowdleriser, but they are better understood as further evidence for his edition's textual representation of a particular understanding of perform-ance, one based on transition and crystallised by Hill.[81] Gentleman even extends this representational strategy to plays without stage traditions: volumes 7 and 8 offer versions of the second and third parts of *Henry VI* (never performed as such in the eighteenth century) and of *Titus Andronicus* (last performed for a single night at Lincoln's Inn Fields in 1724).[82] The part of Aaron, with its 'unprovoked villainy' against the Andronici (VIII, p. 23), we are told, should be given to 'an actor of strong ideas, and adequate powers of execution' (VIII, p. 55). This is a remarkable statement for two reasons. First, it is an echo of Hill's own advice to actors to summon, before anything else, a *strong idea* of the passion' to be represented, and so indicates the extent to which such a way of thinking about how to act endured across the eighteenth century. Second, this statement establishes an unequal relationship between idea and execution: providing that the ideas of the actor playing Aaron are strong enough, their powers of execution, their physical performance, need only be adequate. Hill would argue that the strength of the idea guaranteed the power of the execution, but the phrasing of Gentleman's note opens the path to a different interpretation, and one which risks the very power of perform-ance that Hill wished to recover from the pantomime. If ideas matter more than execution and such ideas have their source in an imaginative engage-ment with text, then the wonders of Shakespeare and the beneficial powers of the stage are as available to the careful reader as to the actor or theatregoer. Macbeth's dagger soliloquy, Gentleman tells us, will 'act powerfully, even in the closet, as well as on the stage' (1, p. 82).

* * *

There is a Faustian pact emerging here between page and stage. Such a pact is the third of three such bargains present in this chapter. The first, with its demons and fire-breathing dragons, is the spectacular opening of the Doctor Faustus pantomimes of the early 1720s, whose immediate and enduring success proved the power of an art that juxtaposed extremes of emotion.

The second is the trade Aaron Hill brokered with the pantomime. He believed that the actor could offer a refined version of pantomime transition through the use of a *strong idea*. These ideas, summoned in a pensive pause, would trigger physical changes in the performer and so produce a spectacular display of emotion, one performed to the very instant of the changing passion and capable of carrying the moral message of the drama. By being founded in such strong ideas, this spectacle distinguished itself from those unthinking but entertaining displays of pantomimic transformation exemplified by the Faustus enter- tainments of Rich and Thurmond. Later writers, active during the career of Garrick, offer a similar understanding of performance: scientific paradigms may have changed, but the sense that audience attention could be maintained and directed through the rhythmic exhibition of those passions that the expression of an idea dictated did not. Pauses and their transitions were the subject of praise and blame, and negative criticism was quick to connect such acting back to the style of panto- mime and so reveal Hill's theory for the infernal bargain it was. Yet rich transitions, for all their dangerous associations with pantomime, remained moments in which the actor could assert their artistic autonomy.

The third pact emerges from this situation and risks binding the actor to the scholar rather than the Harlequin. The new emphasis on the play of passions that the actor should bring to life as a reformed pantomime required that each performer undertake a close study of their text rather than of those established performance traditions judged by Hill and others as inadequate. This meant that the very thing that Hill intended to redeem the performance practices of serious theatre also encouraged the appreci- ation of the written word over its rendition before an audience and so undermined performance from a new direction, dematerialising it in favour of purely intellectual appreciation.

Such dematerialised appreciation, still nascent in Gentleman, is the subject of Chapter 5, but there remains one other, Faustian, point to be made here. Every example and metaphor I have employed so far points to the power of transition to induce critical cynosure. At its most extreme, a critic's focus on the individual's transitions between passions risks trans- forming dialogue into soliloquy and dramatic action into lyric expressions of feeling. Faustus is everything. The pantomime re-tellings of his story follow a single Harlequin scholar. Hill's letters of advice and worked examples only ever concern themselves with the performance of one person's part. Gentleman considers the Tubal-Shylock scene in *The Merchant of Venice* as a 'rhapsody' rather than a conversation: its 'finest transitions' are for 'an' actor, not both of them. Burgh, for his part, ascribes all of this passage's emotion to Shylock, merely noting 'Narration' next to each of Tubal's lines. Macklin recalls only his performance here and, when designating the scene 'a fine field for an actor's powers', again makes a revealing use of the singular. The captivating rendition of the passions is thus the work of the star, taming the audience by focusing their attention on a single figure.

Lichtenberg sees only Garrick on the battlements of Elsinore, and Claudius, for Murphy, is no more than a target for the contempt of this actor-manager's Virginius. At the same time, the misplaced pauses of Hamlet are Hamlet's only, the claptraps of *King Lear* make only Garrick a two-bit conjuror, and in Cibber's unflattering portrait of this man, it is 'his pantomimical Manner of Acting', with 'his unnatural Pauses' and 'his wilful Neglect of Harmony', that are at issue. Transition emerges from such critical analysis as the property of a single man or woman. And few plays show this aspect of transition, or those other aspects discussed here, as well as the subject of Chapter 2: Aaron Hill's *Zara*.

Zara

Theatrical *Experiment*

In the opening chapter of this book, I showed how Aaron Hill put the imagination of the actor, as the true 'FAUSTUS for the *Theatres*', at the heart of his acting theory.[1] In Hill's writings, a performer must use their imagination to undertake a sensitive study of the emotions of a role so that they may then work 'to the very *Instant* of the *changing Passion*' and produce iconic and dynamic performances to capture audience attention. Hill's publications crystallised a set of concerns that came to dominate writing about acting during the career of the actor-manager David Garrick (1740–76). Although scientific paradigms changed, an emphasis on the power of what Hill called '*strong*' ideas to trigger striking shifts of passion remained. Actors and theorists such as James Burgh, Charles Macklin, John Hill, and Francis Gentleman all held that the rapid sequencing of contrary emotions could create compelling, spectacular performances and used such sequences to prove the merit of particular performers. Such extensive attention led to a specific approach to drama: the pauses and their transitions within a work of theatre became the property of a single performer and moments of spectacular cynosure, to the point that dialogue resembled soliloquy and the dramatic flirted with the lyric. These new biases risked compromising the work of actors entirely, as an increased demand for the emotional analysis of a single character encouraged greater study of the printed script than of its ephemeral instantiation on the stage.

No play of the eighteenth century better reflects these theoretical developments than Hill's own *Zara*, a translation of Voltaire's *Zaïre* (1732), which he presented as an '*Experiment*' to prove his ideas about acting.[2] Hill began translating the work shortly after the text became available in early 1733,[3] at a time when he was still deeply engaged in his critique of pantomime's dominance on the English stage, having written to Barton

Booth (the manager of Drury Lane) in December 1732 to wish that 'the tricks of *Harlequin* were connected into a *thread*' if only to 'give *pleasure without shame*'.[4] The translation of *Zaïre* did not take long: Hill's text was presented to and refused by John Rich for staging at Covent Garden as early as March 1733. Christine Gerrard suspects that Hill then tried to have the work performed at Drury Lane, only to fall foul of a change of management in February 1734.[5] These failed attempts to get *Zara* onto the patent theatre stage only slightly precede Hill's writing for his period-ical *The Prompter*, including a number of his reflections on the state of English theatre and on the best techniques for acting.[6]

With *Zara* refused a place at Drury Lane and Covent Garden, Hill prepared his own London production in the Music Room at York Buildings, Villiers Street for the spring of 1735. His actors were all ama-teurs, trained by Hill according to the principles being laid out at this time in *The Prompter*. His nephew, also called Aaron Hill, took the role of Osman, the Turkish sultan and lover of Zara. The preface to the play's earliest printed edition recalls how Osman's success, as that of a performer free from 'Custom, and obstinate Prejudice', would 'supply one Part of the Proof, that, to imitate Nature, we must proceed, upon natural Principles' (p. iii). Following the well-received amateur production, *Zara* transferred to Drury Lane in January 1736 and ran for an impressive fourteen nights.[7] Susannah Cibber, in her theatrical debut, took the title role and received extensive training from Hill, becoming one of many performers who received marked scripts from him. Thomas Davies records that the script given to Cibber contained particularly heavy annotations, with 'every accent and emphasis, every look, action and deportment proper to the character, in all its different situations'.[8] Whether because of Hill's drilling or because of her own natural talent (Hill writes of 'her Face, so finely dispos'd, for assuming and expressing, the PASSIONS'), Cibber shone as Zara and went on to perform the role throughout her career (p. iii). The same could not be said for Hill's nephew, who was driven from the Drury Lane stage by repeated booing on the opening night and thereafter replaced by the veteran William Mills.[9] Hill answered the apparent failure of his protégé with a number of *Prompter* articles defending his performance and arguing that the other actors had conspired against him. Rather than causing Hill to question his methods, such a turn of events only confirmed his vision of the deplorable state of English theatre in the 1730s. He concludes *Prompter* 129 by admitting that his recent experiences have led him 'to look upon the *Stage*, as a DEAD BODY, *without Hopes of Resurrection*'.[10]

At first, it seemed that *Zara* itself might be no more than a failed attempt to resuscitate English theatre, as the play fell out of favour in the 1740s. However, the work returned in 1751, one year after Hill's death. The play, now at Covent Garden but still with Susannah Cibber as Zara (for whose benefit it was staged), succeeded once again.[11] In 1754, David Garrick had his Drury Lane company follow Covent Garden's lead and organised a performance of the play as a benefit for the Irish actor Henry Mossop. Garrick played Lusignan, Zara's long-lost elderly father, while Cibber – having switched theatres – assumed the role of Zara once more. The performance drew a house of £225 and established *Zara* as a popular choice for benefit nights.[12] The work also became a staple of the Drury Lane repertoire, going on to appear in twenty-three consecutive seasons during Garrick's management (a tally beaten only by *Hamlet* and *The Suspicious Husband*).[13] At some point in this run, Garrick made a number of minor alterations to Hill's original text, largely in the form of cuts and small modifications in phrasing, which – as I shall show – reflect the elaboration and development of Hill's ideas in Garrick's practice. Fredrick Bergmann suggests early 1766 as the most likely period for these changes, timed to coincide with the retirement of Susannah Cibber at the end of the 1764–65 season and the visit of Jean-Jacques Rousseau to see the play at Drury Lane on 23 January 1766.[14] The modified text was edited and published by Francis Gentleman (another theatre professional indebted to Hill's thinking) in 1776 alongside *Venice Preserv'd, Jane Shore, The Siege of Damascus*, and *The Distressed Mother* as the first volume of *Bell's British Theatre*.[15]

Gentleman's edition contains the prologue written by Colley Cibber for the play's first performance at Drury Lane, along with the text of Hill's specially designed interval entertainments.[16] It does not, however, include Hill's preface to the play, which presented it as an '*Experiment*' (p. ii). Such an experiment had a clear aim: to test, in Hill's words, 'whether our Taste, for *true Tragedy*, is declin'd; or the true *Art*, of *Acting* it, is forgotten' (p. iii). The following analysis of *Zara* takes Hill's characterisation of his work as its starting point: it draws on the play's context to understand what attracted Hill to this '*true Tragedy*' and it demonstrates that this tragedy contains numerous features to instruct its performers (and their audiences) in the all-but-forgotten art of expressing the passions. As a theatrical experiment, this play offers us a window into eighteenth-century performance reception, practice, and theory. Hill's translation echoes both his own theoretical work and that of his forebears, while Garrick's later alteration of *Zara* is in line with the ways in which his achievements elaborated and refined an earlier understanding of drama crystallised by Hill. *Zara* thus emerges as both a successful eighteenth-century translated tragedy and a work whose textual and performance transmission bears the traces of over fifty years of thinking about theatre.

Enthusiastic Passions

Voltaire's *Zaïre* takes place in Jerusalem during the Crusades. It tells the story of a young Christian woman, raised as a Muslim and kept captive in the seraglio of the Turkish sultan Orosmane. Despite the religious tensions of her life, Zaïre falls in love with her captor. Meanwhile, another Christian prisoner, Nérestan, has obtained permission from the benevolent Orosmane to return to France and seek a ransom for all the sultan's captives except for their leader, Lusignan. Nérestan succeeds in his mission and returns with funds to free all the Christians, including Zaïre, who, deeply in love with Orosmane, has a difficult choice to make. Using her influence over Orosmane, Zaïre obtains the freedom of Lusignan, now a frail old man. Upon his release, Lusignan recognises a crucifix that Zaïre has worn about her person all her life and so identifies her as his daughter. Thanks to a distinctive scar, he also realises that Nérestan is his son. Her newly discovered family places heavy pressure on Zaïre to reject her upbringing and convert to Christianity, even if it will jeopardise her relationship with the sultan. She agrees, and – with her resolution hardened by news of Lusignan's death – promises to meet Nérestan late one night for a secret baptism. Yet Orosmane is suspicious and, knowing nothing of their true relationship, believes Nérestan and his future wife to be lovers. An intercepted letter appears to confirm this jealous hypothesis, and, on the night of the planned baptism, he captures Zaïre and murders her. Nérestan, detained by the sultan's troops, then appears and reveals Orosmane's error. Consumed with guilt, the sultan orders the release of the remaining French captives before committing suicide.

Gerrard offers a number of reasons for Hill's decision to bring this tale to the English stage in the 1730s, anglicising Orosmane as Osman and Zaïre as Zara.[17] The religious tensions of Voltaire's Middle Eastern setting were analogous to those that Hill himself had experienced when visiting his distant relative, William, sixth lord Paget, in Constantinople between 1700 and 1703. That journey and subsequent research had provided Hill with the material for his *Ottoman Empire* (1709) and a knowledge of Turkish culture and history that could well have exceeded Voltaire's. As well as personal familiarity with the subjects of *Zaïre*, the play also appealed to Hill's theatrical interests: Voltaire's choice of a Crusades setting and a heavy emphasis on pomp and spectacle dovetailed with Hill's own preferences, particularly visible in his production of Handel's *Rinaldo* in 1710. Furthermore, Hill's own articles in the *Weekly Miscellany*'s 'Foreign Literary' section praise Voltaire for achieving something that he and other English playwrights could only dream of, a situation in which French audiences 'support, and applaud, the gravest, the most moral, and sublimest, tho' plainest, Tragedy'.

Yet Hill's familiarity with Ottoman culture and *Zaïre*'s remarkable mix of the spectacular, the popular, the moral, and the tragic do not fully account for the play's appeal to him. A crucial element of this drama, for Hill, was also the way in which Voltaire's *Zaïre* exploits the passions of its characters. For this reason (in addition to all those cited by Gerrard), there were few plays better suited for Hill to use for an '*Experiment*' on English acting and appreciation of tragedy. The performance of *Zaïre*'s passions had made morally engaged tragedy popular in Paris: could not *Zara* do the same in London? Audiences in both cities would hear, in the drama's very first speech, Selima, Zara's lady-in-waiting, remark on her mistress's current emotional state and her own.

> SELIMA. It moves my Wonder, young, and beauteous *Zara*,
> Whence these new Sentiments inspire your Heart!
> Your Peace of Mind increases with your Charms;
> Tears, now, no longer shade your Eyes' soft Lustre:
> You meditate, no more, those happy Climes
> To which *Nerestan* will return to guide you: (p. 1)

This opening attention to the current and past emotional states of the play's heroine continues throughout the first scene. As Selima slowly extracts from Zara the information that she is now in love with Osman, Hill departs slightly from Voltaire to provide his main character with additional opportunities to mark the nuanced expression of her love. Whereas Voltaire has Selima interrupt her mistress once, Hill's confidante does so twice, dragging out the moment that reveals the identity of Zara's lover to produce what this translator called the 'very *Instant* of the *changing Passion*' in his *Prompter* articles.[18]

> Zar. [...] This mighty *Osman*!
> Sel. What of him?
> Zar. This Sultan!
> This Conqu'ror of the Christians! Loves —
> Sel. Whom?
> Zar. *Zara*! —
>   (p. 3)

This exchange, however, serves only as a prelude to the scene's most striking moment. Having learnt of the affection between Zara and Osman, Selima cannot help but mention what her mistress will not: the difference in the lovers' religions. At first wondering whether 'Heaven [. . .] will permit this Marriage?', a four-line speech from Selima articulates Zara's quandary with increasing insistence, finishing by asking the heroine 'Have you not forgot, you are of Christian blood?' (p. 3). These iterative lines, with less exclamation and greater brevity than Hill's French source, represent the final crescendo to the moment when Zara realises her predicament and bursts out in a mix of despair and anger.

> *Zar.* Ah me! What hast thou said? Why wou'dst thou, thus,
> Recall my wav'ring Thoughts? — How know I, what,
> Or whence I am? Heaven kept it, hid, in Darkness,
> Conceal'd me from myself, and from my Blood.   (p. 3)

It was to moments such as this, when a religious subject causes a flare of powerful emotion, that Hill referred in several *Prompter* pieces intended to defend his play's amateur staging at the York Buildings. The issue for 13 June 1735 chastises, for example, the managers of Drury Lane and Covent Garden for having refused the translated tragedy. Hill claims this was because both theatres, in a cowardly and ultimately self-harming move, had '*agreed*, in one ridiculously mistaken Opinion, "That *Zara*, tho' an Excellent tragedy to READ, wou'd hardly *please*, *upon the* STAGE, because Abundance of its warmest Strokes, turn'd more upon RELIGION than the Spirit of our Times *has Taste for*."'

> – Men who were *weak* enough to think in this *light* manner, ought to *blush*, at their *Correction*, in those Loudest, and most general, *Applauses*, which distinguish'd, in the Action, those *objected Passages*. – All *Poetry* depends on *Passion*. – The most powerful *Mover* of our Passions, is *Enthusiasm*: and the warmest, and most spirited Enthusiasm, is imprinted by *Religious Sentiments* – I quite exclude all Flatness of cold *Cant*, and *formal Habitudes* of Sanctity: to which *Few* Religious Strokes in *Zara* bear no manner of Resemblance; but draw their Warmth, from the *touch'd Heart*, describing strongly what it feels sincerely, and *compelling* the attentive Hearer, to *participate* in its Emotions.[19]

When Zara cries 'Ah me!' and answers Selima's interrogation with her own bewildered questions, the theatre audience enjoys a 'Religious Stroke': Zara's heart is powerfully '*touch'd*', and, as Hill makes clear here, so too should be that of every theatregoer. This paragraph also explains that a great deal of the power of this scene comes from the fact that it deals in religious sentiments: these sentiments, such as Zara's half-realised Christianity, cause enthusiasm, and enthusiasm moves the passions of part, performer, and public more powerfully than anything else.

Hill's argument here owes a great deal to the work of the critic John Dennis, who wrote to defend the stage against Jeremy Collier in the later 1690s and went on to publish a number of works on the religious sublime.[20] In Gerrard's analysis, Hill became 'largely responsible for [Dennis's] rehabilitation in the 1720s after the decade of neglect into which Scriblerian irony had plunged him'.[21] Dennis and Hill had supported one another throughout the early decades of the eighteenth century, until Dennis's death in 1734: Hill's play *The Fatal Vision* (1716) was dedicated to Dennis and Charles Gildon, a letter from Dennis to Hill in 1724 indicates that they were frequent companions, and Hill quotes frequently from Dennis's verse in *The Plain Dealer* (as well as employing Dennis as a sometime contributor to the periodical).[22] Such proximity manifests itself in the way Hill's writing about the theatre echoes Dennis's critical writings, both in the *Zara* puff and elsewhere. In *The Advancement and Reformation of Modern Poetry* (1701), for example, Dennis had defined poetry generally (so as to include the subcategories of the epic and dramatic) as 'an imitation of Nature by a pathetick and numerous Speech'.[23] The key word here is 'pathetick', for it is the passions that are 'the Characteristical mark of Poetry [...] for where-ever a Discourse is not pathetick, there it is Prosaick' (p. 24). A few pages on, Dennis then repeated this point even more forcibly, arguing that 'Passion is the chief thing in the Body of Poetry, as Spirit is in the Human Body. For without Spirit the body languishes, and the Soul is impotent' (pp. 26–27). Such an understanding of poetry as prose vivified by passion lies behind Hill's own description of the moribund stage in *Prompter* 129 (quoted above), his puff for his own play *Alzira* in *Prompter* 159 (which asserts that 'THAT which Life is to the human *Body, That,* is SENTIMENT to Dramatic *Poetry*'),[24] and his statement, when defending *Zara*, that 'All *Poetry* depends on *Passion*'.

It is, however, Dennis's theories about the place of religion that are most relevant to understanding *Zara*'s relationship to Hill's thinking about passion and dramatic poetry. When Hill states that 'The most powerful *Mover* of our Passions, is *Enthusiasm*: and the warmest, and most spirited Enthusiasm, is imprinted by *Religious Sentiments*', he is paraphrasing an argument that runs through a number of Dennis's critical works. The titular '*Advancement and Reformation*' proposed by Dennis in 1701, for example, is that modern poetry should follow the example of the ancients and turn to religious subjects. The reasons for this are clear. Although all poetry depends on passion, not all the passions are of the same kind. There are, according to Dennis, in fact two kinds of passion: 'ordinary' (or 'vulgar') and 'enthusiastic'. These two kinds can be distinguished on cognitive grounds, for Dennis, as Margaret Koehler notes, 'introduces the possibility that the sublime involves an exercise of voluntary attention'.[25] An ordinary passion is one 'whose cause is clearly comprehended by him who feels it' and enthusiastic passions occur 'when their cause is not clearly comprehended by him who feels them' (p. 26). Because the greatness of a passion is proportional to the idea that inspires it, Dennis holds that religious subjects are a major source of the greatest and most enthusiastic passions, 'For all which is great in Religion is most exalted and amazing, all that is joyful is transporting, all that is sad is dismal, and all that is terrible is astonishing' (p. 33). Ancient poetry bears this out, and modern poets would do well to incorporate more religious material, so as to achieve the same kind of powerful emotional response.[26]

When Hill writes, therefore, of the 'Religious Strokes' of *Zara* and of their ability to compel an audience to participate in the drama, he stakes an implicit claim for his translation to have achieved Dennis's aspirations for modern poetry. This claim, along with the other similarities between Hill's and Dennis's understanding of poetry, indicates that *Zara* itself should be susceptible to the same kind of analysis that Dennis performed on ancient poetry in order to show the critical role played by religion in the emotional patterns of the text. A particularly useful example of this analysis occurs when Dennis examines the following extract from Horace's third ode.

> Justum, & Tenacem propositi virum,
> Non civium ardour prava Jubentium,
> Non vultus instantis Tyranni
> Mente quatit solida; neque Auster
> Dux Inquieti Turbidus Adriae;
> Nec fulminantis magna Jovis manus,
> Se fractus Illabatur Orbis
> Impavidum ferient Ruinae.
>
> (pp. 34–35)

Dennis translates:

> *The Man, the brave Man, who is resolv'd upon a right and a firm principle, is sure never to have his solid Vertue shaken, neither by the Rage of the giddy Multitude, nor by the Frowns of an insulting Tyrant, nor by the Fury of the*

Roaring South, that Turbulent Ruler of the Tempestuous Adria; no, nor by the
Red Right Hand of Thundring Jove: Nay, should the World's disjointed Frame
come rushing down with a Dismal Sound upon him, its Ruins might Crush, but
they could never Shake him. (p. 35)

Dennis's analysis of this poem focuses on its deployment of the passions.
He begins by inviting the reader to observe Horace's 'admirable gradation
of Thought' as he 'rises from something that is Terrible, to something that
is more Terrible, till he comes to something Astonishing and Amazing'
(p. 36). This tripartite structure reveals two things. First, in a reiteration of
Dennis's earlier arguments about the centrality of passion to poetry, he argues
that the way in which 'the Spirit of the Poet rises with his Thoughts [. . .] is
a sure sign, that one is nothing but the passions that attend on the other'; in
other words, as grander thoughts are expressed, so the emotional temperature
of the moment rises (p. 37). Second, Dennis identifies a step change within this
structure: while parts one and two concern thoughts of the 'Terrible' and their
attendant passions, the third section astonishes and amazes. This transition
occurs thanks to a change in subject, with the reference to the divine in 'Nec
fulminantis magna Jovis manus'. For Dennis, this line unlocks Horace's final
global vision of 'the World's disjointed Frame'. As Dennis puts it, 'the Poet
could not carry his Enthusiasm higher after the second thought, without
having recourse to Religion' (p. 37).

In this example, Dennis's approach requires a close attention to the
emotional charge of every line's 'thought'. When Horace is read through
such a lens, this ode's crescendo becomes clear, as well as the way in which
such a build-up climaxes in a shift from terror to amazement, simultaneous
with a broadening of the speaker's vision. That transition is enabled
through the use of religion, and so validates Dennis's broader argument
about the ancients' use of the spiritual to supercharge their poetry. This
analysis of Horace shares much with Dennis's critical practice elsewhere in
his writing, which always looks closely at the dynamic gradations of
thought that run through verse and trigger passions as they go. He
presents, for example, Milton's description of Lucifer (in book one of
Paradise Lost) as 'stately and majestic till the last, and then it grows
vehement, because the Idea which causes it ['his Face | Deep Scars of
Thunder had intrench'd'], is not only great, but very terrible' (p. 38). When
studying Sophocles's *Oedipus Rex*, Dennis marvels at how 'instrumental
the Poetical Art is in leading [the audience] from Surprize to Surprize, from
Compassion to Terror, and from Terror to Compassion again' ('Epistle
Dedicatory'). Elsewhere, Virgil's comparison of the fall of Troy to the

hewing of a mountain ash (in *Aeneid* book two) constitutes a moment in which 'the Poet raises his Spirit, as soon as he sets his Image in Motion, and brings in Terror to his Relief' (p. 40).

In addition to demonstrating the pivotal role played by spiritual material in the sudden transformation of emotion, Dennis's tracing of the 'gradation of Thought in each of his examples and the emotions they inspire also reveals the iconic and dynamic qualities of these passages.[27] As Sara Landreth has shown, Dennis's analysis of his examples in *Advancement* and *Grounds* establishes a critical fascination with what he calls an 'Image in Motion', and especially the way in which that motion lends to an image a greater force: Virgil's description of Troy's destruction is thus the case of an instant where 'The Poet hereby setting his Image in motion, had set it before his Eyes, and so made it the more terrible'.[28] Landreth notes here the echo of Aristotle's notion of 'bringing-before-the-eyes', later theorised by Quintilian as *enargia*, but she also underscores how Dennis's essays make use of the work of moderns like Isaac Newton in an effort to understand why a moving object is more easily visualised than a static one.

Dennis's approach to poetry, with its sensitive exploration of the emotional charge that poet and reader must feel in every line and its attentiveness to the motion of an image, shares much with Hill's writing on acting. The 'Image in Motion' that Virgil exemplifies is very similar to the 'active *Image*' Hill hoped that aspiring performers would use to fire their imaginations.[29] As for the gradations Dennis repeatedly discerns, Hill often operates in a similar fashion when discussing a performer's transitions. In the dedication of *The Fatal Vision* to Dennis and Gildon in 1716, Hill had praised Booth as the sole actor able to express passions 'in their Variations and Degrees' thanks to his use of 'thrilling *Breaks*, and *Changes* of the *Voice*'.[30] In other words, Booth's transitions made the gradations of his script visible, and so produced the same kind of rhetorical effect – a striking moving image, a compact of iconic and dynamic qualities that Dennis praised in the writing of Milton, Virgil, and Sophocles.

And nowhere are such images, for Dennis, more forceful than when religion enters the equation and produces an unprecedented gradation of thought. We have already seen how Selima's mention of Zara's Christian heritage provokes a new outburst of anger and despair, more forceful than anything prior to it in the play's opening scene. Yet this outburst is in fact but one step in a larger sequence of thought and passion. Zara's outburst (like Horace's mention of Jove) is the moment of dramatic gear change, a powerful transition, but this, after a brief speech from Selima, then opens up a new level of poetic vision and emotion.

Zar. Can my fond Heart, on such a feeble Proof,
Embrace a Faith, abhorr'd by him I love?
I see, too plainly, Custom forms us All;
Our Thoughts, our Morals, our most fix'd Belief,
Are Consequences of our Place of Birth:
Born beyond *Ganges*, I had been a Pagan;
In *France*, a Christian; —— I am, here, a *Saracen*:
'Tis but *Instruction* all! Our Parents Hand
Writes on our Heart the first faint Characters,
Which Time, re-tracing, deepens into Strength,
That nothing can efface, but Death, or Heaven! ——

(p. 4)

Sweeping from the cradle to the grave, from Asia to Europe, and from the personal to the political, the grandeur of this speech is undeniable. What the application of Dennis's methods to this scene allows us to spot is the way that such a powerful, emotional vision arrives following the appeal to religious material. This is another one of the 'Religious Strokes' that Hill referred to when he defended the play, and a moment too where Voltaire would seem to channel what Dennis considered the greatest strength of the ancients.

Yet Hill has done more than put a Dennisean passage of Voltaire's play into English. His translation also helps to bring out the gradation of thought with greater clarity than in the French original. In part, this is done by the cutting of a pair of lines ('La coutume, la loi plia mes premiers ans | A la religion des heureux Musulmans') so that Zara reaches her vision of 'Custom' immediately after the restatement of her 'Faith, abhorr'd by him I love'.[31] At the same time, Hill also seems to depart from his source in more subtle ways, which are not always captured by modern editions.[32] Just as in Hill's dramatic quotations (in *The Prompter* and *The Essay on Acting*), so too does this speech rely on dashes, punctuation, and italics to mark out the contours of the speech and bring about, as Anne Toner has argued with regard to signs of ellipses in particular, 'the submission of the text to external definition'.[33] The text above transcribes the earliest printed edition of *Zara* (1736), which, while lacking Hill's signature use of small capitals, nevertheless has a distinctively Hillian use of italics, punctuation, and dashes to mark out the patterns of the passions, perhaps reflecting Hill's own marking of the text. Meditating on her newfound happiness earlier in this scene, Zara's lines in this edition contain, for example, italics for emphasis and a dash at the point she comes perilously close to confronting the problem of religion: 'His whole Regard is fix'd on *Me* alone: | He offers Marriage —— and its Rites' (p. 3).

As for this climactic speech, the long dash after 'Christian' marks out a complex transitional pause, where anger and despair fight for supremacy and the audience could eagerly anticipate the heroine's next move. In the following line, the italics of "'Tis but *Instruction* all!' (absent from nineteenth-century and modern editions of the play) indicate the key emphasis of Zara's entire discourse.[34] Later on, the dash that follows 'Death, or Heaven! –' (also absent in later editions) leaves room for another pause, a time for the performer to prepare, in the next line, to address Selima in a tone of wearied envy, and a time too, as Hill wrote in a letter to James Quin, for the central idea of the speech 'to descend perfect, from the *ear* to the *understanding*' (1, p. 219).

Voltaire's *Zaïre* tells the tragic tale of a woman caught between love and religion. Its crusades setting, its success with Parisian audiences, and its spectacular stagecraft all, as Gerrard shows, appealed to Hill. Yet the work also had a theoretical significance. At the heart of *Zaïre*'s spectacular tragedy lie the passions, and it is the work's emphasis – from its opening lines – on the emotional state of its characters that help it to serve as an '*Experiment*' to test the calibre of English acting and English taste. When defending his translation, Hill focused on the passions of the play, arguing that it contains 'Religious Strokes' capable of producing not just any emotions but powerful, 'enthusiastic' passions in particular. This line of argument echoes the writings of Hill's friend and collaborator, John Dennis, an echo which implies that Voltaire's play may also have appealed to its English translator as a proof of Dennis's belief that modern poetry should imitate the ancients' use of religious subjects to increase its emotional force. If we apply Dennis's own techniques for the study of poetry (techniques which share many similarities with Hill's advice to actors), then the patterns of passions in the opening sequence of *Zara* become clear. The dialogue between the heroine and her confidante explodes with the explicit mention of religion, an outburst which then clears the way for Zara's grand vision of the power of '*Instruction*' in our lives. While such a pattern is present in Voltaire's text, Hill's English translation reinforces it. Along with some cuts, dashes and italics (perhaps the printed vestiges of a marked script) indicate the positions of pauses and transitions, emphases that would allow the work's enthusiastic passions to capture audience attention, testing, in the process, the English theatregoer's capacity to receive tragic instruction from a work which Hill claimed to be ceaselessly '*compelling* the attentive Hearer, to *participate* in its Emotions'.

Dramatic Passions

Zara's realisation that only 'Death, or Heaven!' can erase '*Instruction*' does not end her speech, although it does represent a climax in it. Her next lines turn reflective, comparing Selima's fortune at having only been 'made a Pris'ner in this Place, | Till, after Reason, borrowing Force from Years, | Had lent its Lustre, to enlighten Faith' to her own unlucky situation as one 'who in my Cradle was their Slave' (p. 4). While Selima has thus always been a Christian, Zara suffers, particularly as her Muslim upbringing does not prevent her feeling 'a kind of awful Fear!' every time she catches sight of the crucifix about her neck (p. 4). She concludes with praise for 'Christian Laws' and the observation that 'Christians are happy; and, 'tis just to love 'em' (p. 4). Seeing her chance, Selima offers another variation on the question she has asked throughout this scene and begs Zara to answer: 'Why will you join your Hand, with this proud *Osman*'s? Who owes his Triumphs to the Christians Ruin!' (p. 4). Whereas before, this line of interrogation had led her mistress to rhapsodise on religion rather than romance, it now leads Zara back the other way.

> *Zar.* Ah! —— *Who* cou'd *slight* the Offer of his Heart?
> Nay, —— for I mean to tell thee all my Weakness;
> Perhaps I had, ere now, profess'd *thy* Faith,
> But *Osman* lov'd me —— and I've lost it All: ——
> I think on none but *Osman* —— my pleas'd Heart,
> Fill'd with the Blessing, to be lov'd by *him*,
> Wants Room for other Happiness : ——   (p. 4)

As Zara speaks and pauses, pauses and speaks, the strength of her love grows all the more apparent. It is, however, hard to account for such a development with an appeal to Dennis's categories of vulgar and enthusiastic passions. If the former come from ideas whose causes are known and the latter from ideas whose causes are not, what is Zara feeling? Her passions, clearly inspired by thoughts of Osman (whose name and pronouns echo through this speech) might be vulgar, were it not for the obscurely articulated connection between such feelings and her religion, the 'other happiness' that acts as a foil to her love of the sultan. Partly explicable, partly not, Zara's pauses and emphases ('*lov'd*', 'by *him*', and so on) require more than Dennis's distinction between vulgar and enthusiastic passions. This is because Dennis, writing of all kinds of poetry, operates mostly at the level of kinds of passion and not that of specific passions. To demarcate different kinds of passion, he concentrates on their inspiration: on the idea and not on the specific feelings that such an idea could – as it animates the Cartesian machinery of man – awaken in the character or performer. He mentions, of course, the emotions present in passages of Virgil or Milton, but his emphasis clearly lies upon the source of such emotion (the divine or the ordinary) rather than on the emotion itself.

This is an area, therefore, where Hill goes beyond his friend. Hill, when writing specifically for the theatre, developed a way of talking about the instantiation of specific passions. Rather than deal in enthusiastic or vulgar passion (where the emphasis falls on the idea that inspires the emotion), Hill writes in his *Essay on Acting* of the 'dramatic passions', passions which 'can be distinguished by their outward marks': 'Joy, Grief, Fear, Anger, Pity, Scorn, Hatred, Jealousy, Wonder, and Love' (IV, p. 357). While his *Essay* gives many examples of each '*strong idea*' that can cause such passions, Hill is thus also interested (far more than Dennis) in how such passions play out, their proximity to one another, and even their combination.

It is Hill's own theory, therefore, that offers the sharpest insight into those lines that follow Zara's speech against '*Instruction*'. In the final chapter of his *Essay*, Hill recognises that love, as well as being in its own right a specific dramatic passion, discernible by 'outward marks', is also capable of coexistence with all the other passions discussed in the work so far.

> And thus we are come, at last, to a Passion, the true name whereof might be *Legion*; for it includes all the other, in all their degrees and varieties. It has therefore been postpon'd, and kept to bring up the rear; tho', from the weight and extent of its influence, it ought to have taken place in the front of the number. (IV, p. 388)

Zara's speech demonstrates the phenomenon described here. Love runs through all her lines, although at every turn it seems to include another emotion: '*Who* could *slight* the Offer of his heart?' blends love and scorn; 'Perhaps I had, ere now, profess'd *thy* Faith, | But *Osman lov'd* me' incorporates wonder; the following thought, separated by dashes – 'and I've lost it All' – has both grief and love; and the final lines reverberate with joy and love. Love is the governing passion here, including all others.

Yet this raises a new difficulty. Love (in combination with much else) is what is felt by Zara at this time, but is it not also what Hill would call the '*strong idea*' of this speech too? This is a speech that is as much about love as it is an expression of it. Dennis is able to keep a strict division between idea and emotion: spiritual thoughts result in enthusiastic passions. Hill blurs this line: love can be the subject of a speech and the passion at its heart. Such a difference between Hill and Dennis comes, in part, from the fact

that Hill is writing with performance in mind: by speaking of an emotion –
as well as manifesting its physical symptoms – an eighteenth-century actor
is able to communicate the state of their character twice over, with a clarity
often necessary in the crowded theatres of the time. As well as being helpful
to the audience, such speeches, which descant on their own emotion, are
also helpful to the actor. Along with Hill's italics and dashes, his repetition
of love and its cognates in this speech by Zara clearly signals to the
performer what both the idea and the passion of this moment are, with
all other ideas (such as her faith) and passions (her grief, joy, and wonder)
bound within it.

When writing on love in the *Essay*, Hill gives ten examples (one for each
dramatic passion) of this passion's ability to include all others. Almost all of
these passages are drawn from Hill's own plays, and many of them deal with
both what is felt and what is at stake: love and wonder are, for example, both
the passions and the subjects of the extract Hill takes from *Zara* for this
section. Desperate to be baptised a Christian before her marriage to the
sultan, Zara tells Osman to delay their wedding while refusing to explain her
reasons for it. She exits '*disorder'd*', torn between her love and her faith,
leaving Osman to express his wonder at this turn of events (p. 26).

An *Example of* WONDER, in Love.

I STAND *immoveable* – like senseless *marble!*
Horror had frozen my suspended tongue:
And an astonish'd silence robb'd my will
Of power, to tell her – that she shock'd my soul.
Spoke she to *me!* – sure, I misunderstood her!
Cou'd it be *me*, she left! – what have I seen!
Orasmin! what a change is here! she's gone!
And I permitted it – I know not *how*.

(IV, p. 399)

I transcribe here the version of this speech printed in Hill's *Essay*, which
carries, further to the capitals with which Hill starts all his examples,
additional italics (on '*marble*', '*immoveable*', and '*how*') to those printed
in the 1736 text of the play.[35] The typographical similarities between the
two printings support the idea that the italics and dashes of the 1736 edition
are Hill's, but the differences here are also a warning that, even if the
markings in the published script came from his hand, they are subject to
other influences and have either varied over time or have not been rendered
fully, so that a crucial part of a translation so deeply concerned with
directing performance remains elusive. Indeed, such dashes, known to

printers as a slash or 'scratch' comma when used to indicate a pause, can be found in printings of early eighteenth-century drama too.[36] As for Hill's choice of words, there is already much to say, for Osman's speech is both a reflection on love and wonder and an expression of those feelings, both instruction (to audience and actor) and spectacle.

In these lines, the character describes himself, hinting at the position he now holds (he stands '*immoveable*') while, at the same time, recalling the silence he has just broken. Osman's lines, in other words, draw our attention to the physical effects of his passion. They are also peppered with a number of words that help to cue the actor (and reader or theatre-goer) sensitive to eighteenth-century categorisation of emotion: Osman speaks of his 'astonish'd silence', of his 'shock'd [...] soul'. All of these terms, none of which appear in Voltaire's French, help to categorise the sultan's feelings within a Cartesian framework.[37] Indeed, Descartes himself had written of how, in shock, the body freezes, as the animal spirits pool in the eyes and are 'so much preoccupied in preserving this impression that there are none which pass from thence into the muscles [...] and this causes the whole body to remain immobile as a statue' – or, as Hill's Osman puts it in another departure from his French source, '*immoveable* – like senseless *marble*'.[38]

Osman's stunned response to Zara's abrupt departure is far from the only example of a speech where the character describes the very passion (or passions) they are feeling, often in programmatic Cartesian terms. The very first line of the play, Selima's announcement that Zara's new behaviour 'moves my Wonder', does this. Towards the end of the first act, Osman descants on 'Jealousy', repeating the word over and over as this passion mixes with the fact that he is one who must, to use his own self-descriptive words, 'love with Warmth' (p. 9). Right at the end of the tragedy, when Osman believes his worse suspicions confirmed, he speaks of how 'ev'ry mortal Aspect moves my Hate' (p. 42). In each of these cases Hill's translation nominalises either adjectives (*jaloux* into 'jealousy') or verbs (*je hais* into 'my Hate'), as though he were bringing the dominant passion of each moment more clearly into view.[39]

Hill's nephew, who performed the part of Osman with no prior experience, could have been guided by these passages, or at least helped by his uncle to read their cues to him. But this phenomenon is not restricted to the sultan's speeches. Zara, in one of her interviews with Osman, cries 'O Grief! Oh, Love!', offering an index of her feelings to the performer and the audience (p. 24). Later in the play, and moments before her death, Zara crosses the stage and speaks of walking 'in Terror' (p. 44). These passages and many others in the drama bear a distinct resemblance to those extracts Hill chose to illustrate his *Essay on Acting*, which frequently name the very passion Hill uses them to demonstrate, such as Torrismond's joyful speech, from John Dryden's *Spanish Friar* (1681), with its concluding 'And thou, my heart! Make room — to entertain the flowing joy!' (IV, p. 359). More generally, such lexical choices chime with a style of eighteenth-century performance that Dene Barnett has described as acting 'by the word rather than by the paragraph or by the pervading emotion', with the caveat that the 'pervading emotion' of the scene should be read as a product of its dynamic and iconic transitions between those emotions named by individual words.[40]

The way in which *Zara*'s characters speak of what they feel allows the play to operate as both compelling performance and instruction. Each function was as important as the other, for both were needed to make the play an '*Experiment*' in the capacities of the English stage: both audience and actors, Hill feared, had sunk too low to identify tragic passion and be moved and improved by it. They needed guidance, and such speeches offered both a helpful frame and moving content. Other sections of *Zara* take a different approach, having a speaker give – without much feeling of their own – a description of a passion. This is the case for Melidor, a slave sent by Osman to observe Zara reading a letter from her brother Nerestan (whom Osman believes to be his rival). Melidor reports back to his master with a description of the kind of spectacular performance of the passions that Hill frequently dreams of.

> *Mel.* She blush'd, and trembled, and grew pale, and paus'd;
> Then blush'd, and read it; and again grew pale;
> And wept, and smil'd, and doubted, and resolv'd:
> For, after all this Race of vary'd Passions,
> When she had sent me out, and call'd me back,
> Tell him, (she cry'd) who has intrusted thee,
> That *Zara*'s Heart is fix'd, nor shrinks at Danger;
> And, that my faithful Friend will, at the Hour,
> Expect, and introduce him to his Wish.   (p. 41)

This detailed speech describes a set of transitions that the audience has already seen, and therefore operates both as a way of shaping theatregoers' memory (and analytic skills) and as a guide to the actress playing Zara. Melidor's description of the play of passions here is a version of a kind of speech that Hill had praised extensively in his *Essay*: those which contain instructions for the performance of the passions. Shakespeare, in Hill's view, offered an excellent example in *Henry V* when the king urges his troops 'Once more unto the breach' at Harfleur. Henry's advice to 'stiffen the sinews' and 'set the teeth and stretch the nostril wide' was so precise (and useful for performers) that Hill included it in the *Essay* with the comment that 'It were impossible to draw [...] an instruction more compleat and clear, for expressing it!' (IV, pp. 369–70). It seems, in *Zara*, that Hill wanted to provide similar material. Melidor's retrospective description of Zara is one such case, but so is Osman's astonished speech about his own astonishment.

Angelina Del Balzo, in one of only a handful of recent critical studies of *Zara*, analyses Melidor's speech as part of a number of 'metatheatrical' passages in the play that increase the potential for 'sympathetic exchange' between stage and audience.[41] To strengthen her argument, Del Balzo adopts David Hume's theories about the pleasure to be drawn from tragedy when an audience's sympathy is tied to their awareness of the double presence of both actor and character.[42] So-called metatheatrical passages, such as Melidor's replay of an earlier scene or Osman's descriptions of himself, make performer and part simultaneously visible, enriching the theatrical experience. Further evidence for Del Balzo's argument occurs in Hill's use of the word 'start' in his translation of Voltaire. Without precedent in the French, Hill has his heroine use the term twice, in its theatrical sense of an abrupt transition between emotions. In a passage from the play's first scene, already examined above, Zara asks Selima if she thinks that her outburst of love and righteous anger are 'Starts of Passion' (p. 5).[43] In the second act, when Zara appears to tell Nerestan that she has obtained Lusignan's freedom, she begins her speech with the words 'Start not, my worthy Friend!' (p. 12).[44] Both these examples fit Del Balzo's hypothesis. Zara's use of 'start' achieves several things: it makes the audience aware of the performance as performance, but it also uses that awareness to insist on the emotional force of such moments. Zara denies that her fulminations were mere 'starts', while her order to Nerestan recognises that her revelations about Lusignan are worthy of a shocked response.

Del Balzo's argument is thus capable of extension into other aspects of Hill's translation and provides us with an important reminder that what we nowadays call metatheatricality was, in the eighteenth century, good theatrical practice, a way of activating audience sympathies. However, by relying on Hume and other writers on sympathy (such as Henry Home, Lord Kames) who wrote after *Zara*'s first performances, Del Balzo does not capture the extent to which Hill's translation integrates with Hill's own theories for performance, instruction, and the improvement of the theatre. More than a work rich in what Dennis called 'enthusiastic' passions, Hill's *Zara* is also an exposition of Hill's 'dramatic' passions. These passions are not just the product of particularly powerful ideas but ideas in their own right: characters speak of what they and those around them feel, and the line between the idea that inspires the passion and the passion itself, so firm in Dennis, weakens. Furthermore, Hill's dramatic passions are present as instruction as well as entertainment. Love is the supreme example of this, an idea and an emotion capable of including all others, and one which Hill's English – through the nominalisation of French adjectives and verbs, or through the use of typography – took care to trace. Indeed, Hill's efforts to map the crucial gradations of thought within all his translated speeches, and thus inscribe his ideas about theatrical practice into his translation, allowed inexperienced performers to find 'those thrilling *Breaks*, and *Changes* of the *Voice*' that Booth once found, so that those who saw *Zara* could then witness the outward marks of many passions and trace on stage their performance to the very instant. Such opportunities made the play perfect for an '*Experiment*' on taste and acting in England in the 1730s.

Garrick's Passions

In January 1779, Thomas Rackett paid a visit to David Garrick. The actor had less than a week to live and was sinking fast.

> But oh! how changed! from that vivacity and sprightliness which used to accompany every thing he said, and every thing he did! His countenance was sallow and wan, his movement slow and solemn. He was wrapped in a rich night-gown, like that which he always wore in Lusignan, the venerable old king of Jerusalem; he presented himself to the imagination of his friend as if he was just ready to act that character. He sat down; and during the space of an hour, the time he remained in the room, he did not utter a word. He rose and withdrew to his chamber.[45]

Rackett's account of his visit, published in Thomas Davies's *Memoirs of the Life of David Garrick*, strikes a melancholy note: it remembers the actor-manager's 'vivacity and sprightliness', the qualities that made him, more than any other performer, the greatest exemplar and elaborator of a Hillian style of pause and transition; yet it also regrets how such qualities are no longer present, the mobile face now 'sallow and wan' and every gesture 'slow and solemn'. Rackett's regret and remembrance meet in a revealing detail: that Garrick appeared that winter's day 'in a rich night-gown, like that which he always wore in Lusignan, the venerable king of Jerusalem'. On one level, this is another recognition of Garrick's status, still performing a 'venerable king' even when confined to his apartments. On another, though, this reference has more sinister implications. Lusignan only appears in a single scene of

Zara and dies off-stage shortly afterwards. It is the part of a man at the very end of life. Readers of this section of the *Memoirs* may even have known the story of the very first Lusignan on the English stage, William Bond, who, in declining health, performed the role on *Zara*'s opening night to raise money for his family. Bond died the next day, leaving Hill's nephew to double Lusignan and Osman, performing the contrasting parts, in the words of his uncle at least, with 'elevated Grace of *Nature, Attitude, Force, Glitter* and *Perfection*'.[46]

Even if the readers of Davies's biography did not know the stage history of *Zara*, they would certainly have been familiar with Lusignan. Garrick himself had made the part his own, acting it in almost every season of his theatrical career from 1754 onwards. In addition to this, Garrick had also modified the text of the play, so that Rackett's audience would have been better acquainted with the Garrick-Hill version of *Zara* than that composed in the 1730s. As Bergmann has shown, most of Garrick's alterations were minor. He trimmed around three hundred lines from across the play, largely in the interest of raising the pace of the performance.[47] He also modified a few passages here and there, either to bring the English version closer to the French or, in a departure from both Voltaire and Hill, to harden Osman's character, who no longer, for example, claimed to love Lusignan (his captive enemy) 'for his virtue and his blood'.[48] Perhaps unsurprisingly, the majority of Garrick's alterations occur in the second act of *Zara*, during which he would take the stage as Lusignan.

Zara herself announces to Nerestan and Chatillon (another captive French soldier) the pardon she has obtained for Lusignan, a pardon which means that the old soldier will soon appear before them. I quote now from a modern edition of Garrick's adaptation of Hill's translation.

> ZARA. To bring him freedom you behold me here;
> You will in this moment meet his eyes in joy.
> CHATILLON. Shall I then live to bless that happy hour?
> NERESTAN. Can Christians owe so dear a gift to Zara?
> ZARA. Hopeless I gathered courage to entreat
> The sultan for his liberty – amazed
> So soon to gain the happiness I wished!
> See where they bring the good old chief, grown dim
> With age, by pain and sorrows hastened on!
> CHATILLON. How is my heart dissolved with sudden joy!
> *Enter* Lusignan, *led in by two guards.*   (VI, pp. 161–62)

As elsewhere in Hill's translation, these lines (untouched by Garrick) contain a quantity of emotional direction for the actors. Whereas Voltaire has no character mention their 'joy', the word appears twice in this brief exchange, alongside other proximate terms like 'dear' and 'happy'.[49] A single passion of joy seems to animate all three figures, leavened only with an undercurrent of amazement. In Hill's original text, this undercurrent grew as Zara's mention of how 'amazed' she was at Osman's pardoning of Lusignan was echoed by Chatillon at the moment of his former leader's entrance, with a cry of 'Amazement! — Whence this Greatness, in an Infidel!' (p. 13). Chatillon's line, along with six more from Zara (all of which also depart from Voltaire), are omitted by Garrick. As Bergmann argues, this increases the tempo of the play and brings Garrick's character to the fore with greater efficiency, yet it also – from the point of view of the passions – does one other thing. If Hill's preparation for Lusignan's arrival was a mix of joy transforming into amazement at Osman's clemency, Garrick keeps the emotions of the on-stage audience of Zara, Nerestan, and Chatillon much more uniform: they are simply joyful. This means that there were no transitions to compete with Garrick's own complex rendition of Lusignan's passions, and so instead helps form the theatrical cynosure so characteristic of his acting style.

Framed by two guards, Lusignan begins by speaking the following lines.

> LUSIGNAN. Where am I? From the dungeon's depth what voice
> Has called me to revisit long-lost day?
> Am I with Christians? – I am weak – forgive me,
> And guide my trembling steps. I'm full of years;
> My miseries have worn me more than age.
> Am I in truth at liberty? (*Seating himself*)   (VI, p. 162)

Lusignan's questions have no specific addressee and work instead to draw all attention, from the stage and from the auditorium, to him. Hill's original speech began by elaborating on Voltaire's 'Du séjour du trépas quelle voix me rappelle?' with 'What forgiving Angel's Voice | Has call'd me, to visit long-lost Day?' (p. 19).[50] Garrick brings the English closer to the French, which has the additional effect of minimising the risk of redirecting the gaze of the audience to Zara (a potential candidate for Lusignan's 'Angel'), especially when, in Hill, Lusignan first speaks of 'forgiving', then asks his listeners to 'forgive me'. Thus, while Lusignan's speech recognises that he is not alone, its lack of direction means that it engrosses rather than re-directs attention. All eyes and ears would thus catch the pause (marked here with a dash) as, after three questions, Lusignan's energy fails him and Garrick can execute a transition from wonder to sadness and regret. 'I am weak', the old man declares, and then another pause, in which the tableau of a frail old man can leave its impression on an audience, before this figure reaches out and asks for help to guide his 'trembling' steps.[51]

For all his weakness, Lusignan (which is to say Garrick as Lusignan) dominates the script of this moment. It is he who signals an elevation of tone as he speaks of 'years' and 'miseries' ('*misery*' in Hill (p. 14)) and 'liberty', and it is he whose voice is heard most throughout the remainder of the act as he discovers the true identity of Nerestan and Zara, his long-lost children. This revelation breaks through what remains (despite Garrick's best efforts) a considerable quantity of exposition to trigger a series of emotional outbursts, all of which, again, focus on the old man. When Zara unwittingly mentions that she has owned the crucifix about her neck since birth, the dash that truncates the line gives Lusignan time to express shock, an emotion Zara then underlines when she speaks of how 'You seem surprized!' and, resigning her role as story-teller, asks 'Why should this move you?' (vi, p. 165). Zara is not totally eclipsed here – she has a pair of lines announcing that 'Rising thoughts | And hopes and fears o'erwhelm me' – but she is far from the main focus of the scene (vi, p. 165). Indeed, Lusignan seems almost to talk to himself as his excitement and wonder builds: 'Oh failing eyes, deceive ye not my hope? | Can this be possible? | Yes, yes – 'tis she!' (vi, p. 165).

Lusignan's other newfound child, Nerestan, has even less of a role here than Zara. He bares his chest to show a distinctive scar, but the line on which he does so – 'Sir, the mark is there!' – actually serves as a cue for an emotional tableau, without precedent in Voltaire, that again enshrines Lusignan, repeating the triangular form of his entry flanked by Osman's guards.

> LUSIGNAN. Nerestan, hast thou on thy breast a scar
> Which, ere Caesarea fell, from a fierce hand,
> Surprizing us by night, my child received?
> NERESTAN. Blessed hand! I bear it. – Sire, the mark is there!
> LUSIGNAN. Merciful heaven!
> NERESTAN. (*kneeling*). Oh sir! – Oh Zara, kneel. –
> ZARA. (*kneeling*). My father! – Oh! –
> LUSIGNAN. Oh! My lost children!
> BOTH. Oh!   (vi, p. 165)

This exchange is hard to read in print. On the stage, the image is crystal clear, an acme of familial love that passes beyond verbalisation. Yet, in what must have been a thrilling twist, the scene does not end here. Instead, as Dennis had advised, it turns to religion to reach new heights as Lusignan attempts to persuade his newfound daughter to convert to Christianity. While Zara's earlier speech on '*Instruction*' had already used a similar thematic shift, the fact that that speech turned on an enlightened questioning of what constitutes faith, rather than an evocation of the Christian divine, means that it is Lusignan's words in this moment that most fully correspond to Dennis's ideas and their echoes in Hill. Indeed, having established the importance of religious ideas for the generation of enthusiastic passion, Dennis himself had drawn a distinction between Greek and Roman religion on one hand and Christianity on the other, a distinction Hill later summarised in *The Plain Dealer*.[52] The former is limited by pretending 'either to set up our passions above our Reason, or our Reason above our Passions', while Christianity 'exalts our Reason by exalting the Passions' and so achieves the status of a 'True Religion' (p. 159). Such 'True Religion' (a phrase in which one hears Hill's concern for 'true *Tragedy*') is a better foundation for the best possible poetry, which, like such a creed, also seeks to please 'the Reason and Passions and Sences [*sic*] [. . .] at the same time superlatively' (p. 169). One has only, argues Dennis, to compare Homer, Virgil, and the Psalmist to see that the last of these surpasses the other two when it comes to describing the power of God, or, alternatively, to compare Milton's account of the Creation to similar passages in Ovid and Virgil to realise his superiority. That superiority comes not from 'the continual harmony' of Milton's verses nor from 'the constant Beauty of his expression' but 'purely by the advantage of his religion' (p. 201).

When Zara thus admits that 'Osman's laws | Were mine – and Osman is not Christian', her father rises up and, in a whirlwind of passion, carries his daughter to repentance with a speech that relies on what Dennis called 'True Religion' for a series of transitions that Hill hoped would test an audience's taste for 'true *Tragedy*' (VI, p. 167). In Garrick's theatre, this speech is retained with only minimal changes. The actor-manager reintroduces Voltaire's decision to have Lusignan begin with a description of his daughter's words as 'thunder bursting on my head' (VI, p. 168). After this, Lusignan recounts how he has 'fought the Christian's cause' for sixty years and spent 'Twenty a Captive in a Dungeon's depth'. Throughout his long imprisonment, Lusignan has been praying; 'never for myself' but 'All for my children' have his 'Tears sought Heaven', and it is with this word, soon repeated, that his speech begins to take flight, rising from the domestic to the divine (VI, p. 168).

> I have a daughter gained, and Heav'n an enemy.
> Oh my misguided daughter – lose not thy faith,
> Reclaim thy birthright – think upon the blood
> Of twenty Christian kings that fills thy veins;
> 'Tis heroes' blood – the blood of saints and martyrs!
> What would thy mother feel to see thee thus!
> She and thy murdered brothers! – Think, they call thee!
> Think that thou seest 'em stretch their bloody arms
> And weep to win thee from their murd'rer's bosom.
> Ev'n in the place where thou betray'st thy God,
> He died, my child, to save thee. –
> Thou tremblest – Oh! Admit me to thy soul;
> Kill not thy aged, thy afflicted father;
> Shame not thy mother – nor renounce thy God. –
> 'Tis past! Repentance dawns in thy sweet eyes;
> I see bright truth descending to thy heart,
> And now my long-lost child is found forever.
>
> (VI, pp. 167–68)[53]

As well as its opening line, Garrick also modifies this speech by replacing a passage in which Lusignan appeared to weaken and recognise his own responsibility for Zara's Islamic upbringing ('thy father's prison | Deprived thee of thy faith') with a much more forceful injunction for his 'misguided daughter' to 'lose not thy faith, | Reclaim thy birthright' (VI, p. 167). Nothing, it seems, was permitted that could compromise the patriarch and break this figure's rhetorical spell. Instead the dying king paints what Dennis called an 'Image in Motion': Zara's mother and her murdered brothers call to her; her father orders her to 'think that thou seest 'em stretch their bloody arms and weep to win thee'. The final lines of this speech narrate the success of such an image, describing how 'Repentance dawns' in the young woman's eyes. Capitalising on this moment, Lusignan then leads Zara through a catechistic exchange, culminating in a final appeal to God: 'Receive her, gracious Heaven! And bless her for it' (VI, p. 168). This whole sequence, the climax of Lusignan's only scene, stages in miniature what Hill (and Dennis before him) hoped the theatre could achieve. It is the forceful expression of Lusignan's emotions, through an 'Image in Motion', that moves his daughter, returning her to her Christian faith through a series of emotional shifts that he feelingly narrates. It is, in other words, the performance of passion (inspired by great, religious ideas) that causes social change. At the same time, we might also see a vindication of Hill's own theories about acting: the '*strong idea*' that Garrick's Lusignan summons is sufficient to change the feelings of his Zara, allowing us to see both the character's reformation and the actress's inspired transition operating simultaneously.

At the very close of this scene, and the close of the entire act, Orasmin (Osman's second-in-command) enters to announce that Zara has been ordered to bid her 'last farewell to these vile Christians'. She must now, as Lusignan tells her, 'keep the fatal secret' of her parentage and faith, and all is in place for the heroine to be torn between her lover, her family, and her religion (VI, p. 168). Yet Orasmin's entrance, as well as a convenient hook before the traditional eighteenth-century interval between acts, is also part of a wider pattern, one which Garrick (unremarked by Bergmann) also contributed to. *Zara* is full of ironic concatenation. Here, no sooner has Zara found her true faith and family than Orasmin announces that she is to be sequestered from them. Something similar has already occurred on multiple occasions in the earlier acts and scenes: no sooner had Zara spoken of her resolution to 'descend' to Osman in the play's opening sequence than Selima hears 'the wished music' and Osman himself enters with enormous pomp and circumstance (VI, p. 153); a little later, just as Zara tells the sultan of her pride 'To be the happy work of his dear hands!', Orasmin announces Nerestan's unexpected arrival at court (VI, p. 155). On each of these occasions, the entrance of a character offers an unexpected, ironic reversal of events, a kind of structural transition between different emotional environments.[54] The pattern continues beyond Lusignan's scene. Just as Zara tells 'Heav'n' that 'To thy hard laws I render up my soul', Osman enters and – misreading religious paroxysm for amorous timidity – tells his beloved to 'Shine out, appear, be found, my lovely Zara!' (VI, p. 174). In the fourth act, the same situation is replayed, as Osman appears just as Zara worries that she, by behaving so suspiciously, may 'lose his love' (VI, p. 180). Towards the end of the same act, the roles are reversed, and it is instead the sultan who is interrupted by his beloved, just after he has, with the aid of an intercepted (and misunderstood) letter, laid a trap for her (VI, p. 186).

All these ironic entrances occur in Voltaire and are faithfully translated by Hill. Garrick's contribution concerns his cuts, for, on several occasions, he removes the lines immediately preceding each entrance. Some time in the 1760s, Osman stopped exclaiming 'Heav'n! she's here!' when Zara missed by moments the chance of overhearing his plots against her, and, right at the beginning of the play, Zara's resolution to 'descend' to Osman is immediately followed by her beloved's entry, unprefaced by Selima's comment about 'wish'd for music'. Garrick is able to remove such lines because, in performance, they are extraneous: their work is done by the actor's performance of shock and surprise, the execution of transitional pauses so crucial to maintaining audience attention in the theatre of the eighteenth century. This is not to say that Voltaire and Hill's texts lack such transitions: indeed, they may well have used so many ironic entrances because they are such perfect triggers for emotional upheaval. Garrick's work was not to depart from this insight but, as in so much of his interaction with those ideas about performance crystallised in Hill, to refine it. Such refinement amounts, with Lusignan, to a re-distribution of dramatic and enthusiastic passions. More so than in Hill, these emotions spring from a single figure on the stage. They are Garrick's passions, either expressed by him or inspired by him in others through the use of the iconic and dynamic 'Image in Motion', and they remained so associated with him that, even as he lay dying in 1779, his visitors thought of Lusignan.

Cumberland's Criticisms

The pattern of ironic entrances that runs through *Zara* (in all its forms) terminates in the final moments of the play. After dispatching Orasmin to apprehend Nerestan, Osman immediately hears Zara and Selima making their way out of the palace. Yet rather than the usual meeting of characters, Osman instead stands transfixed, torn between contrary impulses. First (in lines truncated by Garrick), he draws a dagger with the words 'Revenge, stand firm and intercept his wishes!' and then drops his weapon as he realises 'I must not, cannot strike' (vi, p. 194). Then, at the last possible instant, Osman stabs his beloved, but the moment remains (after so many moments of dramatic meetings) unbalanced: Zara hardly speaks before she falls, and this silence is in fact typical of a larger shift within the play as Osman, more than the play's heroine, fills out the final section of the drama with his passions of jealousy, anger, and, later, regret. Despite her place in the title, an overview of the emotional patterns in the English *Zara* of Hill and Garrick would indicate that the work's eponymous heroine is, at best, one of three major figures in the work. While Zara opens the play, it is her father, Lusignan, who sharpens both its pathos and its tragic tensions and, in the last act, the sultan Osman whose emotional instability provides a spectacular denouement.

In 1817, Richard Cumberland edited *Zara*, producing an edition that testifies to the play's continuing popularity beyond the eighteenth century.[55] Cumberland's volume contains both Hill's translation and (marked with italics) Garrick's alterations. It also features a preface in which the editor signals his own lukewarm opinion of the play. *Zara* has three key failings. While Cumberland finds Hill's 'versification [. . .] elegant; and his diction flowing and harmonious', he also believes it 'not sufficiently diversified to answer the purposes of tragedy, whose first great object is to move the passions'.[56] As for plot, '*Zara* cannot boast of that intricacy which perplexes and that denouement which surprises'.[57] Indeed, Cumberland is able to summarise the action of the drama in just four sentences.[58] Last, but by no means least, Cumberland takes issue with the play's characterisation. 'Osman and Zara are by no means preserved with the consistency required by tragedy', being subject to a number of contrary passions when it should be the case that 'in tragedy [. . .] one passion alone operates, "like Aaron's serpent swallowing up the rest"'.[59]

Cumberland's criticisms of *Zara*'s plot, versification, and character epitomise a shift in critical attitudes to tragedy. Blair Hoxby locates this shift at the end of the eighteenth century, as a time when an 'early modern poetics of tragedy', long persisting as 'a running conversation', fell out of favour.[60] The reading of *Zara* offered in this chapter, by returning to Dennis, Hill, and Garrick's own aesthetic priorities, follows Hoxby's advice to study drama written before 1790 in its own terms. In so doing, it provides a specific application and elaboration of Hoxby's thinking while answering Cumberland's disparagement of *Zara*'s verse, plot, and character. Against Cumberland's dislike of the plot stands the use of ironic, dramatic entrances throughout the play, culminating in Osman's murder of Zara. Against the accusations of monotonous versification stand, on one hand, Hill's careful use of emotional direction ('joy', 'horror') and vocabulary (such as 'start') drawn from the stage and, on the other, Garrick's revisions to tighten the verse, emphasise his own lines, and, in places, bring the English text closer to Voltaire's original sense. Finally, against the focus on the inconsistencies of characters stands a focus on passion and the kinds of ideas and images that produce it.

The passions are, to use Hoxby's phrase, the 'dramatic units' of *Zara*.[61] I offer three interlocking ways of reading them. First, as 'enthusiastic passions'. Hill (following Dennis) turns to religious material to drive his drama to new heights. Voltaire had done this too – hence perhaps Hill's attraction to Zara in the first place – but the English *Zaïre* adds to the spectacular outbursts of emotion a set of typographical and lexical choices that make such shifts particularly vivid both to the audience and the performers. Indeed, such clarity is part of Hill's experimental emphasis on 'dramatic passions' where what is felt is just as important as the idea it is felt about. Indeed, many speeches in this play are both about a passion and an expression of that passion. Characters speak of their anger, love, grief, and joy (or a combination of them all) even as they feel it. Hill's decision to emphasise this by nominalising or departing from his French source indicates to what extent *Zara* was as pedagogical as it was emotional. Finally, in the years after Hill's death, the passions of this play become Garrick's passions. His revision cuts lines whose effect can be achieved purely by the kind of fluid physical transition Garrick himself epitomised and taught. At the same time, Garrick made his own part of Lusignan an even greater centre of attention, drawing on the full power of transitional pauses to make the old man into a powerful focus for the audience to the extent that, on his deathbed, the shadow of the dying Frenchman fell upon Garrick himself.

The enthusiastic, dramatic, and Garrickean passions found in *Zara* indicate the extent to which this work remained, across the eighteenth century, true to Hill's original characterisation of it as an '*Experiment*'. The images and ideas of this play provided a testing ground for the performance and reception of the passions of tragedy. Cumberland's assessment of the play is part of this. His request for a different kind of verse; for a richer, organic plot; and for consistent character all indicate that, by 1817, the stage was no longer in his eyes a place for testing a nation's capacity for tragedy. Yet this change in attitudes, so influential in the nineteenth and twentieth centuries,[62] should not limit our modern appreciation of *Zara* and its sophisticated techniques – across a variety of media and versions – all, in Hill's words of 1735, aimed at '*compelling* the attentive Hearer, to *participate* in its Emotions'.

CHAPTER 3

Odes

Dramatic and Lyric

At the very front of the stage, with a crowd of performers behind him and much of London society before him, David Garrick pauses and lets an 'awful silence still the air'.[1] In the few seconds that follow, his expression passes from anticipation into wonder, so that when he next speaks, his ringing description of a 'hidden light' that 'bursts' from 'the dark cloud' strikes the listening audience with maximum force (p. 2).[2] James Boswell, writing in the *Public Advertiser*, would later detail Lord Grosvenor's response to this performance, which had, at its conclusion, left the nobleman's 'Veins and Nerves still quivering with Agitation'.[3] Such reports are of a piece with other records, such as Lichtenberg's or Murphy's, of Garrick's effect on audiences at Drury Lane. But Lord Grosvenor did not see Garrick at the Theatre Royal. He saw him on 7 September 1769 in a temporary theatre, hastily constructed near a swollen river on the outskirts of Stratford-upon-Avon. The lines spoken by Garrick were not the lines of a play but the lines of his own *Ode upon Dedicating a Building, and Erecting a Statue, to Shakespeare*, delivered as the centrepiece of the Jubilee he had organised with local dignitaries to celebrate the Warwickshire town's most famous son and consecrate himself as the national playwright's leading interpreter. The performers gathered behind Garrick were a mix of actors, singers, and musicians, all from Drury Lane and now supporting their manager in Stratford: he would speak the recitative sections of his roughly Pindaric ode over string accompaniment while others interjected with sung arias and choruses to complete the performance.[4]

The Stratford Jubilee, with Garrick's ode as its centrepiece, has long been considered an important event in Shakespeare's rise to the status of a national poet.[5] Vanessa Cunningham's *Shakespeare and Garrick* discusses both the events in Stratford and their subsequent spin-offs as evidence for mainstream appreciation of the bard, esteem for Garrick, and the lucrative potential of 'Shakespeare-related products to make money in the cultural market-place'.[6] In addition to detailing what happened on 7 September, Cunningham also examines rival adaptations of the Jubilee festivities for the stages of Drury Lane and Covent Garden, as well as Garrick's own pride in his creation, as he sent copies of his ode to Voltaire and Jean-Baptiste-Antoine Suard and defended his composition in a letter to Charles Macklin.

Another possible sign of Garrick's pride, one undocumented by Cunningham, is the existence of a collection of newspaper cuttings about the ode, supposedly made by the actor-manager himself before being bought by George Daniel of Islington and then donated to the British Library.[7] These cuttings include Boswell's account of Lord Grosvenor's veins and nerves for *The Public Advertiser*, along with another, from *The Public Ledger*, where one 'Musidorus' reflects that 'perhaps, in all the Characters [Garrick] ever played – he never shewed more powers, more judgment, or ever made a stronger impression on the minds of his Auditors than when delivering his ode'.[8] Musidorus's and Boswell's comments point to a significant aspect of the reception of the Stratford Jubilee of 1769, namely that the ode that was at the heart of this event was received as an extension of Garrick's dramatic art and not as a separate achievement in some other domain. The composition of a poem and its delivery to musical accompaniment was, for 'Musidorus', similar enough to Garrick's play-writing and acting at Drury Lane to stand in comparison to them. In other words, there seems to be a critical overlap between what we might now call distinct kinds of dramatic and lyric production. It is the study of the role of transition in such an overlap – at the climax of a ceremony designed to consecrate an Elizabethan playwright as a country's leading poet – that is my subject in this chapter.

Virginia Jackson observes that in the twenty-first century it has now 'become as notoriously difficult to define the lyric as it is impossible to define poetry itself': perhaps the word refers to 'poetry sung to an harp' (the definition in Samuel Johnson's *Dictionary*), perhaps it foregrounds the musicality of language, or the shortness of the verse, or an opposition to narrative, or an utterance in the first person, or even the very essence of poetry itself.[9] What can be recovered, however, is the process by which the lyric acquired so many meanings.[10] As Gérard Genette pointed out in the 1970s, the definition of lyric as, alongside dramatic and epic, one of three distinct 'archigenres' has no solid basis in classical texts, despite many claims to the contrary.[11] Indeed, Quintilian's *Institutio Oratorio* provides a list of seven poetic genres, in which lyric is not only 'one of several nonnarrative and nondramatic genres' but even 'comes down in fact to one form, which is the ode'.[12] The earliest evidence Genette unearthed for the elevation of lyric as equal to dramatic and epic lay in Milton's *Of Education* (1644), yet it was in the pages of the teacher of oratory Charles Batteux's highly influential *Les Beaux Arts réduits à un même principe*, published a century later, that Genette located the key theoretical development. Batteux argued that 'Just as one imitates actions and customs in epic and dramatic poetry, so, in lyric poetry, one sings of feelings or imitated passions'.[13] Dramatic, epic, and lyric are all kinds of imitation, yet while dramatic and epic imitate action, the lyric imitates feeling.

Batteux's treatise first appeared in 1746, five years after Garrick's debut in the London theatres. In the preceding chapters' analysis of Garrick's acting style (and its theoretical precursors), I have suggested that the art of transition, particularly as practised by this performer, focused audience attention on the dramatic expression of the speaker's rich and varying emotional state. This focus on feeling had a number of consequences: the pauses and the transitions within a work of theatre became the property of a single performer and moments of spectacular cynosure, to the point that dialogue resembled soliloquy and the dramatic flirted with the lyric, where 'lyric' is understood as Batteux understood it, as the imitation of feeling rather than action. Neither Genette nor more recent theorists of the lyric, such as Jackson or Jonathan Culler, remark on the proximity between the dramatic and lyric, which we find in everything from the willingness of writers like Gilbert Austin or James Burgh to include lyric and dramatic texts alongside each other in their manuals on public speaking to Jean-Jacques Rousseau's innovative *Pygmalion* (1762).[14] Such evidence indicates that, as the post-Enlightenment establishment of lyric, dramatic, and epic as what Goethe called the three 'natural forms' of poetry began, the nature of what was dramatic also shifted, and Garrick performed throughout the years in which such flux took place, negotiating a situation where dramatic and lyric expression could and did overlap.[15]

While Garrick's transitions, by making drama about feeling as much as about action, are congruous with Batteux's theories, his rendition of the Shakespeare ode – with those very same transitions and a similar emotional impact on his audience as in his dramas – also touches on other definitions of the lyric. Quintilian, as already noted, had positioned the ode as the key example of lyric poetry, and the ancient definition of lyric as a combination of music and poetry is one that Garrick's ode conforms to also.[16] While this definition is useful, it is, however, hardly sufficient, not least because ancient epics were also accompanied on the lyre. Yet rather than make a futile attempt at a precise delineation of our historical understanding of the lyric and the place of an ode within it, this chapter is more interested in the instability and multiplicity of literary categories, since it is from this flux that a general sensitivity to transition emerges. Thus, of all the kinds of ode George Shuster observes in the long eighteenth century (the Pindaric, Horatian, Cecilian, Birthday, Cantata, heroic, festival, religious, and so forth), I take two things.[17] First, I endorse Shuster's view that 'from a distance the boundary lines [between types of ode] cannot be clearly discerned'.[18] Taking Shuster's advice, more recent critics, like Margaret Koehler, have instead focused, as I focus on here, 'the intriguing intersections of categories and dissolutions of boundaries that can occur in a single ode'.[19] Second, I make a deliberately expansive use of Shuster's category of the 'enthusiastic ode'. This category is epitomised for Shuster by the writings of John Dennis and Aaron Hill in the early decades of the 1700s[20] but also, as I will show, might be extended forwards in time as a useful term for understanding Garrick's own enthusiastic invocation of Shakespeare some fifty years later, not least because such a less rigorous approach allows us to see in this work a connection between it and the theories of the passions that this book has already described as underpinning the art of transition.

In order to make such arguments, this chapter relies on another work of 1769. This second work both proposes a set of tools for understanding how the movements of verse and music fit with the passions and offers a conceptual framework for understanding the relationship between the dramatic and the lyric that is particularly wide-ranging in its examples. It is Daniel Webb's *Observations on the Correspondence between Poetry and Music*, the third publication of an Oxford-educated Irish art critic.[21] Following Webb's *Remarks on the Beauties of Poetry* (1762) and his *Inquiries into the Beauties of Painting* (1760), the *Observations* extended this writer's aesthetic speculations into the same mix of media employed in Garrick's intermedial ode. Yet even in his first publication some sixteen years earlier, Webb had already displayed the remarkable sensitivity both to the transitions of drama and to the existence of this phenomenon across the sister arts that makes him such a useful interlocutor for me here. In a section of the *Remarks* discussing a line from *Othello* – 'Farewell! – Othello's occupation's gone' – Webb had, for instance, observed that the way in which the 'contrasts' present here 'succeed each other suddenly' and thus make us 'feel the transitions'.

This meant that, in one of this writer's typically interdisciplinary conclusions, 'the several parts' of Shakespeare's text 'have not only the intrinsic beauties of musical imitation, but likewise a relative advantage from their comparison one with the other; and this may, with some allowance, be called the clear-obscure of harmony'.[22]

Webb frames this comment with the claim that 'The voice of a Garrick cannot lend beauties to Shakespeare; it is no small praise that he can do him justice'. This is the only mention of Garrick in Webb's published output, and my choice of pairing each of the works that these men produced in 1769 is motivated more by critical utility than historical proximity, since each illuminates the other in the general context of fluctuating understandings of the dramatic and the lyric. Specifically, this chapter makes use of Webb's work in two ways. First, it draws from the pages of Webb's treatise a set of eighteenth-century literary critical tools that can still help us to analyse the functioning of Garrick's ode and its use of music and of verse to produce the powerful effects reported by Boswell and 'Musidorus' and so akin to the impact of his stage performances of passions and transitions. Second, it examines Webb's concept of 'dramatic spirit' as a re-definition of the dramatic mode along emotional lines that both connects it to ancient understandings of the lyric and responds to eighteenth-century re-appraisal of this category. This conceptual work then serves to explain Garrick's positioning of both Shakespeare and himself as exemplary artists of emotional transition.

Studying Movement

At the end of the Jubilee ode, Lord Grosvenor's nerves and veins were 'still quivering with agitation'. Boswell's particular turn of phrase for reporting this nobleman's experience would have been of interest to Webb, who could well have added it to the list of expressions with which he begins his *Observations on Poetry and Music*: 'we say, that love softens, melts, insinuates; pride expands, exalts; sorrow dejects, relaxes' (p. 4). These common phrases are important to the critic, for, while 'we have no direct nor immediate knowledge of the mechanical operation of the passions', they offer 'some conception' of it (p. 4). All these phrases indicate 'different modifications of motion, so applied, as best to correspond with our feelings of each particular passion' (p. 4). From such a hint, coupled with their 'known and visible effects', Webb claims that 'there is just reason to presume, that the passions [. . .] do produce certain proper and distinctive motions in the most refined and subtle parts of the human body' (p. 5).

Something in us relaxes in sadness, something in us expands in pride, and
something in Lord Grosvenor quivered in agitation as Garrick performed.

Exactly what this something is and how it is 'fitted to receive and
propagate these motions' constitute, as Webb admits, 'points which
I shall not inquire into' (p. 5). Instead, Webb decides to echo 'received
opinion' and, following Descartes, 'assign the functions in question to the
nerves and spirits' (p. 6). Yet his one-sentence summary of the physiological system he will use as the basis for connecting music and poetry
indicates Webb's debt to thinkers other than Descartes:

> The mind, under particular affections, excites certain vibrations in the
> nerves, and impresses certain movements on the animal spirits. (p. 6)

Webb's use of 'vibrations' here distinguishes his writing from Cartesian
philosophy. By the time of this treatise's publication in 1769, the theory of
vibrations had come to supplant the French philosopher's hydraulic
understanding of the passions as the result of the propulsion of animal
spirits around the body. Nervous vibration had, after all, the significant
advantage over the earlier, Cartesian hypothesis of accounting for the
duration of an emotion. As everyone knew, the strings of a violin, harpsichord, or guitar would continue to oscillate after being struck. The nerves
were just a different kind of instrument. David Hume, in his *Treatise on
Human Nature*, uses such an acoustic model to 'consider the human mind
[...] with regard to passions' as 'a string instrument, where after each
stroke the vibrations still retain some sound, which gradually and insensibly decays'.[23] Indeed, Grosvenor's quivering veins and nerves, still shaking
after the end of the ode, support just such a theory.

Yet Webb's focus is not so much how the passions endure but, like
Cicero's *De Oratore*, how they are aroused, and, even before establishing
his belief in 'certain vibrations in the nerves', his treatise has already discussed
the stimulation of a different kind of vibration: sound.[24] Thus follows
Webb's distinctly physiological explanation for the effect of music on the
passions. It is 'in the nature of music to excite similar vibrations, to communicate similar movements to the nerves and spirits' as those associated with
the passions (p. 6). Both music and passion owe their being to 'motion' (the
vibration of the nerves or the vibration of a musical instrument), and so 'the
agreement of music with passion can have no other origin than a coincidence
of movements' (pp. 6–7). To take an example from Webb himself, a child
will 'cry violently on hearing the sound of a trumpet, who, some minutes
after, hath fallen asleep to the soft notes of a lute' (p. 2).

Webb's next step, after establishing the connection between acoustic and nervous motion, is to observe that 'music cannot, of itself, specify any particular passion' (p. 10). The reason for this is simple: there are, according to an analysis made in Webb's own *Remarks on the Beauties of Poetry*, only four kinds of movement available to music, and each movement corresponds not to a particular passion but to a class of passions.[25] First, we may be '*transported* by sudden transitions, by an impetuous reiteration of impressions' (p. 8). Second, we may be '*delighted* by a placid succession of lengthened notes, which dwell on the sense and insinuate themselves into our inmost feelings' (p. 8). Third, 'a growth or climax in sounds *exalts* and *dilates* the spirits' (p. 9). Fourth, a 'descent' of notes is 'in unison with those passions which *depress* the spirits' (p. 9). Each of these four kinds of movement (abrupt, smooth, growing, and decreasing) enters, as they also do in gesture manuals of this period,[26] into correspondence with a group of passions: abrupt movement, for instance, agitates 'the nerves with violence' and hurries the spirits 'into the movements of anger, courage, indignation, and the like' (p. 9).

The issue, however, is that there remains some difference between indignation and courage. This results, for Webb, in a distinction between the emotional experience of music with words and that without. In a concerto by Francesco Geminiani (to use his own example), 'we are, in turn, transported, exalted, delighted', but, in such a sequence of emotions, we 'have no determinate idea of any agreement or imitation', since 'we have no fixed idea of the passion to which this agreement is to be referred' (p. 11).[27] In contrast, if we 'let eloquence co-operate with music, and specify the motive of each particular impression', we feel not only the 'agreement of the sound and motion with the sentiment' but the song also 'takes possession of the soul, and general impressions become specific indications of the manners and the passions' (pp. 11–12). As one of Webb's contemporaries, James Harris, put it, the union of words and music provides a '*double force*': both the physiological stimulation, through vibration, of our emotional apparatus and the alternate source of sensation to be found in a striking, emotive image.[28]

The relationship between words and music described by Webb and Harris is part of a clear line of eighteenth-century thought, running on to James Beattie and stretching back at least to Jean-Baptiste Dubos, who, in 1719, granted music the ability to evoke 'the natural signs of the passions', which it then 'artfully uses to increase the impact of the words to which it is set'.[29] Building on this position, Harris had conceded in 1744 that in any union of words and music, 'it must be remembered [. . .] that *Poetry* ever have the *Preference*.[30] The composition of Garrick's ode provides an example of this hierarchy in action.[31] A letter from the actor-manager to the Town Clerk of Stratford-upon-Avon, dated 14 July 1769, reported that, with its text complete, the work was now in the hands of Thomas Arne, who 'works like a dragon at it – he is all fire, & flame about it'.[32] Garrick's words come before Arne's music: the poetry has the preference, for all of Arne's fiery contribution. Such a preference may be one reason why no score survives for the string music played when Garrick spoke the recitative sections of the ode, yet Arne's music for the sung sections of the work is still available in an arrangement published by John Johnston for voice and keyboard. Johnston's elegant publication, with its ornamented title page and record of who sung what in Stratford, also allows for a clear demonstration of Webb's ideas about the different expressive capacities of instrumental and vocal music. Arne's settings for the first two songs – 'Sweetest bard that ever sung' and 'When nature smiling' – both contain what Webb calls 'a placid succession of lengthened notes', often sung over smooth *andante* triplets or incorporating melisma, yet each deals with a different subject: the former calls for group celebration of Shakespeare ('Songs of triumph to him raise') while the latter describes the writer's genius ('To him unbounded pow'r was given').[33] The specific emotion of each song is distinct, but Webb's categorisation of classes of music allows us to see how they are nevertheless complementary: both the preparation for celebrating Shakespeare and our wonder at his poetic abilities could share a common emotional ground of delight.

In his treatise, Webb no sooner articulates his distinction between the expressive powers of music (for classes of emotional movement) and verse (for the adumbration of specific passions) than he recasts it in terms of interior and exterior states by adding painting as a third point of reference. He thus extends the judgement of Harris and Dubos by concluding that poetry is a form of expression superior not only to music but to painting as well, since poetry is capable of representing both interior and exterior states, while music only captures our internal sentimental movements and painting merely the external signs of our emotions.

> The process in which we are engaged obliges us to trace the passions by their internal movements, or their external signs; in the first, we have the musician for our guide, in the second, the painter; and the poet in both: it is the province of music to catch the movements of passion as they spring from the soul; painting waits until they rise into action, or determine in character; but poetry, as she possesses the advantages of both, so she enters at will into the

province of either, and her imitations embrace at once the movement and the effect. (pp. 38–39)

Webb's belief in the expressive range of poetry has clear ramifications for his method and the literary critical focus of this chapter. Having stated his hypothesis ('that the correspondence of music with passion springs from a coincidence of movements; and that these movements are reducible to four classes' (pp. 13–14)), Webb tests it, not with extracts from instrumental pieces, but with poetry. The decision to use verse examples is based on the idea that poetry shares with music the ability 'to catch the movements of passion as they spring from the soul'. 'Verse', as Webb puts it, 'is the music of language': if he can trace in this medium those movements that coincide with the movements of the passions and so prove his ideas about the coincidence of movements, then 'we shall have little reason to doubt of their extending to music in general' (p. 14).

As James Malek has pointed out, this method's assumed equivalence of the movements of music and poetry is highly problematic.[34] The claim that 'Verse [. . .] is the music of language' (and the equivalence between the movements of poetry and music it implies) appears to ignore both the influence of the meaning of a poem's words on the dynamic performance of verse and what Webb himself recognises to be poetry's painterly ability to depict outward signs as well as inward movement. Yet this apparent flaw is not as fatal as it might seem. By choosing poetic examples, Webb makes use of passages where a single passion is clearly specified (after all, poetry, and not music, has the power 'to specify'). The treatise then gathers a number of these passages together, each subtly (but clearly) different from the others, to indicate how all nevertheless share a common set of 'movements'. In this way, Webb employs the specificity of poetry to prove the existence of general classes of movement for the passions and thus the existence of that level on which music itself operates. Such a method is at its clearest when Webb explores the class of 'growth or climax'.

This class is closely associated with the passion of pride, yet that passion may manifest itself in several different ways. If Webb is right, though, each specific instance of pride in verse will share a common movement, a movement that music can replicate. With Webb's claim that 'The expansion of pride is constant in its influence, and compels the measures into a corresponding movement', the reader must then trace such expansion in a set of examples from Milton and Virgil (p. 15). First, in the growing phrases of Eve's description of the effects of her sin.

> Op'ner mine eyes,
> Dim erst, dilated spirits, ampler heart
> And growing up to godhead.   (p. 15)

Then, second, in Juno's description of herself at the start of the *Aeneid*, filling one and a half hexameters with epithets in both the Latin and its English translation.

> Ast ego, quae divum incedo regina, Jovisque
> Et soror, et conjux.
>
> ─
>
> But I, who move supreme, heav'n's queen, of Jove
> The sister, the espous'd.   (pp. 15–16)

Webb does not give the metrical and syntactic descriptions I offer here; instead, like an antiquarian presenting objects for our perusal, he trusts his reader to note the expansiveness of each phrase, which gives to each (although the particular situation of Eve and Juno is different) a common movement. He concludes his examples with another quotation from *Paradise Lost*, this time dealing with Satan.

> Thus far these beyond
> Compare of mortal prowess, yet observ'd
> Their dread commander: he above the rest
> In shape and gesture proudly eminent,
> Stood like a tow'r.   (pp. 16–17)

These lines are also analysed by John Dennis in *The Advancement and Reformation of Modern Poetry* as an example of the sublime, and Webb, building on his predecessor, uses them to suggest that 'the pleasure we receive from great and sublime images arises from their being productive of sensations similar to those which are excited by pride' (p. 16).[35] This is because, in both cases, 'we feel the same enlargement of heart' (p. 16) as, once more, the verse takes on an expansive movement (perhaps attributable to Milton's use of enjambment). More than anything else, however, the identification of sensations here that are similar to those in his earlier examples supports Webb's hypothesis that there exists a common class of movement in which a variety of specific passions can be contained. This class is one of expansion and is connected to pride: poetry can enter into the specifics of such a class (whether it is sublime pride or not, for instance), while the music for Eve, Juno, and Satan would remain roughly similar, born from a movement common to all three scenarios. One must, however, imagine such music, for Webb gives no examples of it, and this is one point of many where his treatise's decision to rely on quotations from poetry produces an imbalanced approach to the correspondence between verse and music.

Nevertheless, Webb's analysis of Milton and Virgil provides a model for the analysis of Garrick's ode. This work's opening recitative also contains 'growth or climax', an expansive logic keyed to national pride in Shakespeare. Perhaps this movement is the one that the lost string accompaniment would have highlighted, providing Garrick's speech with a double force. The lines in question accumulate imperatives, culminating in one of the poem's infrequent mentions of its subject's name.

> Prepare! Prepare! Prepare!
> Now swell at once the choral song,
> Roll the full tide of harmony along;
> Let Rapture sweep the trembling strings,
> And fame expanding all her wings,
> With all her trumpet-tongues proclaim,
> The lov'd, rever'd, immortal name!
> SHAKESPEARE! SHAKESPEARE! SHAKESPEARE!
>
> (p. 2)

The imperatives spoken here combine with a heavy use of adjectives and epithets to inflate the verse. In addition to such stylistic choices, the passage itself contains many images of expansion: the choral song shall 'swell', the tide of harmony grows 'full', fame will soon be 'expanding all her wings' and pronouncing Shakespeare's name with 'all her trumpet-tongues'. These lines are repeated moments later as a chorus, but before this occurs, Garrick's voice drops down, providing a contrast to his ringing exclamations with a series of short, rapid orders (an example of. 'abrupt' movement in Webb's terminology): 'Let th'inchanting sound, | From Avon's shores rebound; | Thro' the Air, | Let it bear, | The previous freight the envious nation's round' (p. 2). These short lines separate the two expansive statements of celebration, first by Garrick, then by the chorus. They are also another opportunity for transition, introducing a variety of movements into the recitative to fit with a variety of specified emotions: gratitude, wonder, joy, awe, and rapture are all mentioned in this opening section, and while some lines seem to adhere to the expression of a single class of emotion (as in the 'swell' of choral song), the passage as a whole combines different passions. As such, and with the important caveat of a lack of sources for Garrick's actual practice, his use of recitative bears comparison to one of the two kinds of Italian recitative identified in the period by John Brown, known as *accompagnato* or *obbligato* and now defined by modern critics as 'Distinct from *recitativo semplice* by virtue of its rhythmic and melodic figuration in the accompanimental parts, rapidly shifting character, and imitation of the passions of the text'.[36]

Although Webb establishes only four general classes of movement and even (confusingly) goes so far as to install a single passion 'to preside over, and govern, as it were, the simple movements of music' (pride is expansive, anger abrupt, love smooth, sorrow decreasing), he was also sharply aware of the combinatory possibilities of his system. His essay goes on to explore how each of his four general passions can – like Descartes's primary passions – combine to produce others, whose movements then take something from each of their sources (p. 22). Consider pity, for example, which will 'find its accord in an union of the movements of sorrow and love' (p. 23). Webb has only to turn to the words Milton gives to Adam upon discovering Eve's 'fatal Trespass' for a particularly good example, since it is taken from a speech the poem's narrator explicitly describes as 'inward' sentiment:[37]

> How are thou lost, how on a sudden lost,
> Defac'd, deflower'd, and now to death devote?
>
> (p. 23)

While it is not immediately obvious, the force of this short example of the movements of 'pity' depends on the fact that Webb has already quoted the lines immediately preceding it to illustrate those movements characteristic of the class of love. In this earlier quotation, Milton's use of enjambment, his opening superlatives and concluding string of adjectives combine to create what Webb calls the class's 'soft and insinuating' movements, coupled with love's tendency to dwell 'with a fond delight upon its object' (p. 14).

> O fairest of creation, last and best
> Of all God's works. Creature in whom excell'd
> Whatever can to sight or thought be form'd
> Holy, divine, good, amiable, or sweet.   (p. 14)

> How are thou lost, how on a sudden lost,
> Defac'd, deflower'd, and now to death devote?
>
> (p. 23)[38]

The rhetorical question at the end of this passage transforms it from love to pity by introducing sorrow. Webb does not tell us precisely how this transition occurs. We know from his earlier examples that love's movements are 'soft and insinuating' (p. 14) while sorrow's involve 'a kind of languor or weakness' (p. 17). In Milton's pair of lines, one might consider their density of past participles (lost, defac'd, deflower'd) as a sign of 'insinuating' rhythms, while the repetition and alliteration of many of these words could be symptomatic of 'weakness'. This, however, is conjecture: it is left to the reader to note the symbiotic mix of sorrow's weakness and love's softness in Adam's pity and to appreciate Milton's ability to transform the movements of his verse into it at this particular moment of artful transition. Webb's exploration of pity is followed with a study of several other passions whose movements do not fall within a single one of his classes: joy's 'lively motion of the spirits in ascent' resembles the movement of pride but is more 'prompt' and 'giddy'; terror straddles sorrow and pride, and indignation anger and pride (pp. 23–26).

Having sketched a rough ontology for the organisation of emotion by movement into (and between) classes, Webb returns to 'vibrations' to explore in detail the pleasure to be found in music and verse. Yet rather than using vibrations to examine pitch (the 'grave' and the 'acute' frequencies that produce melody), as his earlier comments may have led the reader to expect (p. 3), Webb instead reflects on the amplitude of the waveform and argues that the *piano* and *forte* of a piece of music can allow that work to become imitative 'when it so proportions the enforcement or diminution of the sound to the force of weakness of the passion' (pp. 42–43). In such cases, powerful noises then arouse powerful responses, for 'the soul answers, as in an echo, to the just measure of the impression' (p. 43). As before, a number of verse examples then illustrate this double observation: that, on one hand, a loud or quiet noise can represent a strong or weak passion; and that, on the other, the loudness or quietness of the representation leaves a correspondingly harsh or soft impression on the auditor. Each of Webb's examples, he claims, contains a change in dynamics between the loud and the quiet, but it is the following lines from Milton that serve as the basis for connecting such changes to the pleasure that verse, as the 'music of language', can give in its movements.

> If thou beest he: but O how fall'n, how chang'd
> From him, who in the happy realms of light
> Cloath'd with transcendent brightness didst outshine
> Myriads, though bright.   (p. 46)

This description of Satan contains 'an even and continued swell from the piano into the forté'. Such a 'swell' is, 'in music, attended with a high degree of pleasure' (p. 45). When Milton's verses are repeated, thanks to the precision poetry offers, 'we discover the source of this pleasure, and find that it proceeds from the spirits being thrown into the same movement as when they rise from sorrow into pride, or from a humble into a sublime affection' (p. 45). Webb calls this movement a 'transition': on one hand, this describes a gradual increase in volume, on the other, it describes the passage from a movement of sorrow (characterised by the short phrases 'how fall'n', 'how chang'd') into one of pride (characterised by the expansive description of Lucifer in heaven) (p. 47). Crucially, it is to transition in general that Webb then attributes the pleasure of verse (and, by extension, music): a later description of Satan 'stood | With Atlantean shoulders' contains a 'descent of sound from the forté into the piano' and has 'a no less pleasing effect', not least because it corresponds 'with the condition of the nerves, when from a state of exertion [. . .] we feel the sweet relief of gradual relaxation' (pp. 46–47).

After re-stating his argument that the pleasure of music (and part of the pleasure of verse) has its source in the corresponding movements created by 'a succession of impressions', Webb extends it by observing that such pleasure is 'greatly augmented' by either 'sudden or gradual transitions from one kind of strain of vibrations to another' (p. 47). Yet whether sudden or not, the success of these transitions produces strikingly dynamic motion; something, Webb notes, that is not exclusive to verse and music. Indeed, he indicates that the painter Raphael excelled because he 'threw his figures much oftner into motions' than into static 'attitudes' (p. 49). Furthermore, and in his treatise's first reference to the stage, Webb suggests that actors would do well to employ such a principle also.

> While an actor is in motion, the mind of the spectator endeavours to keep pace with him; when the action is brought to a point, or determines in an attitude, the progress of the mind is at an end, and this, at a time when the imagination would naturally carry it on through a succession of movements. [. . .] From the moment that a passion falls within the compass of expression, we cannot even conceive it, much less can we represent it, so as to separate from it the idea of increase or diminution. That action therefore which brings the mind to a stop cannot be the representation of a mind in motion. (pp. 49–50)

This paragraph calls for unceasing progress in performance and the abandonment of those 'points' and 'attitudes' most strongly associated, by the 1760s, with a generation of early eighteenth-century actors, such as Barton Booth (who emulated the stylised poses of Italian castrato Nicolò Grimaldi).[39] The kind of motion Webb desires is available in the development of Garrick's ode, as it transitions from expansive to truncated imperatives at the end of its first recitative. Yet Webb's criticism may seem directly applicable to Garrick's spoken delivery also, particularly as someone famous for his dramatic pauses (either in plays or in this ode). Those pauses, as I have shown elsewhere in this book, were paradoxically also moments of movement; they were – to use Aaron Hill's phrase – 'the very *Instant* of the *changing Passion*', and so somewhat like a phenomenon

Webb, in a continuation of his meditation on motion across the arts, identifies in the Laocoön, a statue recommended as a model to actors as much as to other artists.[40] The frozen agony depicted in this iconic statue nevertheless contains 'degrees of action which the artist hath wisely kept in reserve', and so too do Garrick's pauses, hinting – like the marble form – at what has been and what is yet to come, for now held in reserve but still part of a sequence (p. 50).

Webb concludes his thinking on this point with a stirring set of phrases, whose terms echo Dennis's interest in gradations of thought as a way of understanding the impact of a work of art in time, as well as this critic's own ideas about movement.[41] Having added examples from statuary, the stage, and painting to all he has already said of emotional motion in verse and music, Webb asks his reader, 'Is it not from the force of progressive sensations that the vivacity of our conceptions seems, at times, to exalt us above ourselves?' and then answers that this progress, the art of transition, is the source of our 'enthusiastic raptures', born when the 'imagination, hurried through a train of glowing impressions [...] wonders at a splendour of her own creating' (pp. 51–52). In addition to the Dennisean language of enthusiasm, this passage also echoes the terms of Edmund Burke's description of the power of the sublime as that which 'anticipates our reasonings and hurries us on by an irresistible force'.[42]

The move from Garrick's cry of 'SHAKESPEARE! SHAKESPEARE! SHAKESPEARE!' to his swift-spoken request to 'Let th'inchanting sound | From Avon's shores rebound' before the powerful entry of his ode's first chorus exemplifies this Burkean hurrying, and the rest of his enthusiastic ode is full of such sublime moments. Just in the work's first recitative, he expresses, then checks, joy ('He merits all our wonder, all our praise! | Yet ere impatient joy break forth') and sets anticipation against wonder ('Let awful silence still the air! | From the dark cloud, the hidden light | Bursts tenfold bright!') (pp. 1–2). While such dynamic transitions are typical of the recitative sections of the entire ode, these contrasts are almost completely absent from the sung sections of the work. Each short song has a single thought and (to use Webb's terminology) conforms to a single class of movement, with little stylistic variation marked in the published score, although such scores do not record the elaborations usually added in performance. Nevertheless, it is the speaking actor's part that clearly contains a great deal of gradation and internal contrast. Furthermore, it is also the recitative part that serves as a bridge between the emotional content of songs and choruses. Consider, for example, the opening few minutes of the ode: first Garrick's call to celebration, which is reiterated in a chorus and then in an air, originally sung by Maria Barthélemon ('Sweetest Bard'). After this, however, a very different recitative is spoken, which – far from images of 'nature's glory' – suddenly introduces a melancholy Alexander the Great.

> Tho' *Philip's* fam'd unconquer'd son,
> Had ev'ry blood-stain'd laurel won;
> He sigh'd – that his creative word,
> (Like that which rules the skies,)
> Could not bid other nations rise,
> To glut his yet unsated sword: (p. 4)

Garrick's introduction of Alexander hurries an audience through several impressions. The wonder these lines seek soon manifests in a comparison of his ultimately sterile, destructive military legacy to Shakespeare's ability to raise 'other worlds and beings of his own' (p. 4).

Yet Garrick's choice of Alexander as a point of comparison also demands attention, since it seems to have borrowed 'Philip's [. . .] unconquer'd son' from John Dryden's celebrated ode of 1697 about 'Philip's warlike son': *Alexander's Feast*. Set by George Frideric Handel in 1736, the poem tells the tale of how, 'at the royal feast, for Persia won', the bard Timotheus, through the power of his song, woke a series of passions in his monarch.[43]

> Soothed with the sound, the king grew vain:
> Fought all his battles o'er again;
> And thrice he routed all his foes and thrice he slew the slain.
> The master saw the madness rise,
> His glowing cheeks, his ardent eyes,
> And while he heaven and earth defied,
> Changed his hand and checked his pride.[44]

These lines, occurring immediately before Timotheus sinks Alexander to the state of a 'joyless victor', are also susceptible to technical analysis modelled on Webb's writing.[45] The very length and repetitiveness of the line describing the emperor's triple return to his past battles produces an expansion of the verse that could well be read as symptomatic of the 'pride' named four lines later.

However, in addition to illustrating Webb's ideas about classes of movement, this passage also displays two other features examined in his treatise. The first is what Webb calls 'imitative [. . .] signs' (p. 61), words whose sounds constitute an imitation of their object: Dryden's use of 'rise' and 'soothed', with their respective rising and falling intonation, corres-pond to the rise and fall of Alexander's feelings. The second feature concerns rhythm. In a section that is largely iambic, the verse adopts a trochaic meter for the moment at which Timotheus 'Changed his hand and checked his pride', as Dryden imitates the altered state of both the ancient bard's song and (if Webb is to be believed) the sympathetic vibrations of his audience with the form of his own ode. Webb himself finds something similar in Milton, observing how the shift from iambs to trochees around a mid-line break (for example, 'Hail, Son of God, Saviour of men') 'produceth a kind of check or suspension of the movement', a 'transition' with a 'singular dignity' that corresponds to 'an elevation in the sentiment' (pp. 107–08).

The imitative signs and the checks or suspension of movement appear in Garrick's ode, as well as in Milton and Dryden. The former appears in the occasional use of plosives ('Bursts tenfold bright!') or in lines that, conductor-like, offer instructions to the music ('sweep the trembling strings'). As for checks and suspensions, they rarely manifest as shifts from iambs to trochees but appear instead in the work's Garrickean pauses, those moments of potential energy with what Webb called 'degrees of action [. . .] kept in reserve'. One such pause, marked with a dash in the verses quoted above, divides the report of how Alexander 'sigh'd –' from the description of his longing. In the third recitative, another pause (again marked with a dash) splits Shakespeare's 'aweful word' from its effects in the ode's vision of Shakespeare 'sitting on his magic throne'.

> The subject passions round him wait;
> Who tho' unchain'd, and raging there,
> He checks, inflames, or turns their mad career;
> With that superior skill,
> Which winds the fiery steed at will,
> He gives the aweful word –
> And they, all foaming, trembling, own him for their
> 　　lord.　　　　　　　　　　　　　　　　　　(p. 5)

This section of Garrick's poem again invites comparison to Dryden's work, particularly in its use of the word 'checks' to describe Shakespeare's control over the passions, echoing Timotheus's ability to 'check' Alexander's waxing pride. In this image, however, Garrick's Shakespeare is both Timotheus and Alexander, simultaneously a masterful artist and an enthroned monarch. As in the earlier comparison between the Bard of Avon and 'Philip's unconquered son', Shakespeare thus once more comes out ahead: Alexander's victories were sterile, Shakespeare's triumphs creative; Alexander is a slave to his emotions, Shakespeare an emperor over the passions.

The echoes of Dryden's *Alexander's Feast* in the second and third recitative sections of the Jubilee ode both concern the articulation of Shakespeare's power, specifically his power over the emotions. The reference should not be surprising. George Steevens anticipated such echoes when he published, a month before the Jubilee, a poem entitled 'Shakespeare's Feast: An Ode'. This parody of Dryden depicts the mayor of Stratford as Alexander, Voltaire as Timotheus, and tells how the former – after having 'Eat all his Custards o'er again'— gradually loses control of his bowels as he responds to Voltaire's choice of 'a TYBURN Muse | Soft pity to infuse' with the occasional 'backward sigh'.[46] According to Thomas Davies, Steevens paid for this publication with the ending of any 'real terms of friendship' between himself and Garrick.[47] Yet as well as inaugurating another chapter in what was always a turbulent relationship between the two men, Steevens's parody also serves to show the influence of Dryden's work and a willingness in Garrick's contemporaries to connect his ode with that written some seventy-odd years earlier.

An essay by Tom Mason and Adam Rounce on the eighteenth-century reception of *Alexander's Feast* suggests why this ode may have been a reference point for Garrick as much as for those who would mock him. At the start of their survey, Mason and Rounce note a marked difference between the responses of twentieth-century commentators to the poem and those of earlier writers. While the former (following in the footsteps of Steevens, although this is not mentioned in the article) are most interested in the ways by which Dryden's 'Alexander is [. . .] made to seem absurd', it appears 'to have been the sequence, the alternation of passions that most impressed' the majority of eighteenth-century writers.[48] Garrick's ode, when read through Webb's theories, emerges as another work where the 'sequence' and 'alternation of passions' is paramount, both to the performance of the work and its portrayal of Shakespeare. In echoing *Alexander's Feast*, Garrick was thus inviting comparison to a work that both his predecessors and contemporaries understood as a remarkable achievement in the consecutive expression of human emotions. Examples of this view are legion. Mason and Rounce cite Alexander Pope's *Essay on Criticism* (1711), which invites us to 'Hear how *Timotheus*' vary'd Lays surprize', and Jabez Hughes's *Upon Reading Mr Dryden's Fables* (1721), which reminds readers of each of the ode's transitions, as, for example, that moment when Timotheus sings of Darius and 'Relenting Pity in each Face appears'.[49] Later in the eighteenth century, Samuel Richardson also seems to have appreciated the poem's sequential display of emotion: Lovelace praises it in *Clarissa* (1748), while Harriet Byron comments on both Dryden's ode and

Handel's setting of it when she is encouraged by Sir Charles Grandison to play some music for the company.

> As you know, said I, that great part of the beauty of the performance arises from the proper transitions from one different strain to another, and one song must lose greatly, by being taken out of its place[50]

Joseph Warton, in his *Essay on the Writings and Genius of Pope* (1756), shared Harriet Byron's position, singling out for praise the 'transitions from one [passion] to another', which are 'sudden and impetuous'.[51] Mason and Rounce's last example of eighteenth-century appreciation of *Alexander's Feast* is taken from Samuel Johnson's 'Life of Dryden', published ten years after Garrick's ode. Here Johnson 'presents himself as endorsing the common view', namely that 'The ode [. . .] has been always considered as exhibiting the highest flight of fancy and the exactest nicety of art'.[52] Citing Johnson's *Rambler* articles, Mason and Rounce claim that he 'presumably included the versification of the poem in the phrase "the exactest nicety of the art"', although they do not examine exactly how such art captured the passions in transition.[53] With the help of Webb's treatise, this chapter offers a method for understanding such a process as the production and contrasting of different movements through transition.

Webb begins with the belief that passions 'produce certain proper and distinctive motions in the most refined and subtle parts of the human body'. This allows him to explain the power of music, since it is 'in the nature of music to excite similar vibrations, to communicate similar movements to the nerves and spirits' as those communicated by our passions. These movements fall into four classes (abrupt, smooth, growing, and decreasing), but this kind of general expression is all that instrumental music is capable of. Once words are added, however, specific passions can be portrayed, and this union of verbal and non-verbal sound acts upon an audience with a '*double force*'. That force is fully evident in Garrick's ode and in the many poetic examples cited by Webb. With such examples, justified with the claim that 'Verse is the music of language', the theorist demonstrates not just the existence of emotional classes of movement but also the potential effects available through either the combination of such sentimental motions or the transitions between them. Such classes, such combinations, and such transitions are everywhere in Garrick's recitative, as his verses expand with pride, suddenly contract with excitement, or introduce a new mood altogether, often one in direct contrast with the emotionally monolithic sung sections of the work. Webb's own examples of the power of emotional movement (whether immediate or held in

reserve) range from Raphael's paintings to the Laocoön, passing through
the art of acting, but in every case he finds the same crucial principle that it
is by 'the force of progressive sensations that the vivacity of our conceptions
seems, at times, to exalt us'. Garrick also aimed for such sublime exaltation,
hurrying Lord Grosvenor and others in the audience for his ode through
a progression of emotive transitions whose subjects resemble those of
Alexander's Feast, a work famed in the period for its ability to imitate
sequences of feeling. A comparison of Garrick and Dryden shows, however, that Garrick's Shakespeare acquires a particularly exalted status as
both monarch and master musician. That status helps to position Garrick's
Bard of Avon as both lyric and dramatic at a time when the definition of
both these terms was in flux. To understand the intricacies of such
a position is the concern of my next section.

Dramatic Spirit

In ancient times, poets were musicians and musicians poets. As Webb tells us,
'no man could be distinguished by his genius, without an ear for music, and
a talent for versification' (p. 82). The now separate forms then shared
a common Rousseauist 'principle of imitation', whereby the movements of
expression mirrored the movements of emotion (p. 82).[54] Operating under
such a principle, 'the characters of poet and musician would of course be
united in the same person', shaping the patterns of his creation to the motion
of human feeling (p. 82). Yet such figures live no longer, and Webb spends the
latter pages of his treatise enquiring how English writers, particularly writers of
lyric (the form Batteux defined as an imitation of feeling), can return to such
a world and unite in their person the musician and the poet. Webb's thought-
provoking answer is that 'a dramatic spirit must be the common principle' of
a new 'union' between the sister arts of verse and music (p. 132).

Webb struggles, however, to define what is meant by a 'dramatic spirit',
and his attempts to explain the concept both demonstrate a distinctive way
of thinking about drama and illuminate the literary critical claims at the
heart of Garrick's Jubilee ode. First of all, Webb states that 'This spirit is not
confined to the regular drama': one can find the dramatic spirit both on the
stage and off it, so it is not tied to a particular form of expression (p. 132).
Instead, the dramatic spirit 'inspires the lover's address, the conqueror's
triumph, the captive's lamentation', and so 'may govern every mode of
composition in which the poet assumes a character and speaks in consequence of that character' (p. 132). Invoking the dramatic spirit thus entails
assuming a character in order to channel that character's emotions. The poet

becomes a lover to express love, a captive to express sorrow, a conqueror to express pride. Such a transformation returns the writer to the state of the ancient composer: the movements of a passion (sorrow, love, pride) are now their guiding principle, and 'the sentiments which spring from character and passion' are there to be expressed as a union of music and poetry (p. 133).

Webb believed that modern lyric poets had failed to adopt this dramatic spirit fully. Instead of finding 'images productive of sentiment and passion' with which to aid the expression of a character's emotions, they instead had turned to images of 'objects in repose, or the beauties of still life' (p. 133). This material, however, was fatally static, and so did not 'fall [. . .] within the province of musical imitation' (p. 133). The images of contemporary lyric did not contain the dynamic objects that music needs to imitate in order to arouse a response in an audience through the coincidence of musical movement and internal motions of feeling. Webb illustrates this point by comparing the depiction of pity in William Collins's *Ode to Pity* to Dryden's *Alexander's Feast*.

> Long, pity, let the nations view
> Thy sky-worn robes of tenderest blue,
> And eyes of dewy light!   (p. 135)

These lines from Collins focus on what Webb calls 'beauty as a visible object' rather than its 'energy as a source of pathetic emotions' (p. 135). It is poetry that appeals to the eye and not to the heart: there is no dynamic emotion here, just a painterly dwelling upon a pair of shining eyes and a pretty dress. Those lines in which Dryden's Timotheus checks his ruler's pride with a description of his fallen adversary, Darius, king of Persia, are much more successful.

> Deserted at his utmost need
> By those his former bounty fed,
> On the bare earth expos'd he lies
> With not a friend to close his eyes.
>
> (p. 136)

The power of Timotheus's image lies in its use of past participles, which do two things. First, they present a series of actions (present and absent) to be pitied: the abandonment of Darius by his troops, the exposure of the king's body, and the lack of someone to tend the corpse. Second, they may act like the past participles Webb quoted earlier in a Miltonic example of pity, serving there as an example of the soft and weak movements characteristic of pity's combination of love and sorrow: 'How are thou lost, how on a sudden lost, | Defac'd, deflower'd, and now to death devote?' (p. 14).

Yet Dryden's verses present a new difficulty for Webb. This is not a straightforwardly dramatic situation where the poet assumes a character to express that character's emotions as their own. Accordingly, Webb's definition of 'dramatic spirit' as the key principle for the successful union of verse and music must be enlarged.

> If, instead of expressing our own, we describe the feelings of others, and so enter into their condition as to excite a lively sense of their several affections, we retain the spirit of the drama, tho' we abandon the form. (p. 136)

This revision of what constitutes the 'dramatic spirit' expands Webb's previous, Aristotelian definition of drama as *mimesis* (assuming a character) to include the distinctly un-Aristotelian idea that plain *diegesis* (describing the feelings of others) can also be dramatic. The essence of the 'dramatic spirit' thus no longer lies in the kind of imitation involved but in the poet's ability to express dynamic emotion. That emotion can be accessed either through the wholesale, first-person assumption of a character or the third-person description of that character: the key criterion is that this emotion be sufficiently forceful, creating what Hume called, in words that Webb perhaps echoes, a 'lively impression'.[55] A dramatic spirit obtains with a 'lively sense' of another's 'several affections', and Dryden's *Alexander's Feast* is, for Webb, 'the most perfect poem of this kind, in our language' (p. 136).

Webb crowns Dryden's ode as a supreme example of the dramatic spirit because, in its verses, 'music unites with poetry in the character of a descriptive art; but then the objects of her descriptions are her own impressions' (pp. 136–37). Unlike Collins's *Ode to Pity*, which describes painterly, static objects and thus denies music suitable material, the descriptions of *Alexander's Feast* are descriptions of the effect of music, an object eminently suitable for musical representation, since, as Webb has shown at length, the dynamic emotional effects of music correspond to the dynamics of the music itself. It is, in other words, the reflexive qualities of Dryden's work that allow it to achieve those qualities essential to a union between verse and music, a 'lively' expression of the cause and experience of emotion. The movements of music and poetry together describe the emotional motion that is the effect of music and poetry: the movements of the writing describe the emotional movements of Timotheus's audience even as they awake similar movements in those who appreciate the work today.

Two aspects of Webb's attempts to define a 'dramatic spirit' with reference to Dryden and to Collins may guide our analysis of Garrick's ode. The first concerns the extent to which the concept of dramatic spirit constitutes a sublimation of drama: as 'spirit', it is no longer tied exclusively to the representation of action through the assumption of a character, and instead becomes an emphasis on dynamic emotion. The spirit of drama is the communication of passion, something which brings Webb's definition of 'dramatic spirit' into alignment with Batteux's definition of lyric as the imitation of feeling. A work can thus be lyric in form and dramatic in spirit, and, indeed, the lyric form – which Webb mostly defines as any form which combines music and verse – should be, as a dramatic spirit facilitates such a union. The second aspect of Webb's argument that is significant for the study of the Jubilee ode is the way in which he presents the excellence of Dryden's writing. Dryden's ability to create 'lively' description, description that communicates emotion (and thus possesses a dramatic spirit), depends on a high level of reflexivity whereby the movements of his verse and music both describe and imitate the very emotional movements they arouse: as Timotheus stokes Alexander's pride, Dryden's verse expands; as the musician sinks his monarch's spirits, he adopts words with a falling intonation.

These two aspects – sublimated drama and reflexive expression – are key to understanding Garrick's writing about Shakespeare. While Webb's theories about verse and music turn on the distillation of drama into the communication of passion, Garrick's ode exalts Shakespeare by framing his achievement as not just the composition of stage drama but the exercise of a magical power over the passions. This is Shakespeare sublimated: no longer a playwright but a 'blest genius' (p. 1), a 'demi-god' (p. 1), a '*Magician*' (p. 7), a 'Monarch' (p. 8), a 'Bard' (p. 9), and even – in the final recitative of the work – a 'SPIRIT' (p. 14). Garrick's echoes of *Alexander's Feast*, presenting Shakespeare as both Alexander and Timotheus, exalt Shakespeare, claiming for him the status of monarch and musician. Yet another set of parallels, however, make an even stronger claim for Shakespeare's status. The second recitative's vision of the play-wright as a divinity surrounded by 'foaming' and 'trembling' passions is highly reminiscent of an ode as well known to eighteenth-century audiences as Dryden's *Feast*: Collins's *The Passions, An Ode for Music* (1746).

Collins's work opens with a scene from 'early Greece', when 'The Passions [...] throng'd' Music's 'magic Cell' to hear her sing.[56] 'Exulting, trembling, raging, fainting', these personified emotions were 'Possest beyond the Muse's Painting', 'Till once [...] when all were fir'd, | Fill'd with Fury, rapt, inspir'd', they 'snatch'd her Instruments of Sound' and begin to take turns playing their own melodies in a sequence of performed emotions that became famous throughout the eighteenth and nineteenth centuries.[57] The opening of this work, its description of Music surrounded by the Passions, contains the same organisation of figures as Garrick's poem: Shakespeare occupies the place of Music and is surrounded by highly agitated passions. The crucial difference is that the passions in Garrick's work are 'subject passions', and even as they are 'all foaming, trembling', they also 'own [Shakespeare] for their Lord' (p. 5). These personifications will never usurp Shakespeare's place in the way that Collins's figures, for one hour of 'Madness', snatch the lyre from Music's hands. Shakespeare is more powerful than Music.[58]

While the similarity of situation is striking, Garrick may or may not have been inspired by Collins's vision of Music surrounded by the passions.[59] Shakespeare's mastery over human emotion was hardly a new theme in writing about the playwright in 1769. Indeed, Garrick's own colleague at Drury Lane, William Havard, had written his own *Ode to the Memory of Shakespeare* in 1756 and performed it to musical accompaniment by William Boyce that same year, with lines describing its subject seated on a 'Throne' as a 'pow'rful Ruler of the Heart'.[60] In such a position, Havard's Shakespeare, also like Timotheus, 'With ev'ry Passion plays; | Now strikes the String, and every Part | The magic touch obeys'.[61] While Havard's work was not performed in Stratford-upon-Avon, Charles Dibdin's cantata, *Queen Mab, or the Fairies' Jubilee*, was a part of the festivities and also contained an image of Shakespeare as 'Master of the Various Passions | Leader of all Inclinations | Sov'reign of the human Heart' to echo that in Garrick's ode.[62]

Sovereign Shakespeare, a 'SPIRIT', one who occupies the place of Music herself, represents a way of thinking about drama that is – like Webb's 'dramatic spirit' – not tied to dramatic representation by action. This critical standpoint is clearest in the central recitative of the ode, when Garrick narrates the parthenogenesis of Falstaff from Shakespeare's mind, impregnated by '*Fancy*, *Wit*, and *Humour*' (p. 9). As Cunningham has pointed out, the character that emerges from this experience, while recognisably the Fat Knight, has little connection to his actions on the stage but instead exists as a compound of human passions.[63]

> With sword and shield he, puffing, strides;
> The joyous revel-rout
> Receive him with a shout,
> And modest *Nature* holds her sides:
> No single pow'r the deed had done,
> But great and small,

Wit, Fancy, Humour, Whim, and *Jest,*
The huge, misshapen heap impress'd;
And lo – SIR JOHN!
A compound of 'em all,
A comic world in ONE.   (pp. 9–10)

In the section of the ode devoted to Falstaff, it becomes clear that it is the communication of the passions that constitutes Shakespeare's pre-eminence. Sometimes such communication takes the form of character creation, while on other occasions it is a more direct or even elemental process. The passions, we learn, are 'slaves' to Shakespeare; he can use them to create new beings or – in his audience – bring about moral reformation by calling forth the 'penitential tear' at will (pp. 5–6). Shakespeare even 'Like *Neptune* [. . .] directs the storm' when he 'Lets loose like winds the passions of the heart, | To wreck the human form' (p. 14).

Yet while this last quotation speaks to the same sublimation of dramatic action to dynamic feeling as Webb's dramatic spirit, so too does it exemplify Garrick's own kind of reflexive expression. The image of Shakespeare as master of the sea is also an image of Shakespeare's Prospero, who has 'called forth mutinous winds, | And 'twixt the green sea and the azured vault | Set roaring war'.[64] While Dryden – in Webb's analysis – used music and verse to describe the creation and effects of music and verse, Garrick's ode works by using Shakespeare's words to describe the creation and effect of Shakespeare's words. There are many examples of this. The first recitative of the ode repurposes lines from *Romeo and Juliet* to call Shakespeare the 'bosom's lord' and 'the god of our idolatry' (p. 1); Theseus's lines about poets stand behind the second song's description of Shakespeare's 'frenzy-rowling eye' (p. 4); and a later song draws on *Macbeth* to describe how our 'Poet wakes the scorpion in the breast' (p. 7). Garrick himself refers to this practice in his letter to Macklin, where he defends his use of 'done' in the lines 'when our SHAKESPEARE'S matchless pen | Like Alexander's sword had done with men' (p. 4) as a quintessentially Shakespearean usage, for he knows of 'no word more emphatical, & Which Shakespeare has made use of more forcibly'.[65] He also identifies Vernon's description of Prince Hal vaulting into his saddle 'As if an angel dropp'd down from the clouds, | To run and wind a fiery Pegasus' rather than Plato's *Phaedrus* as the inspiration for his description of Shakespeare's mastery over the passions, his 'superior skill, which winds the fiery steed at will'.[66]

Webb's concept of a 'dramatic spirit' and his analysis of Dryden's imitative descriptions illuminate two key aspects of Garrick's ode: its elevation of Shakespeare to the status of a 'spirit', defined by his

superhuman ability to communicate passions rather than his talent as
a playwright, for representation through action; and the ode's incorpor-
ation of Shakespeare's own words into its descriptions of how these
passions are conceived and communicated. All this is present in the
opening of Garrick's third recitative:

> O from his muse of fire
> Could but one spark be caught,
> Then might these humble strains aspire,
> To tell the wonders he has wrought.
> To tell, – how sitting on his magic throne,
> Unaided and alone,
> In dreadful state,
> The subject passions round him wait.
>
> (p. 5)

These lines begin with some of the first words of the opening chorus of
Henry V, using Shakespeare's own language to express the speaker's desire
to verbalise his admiration for the writer. The vision of Shakespeare on
a 'magic throne' and 'in dreadful state' figures Shakespeare as Dryden's
Alexander and Timotheus, and the 'passions round him' imitate the
passions that surround Collins's Music: such images contribute to
Shakespeare's status as divine dramatic spirit.

Yet such an analysis, based on Webb's thinking in 1769, has its limits.
Between the invocation and the vision there fall lines that draw attention to
their speaker, to Garrick's own 'humble strains', more than to their subject.
These lines culminate in a transition, a break in the verse after the second
'tell' as, suddenly, the wished-for inspiration arrives and provides the
performer and (one hopes) his public with a revelation of Shakespeare in
all his glory. And Webb has little to say about the role of the performer in
the expression of emotion through verse and music. Indeed, his use of verse
examples to illustrate such ideas as the division of the passions' movements
into classes relies heavily on the assumption that all such verses can only be
performed in one way and that there is consequently no room for poetic
interpretation. Ignoring the role of Garrick in the execution of his own
Jubilee ode, however, is to neglect a crucial dimension of the text.

In the 'muse of fire' recitative, the moment of transition is simultaneous
with the moment of apparent inspiration. Garrick's skill at transition is
here tied to our ability to perceive Shakespeare's quasi-divine power over
the emotions. There is thus an implicit claim at this point for Garrick's
visionary importance as much as for Shakespeare's. This claim was made by
many texts in the period, all of which helped associate the actor and the

playwright in the minds of the eighteenth-century public.[67] One anonymous poem, entitled *A Poetical Epistle from Shakespear in Elysium to David Garrick at Drury Lane Theatre* (1752), even contains verses, supposedly penned by the playwright himself, that might serve as a gloss for this section of Garrick's ode in his honour.

> But know, much honour'd man, my hov'ring shade
> Oft' waits Thee; and, with inspiration strong,
> Pours on thy senses an enraptur'd flow
> Of eloquence, vivacity and force:
> Impell'd by me, thy rushing soul appears
> All-beauteous through thy glowing orbs of sight.
> And, fir'd by me, invigorated moves
> Each nerve, that speaks the language of the heart.[68]

The model of performance offered here is one of rhapsodic inspiration. This same model is present in Garrick's ode when he abruptly transitions from desperate invocation of Shakespeare's 'muse' to awestruck description of him on his 'throne'.[69] More generally, this earlier work also indicates another way of understanding other sections of Garrick's long combination of music and verse, namely that, in each of its many moments of performed transition between the different movements of the passions, Shakespeare is present: he, to borrow terms from both Webb and the *Epistle*, has 'impell'd' Garrick's soul, starting those emotional movements that will, in turn, be communicated to Lord Grosvenor and everyone else in the audience.

Indeed, one might extend the connection between Garrick and Shakespeare beyond a rhapsodic relationship to the point of distinct resemblance and a specific case of what Koehler describes as an ode's capacity to 'defy the boundaries between voice and object'.[70] Garrick, when performing the ode, held a staff in one hand and seated himself during each song, not quite upon an 'ornate throne' but at least upon an ornate chair.[71] Garrick's physical presence – directing the musicians, leading the audience – thus stood for Shakespeare's as much as the on-stage bust of Shakespeare did. If any audience members in 1769 had attended the Society of Artists' exhibition seven years earlier and seen Joshua Reynolds's painting *David Garrick between Tragedy and Comedy*,[72] they may have detected an echo of that image in Garrick's description of Shakespeare turning from tragic 'horrors', making the 'buskin'd warriors disappear' with a smile, and welcoming 'Thalia' and 'Euphrosyne', the muse of comedy and the goddess of joy (p. 7).

In addition to such images on stage and in verse, the two aspects of the ode identified through Webb's treatise – its sublimation of drama as 'dramatic spirit' and its reflexive expression – also apply to Garrick. The trappings of the

Stratford performance already made a mute argument for Garrick's extraordinary capacity (like Shakespeare's) for depicting feeling, and an ode of 1777 even goes so far as to accord the actor the same mastery over the passions that Garrick gave to Shakespeare in 1769, Collins to Music in 1743 and Dryden to Timotheus in 1697. This anonymous work, *An Ode to Mr Garrick, on his Quitting the Stage*, contained an order for those 'Passions which controul' to perform obeisance to the actor. Just as these wild emotions had done to Shakespeare in the Jubilee ode, they should now 'Approach, and bend at Merit's shrine!' In so doing, they would offer yet another example of how, 'Each movement of the human breast | Hath long thy potent sway confest'.[73]

As for the incorporation of quotation, the reflexive tendency to express Shakespeare's influence through Shakespeare's words, a number of the quotations used in Garrick's ode are in fact taken from roles that Garrick was as famous for playing as Shakespeare was famous for writing. A song describing Shakespeare's ability to wake 'the scorpion in the breast' may well have reminded audiences of Garrick's Macbeth, who had stunned audiences with his portrayal of 'scorpions' in his mind since 1744. Garrick also played Hotspur in 1746 (and so heard Vernon's praise of Hal's horsemanship) and, from 1742, had played King Lear.[74] It is when Garrick illustrates Shakespeare's mastery of human emotion with this last figure that he makes a choice of examples, capable of bringing the actor's own performances to the minds of the public, a recollection that was perhaps helped, here and elsewhere, by short cameo performances by the actor in the course of his delivery of the ode. With the passions ('his slaves'), Garrick explains, Shakespeare 'can control, | Or charm the soul':

> Tho' conscious that the vision only seems,
> The woe-struck mind finds no relief:
> Ingratitude would drop the tear,
> Cold-blooded age take fire,
> To see the thankless children of old *Lear*,
> Spurn at their king, and sire!
> With *his* our reason too grows wild!
> What nature had disjoin'd,
> The poet's pow'r combin'd,
> *Madness* and *age, ingratitude* and *child*.
>
> (pp. 5–6)

The single emphasised words at the end of this passage point to Lear's rejection of Goneril. Garrick had rearranged this iconic point in the drama so that this speech concluded the scene, and he placed even more emphasis upon Lear's final lines: 'How sharper than a serpent's tooth it is, | To have a thankless child!'[75] This part of the ode thus offers a multitude of meanings. It is an example of Shakespeare's ability to communicate emotion, to create a character for whom everyone feels sympathy ('with *his* our reason too grows wild!'). At the same time, it is a reminder of Garrick's own performance of that part, echoing the key themes of the play's most famous scene. In such a moment, Garrick is both with Shakespeare and with the audience: the line 'With *his* our reason too grows wild!' describes both the audience's sympathetic identification with the monarch and the actor's necessary assumption of the character when playing the role.

When attempting to describe the 'dramatic spirit' at the heart of *Alexander's Feast*, Webb wrote of how one might, if not by expressing one's own, then by describing 'the feelings of others', still 'enter into their condition as to excite a lively sense of their several affections'. The key phrase is 'enter into', which represents a recognition of sympathetic identification that lies at the heart of the emphasis on dynamic emotion that Webb calls the 'dramatic spirit'. While Webb focuses on how the modern poet – by description or imitation – should enter into the emotional dynamics of his subject and so re-capture an ancient mode of expression that unites music and verse, one can also see what Webb does not acknowledge, namely how the poet's ability to enter into another's feelings is also the model for an audience's emotional engagement with a work and an actor's assumption of a part.

In Garrick's ode, Shakespeare is frequently portrayed as a master who 'exerts his most tremendous pow'r' (p. 7), but rarely as one who sympathises. Instead, it is Garrick's performance that shows most clearly the dynamic of entering into the emotions of a moment, as he acts out the varied emotions of each recitative, at once describing and embodying the power Shakespeare has over the passions. This phenomenon is also observable in the performance potential of Dryden's *Alexander's Feast* and Collins's *Ode to Music*. In the former, the work's performer must become Timotheus, while in the latter, they must embody in turn each passion as it snatches the lyre from Music. Sarah Siddons did this to great success and offered a rendition of Collins's work as part of her own benefit night at the King's Theatre on 26 March 1792, one example in a long performance tradition for these odes, which stretches at least to the mid-nineteenth century and Charles Dickens's decision to have Pip 'particularly venerate Mr Wopsle as Revenge' in *Great Expectations* (1861).[76] One nineteenth-century reviewer, George Knox, went so far as to say that Collins's ode, because of the 'abruptness of the transitions' between each of its passions, risked creating 'an uninteresting pageant', and so relied on the skills of the performer to reach its full potential.[77] Such reliance allows us to 'account for the different between this *Ode* on the stage, and in the closet', and this may well be true of Garrick's oeuvre too, where the printed form – particularly at the distance of well over two hundred years – does not suffice.[78] Relatively few newspaper accounts from 1769 (and none collected in the British Library's cuttings purportedly made by Garrick himself) quote the text of the ode, with its multiple arguments for the positioning of Shakespeare as the greatest dramatic master of emotion, yet all describe the performance of Garrick.

* * *

The final minutes of Garrick's Jubilee ode bring together each element of the work examined in this chapter, producing the concerted effect that, in Boswell's report, supposedly left Lord Grosvenor's veins and nerves trembling in agitation. The final recitative of the ode first begs that Shakespeare 'Look down [. . .] from above | With all thy wonted gentleness and love' and protect his 'native spot' from contemporary attempts 'to parcel out the land | And limit Shakespear's hallow'd ground' through enclosure (pp. 14–15). This local plea is then followed by a rapid change of perspective as Garrick shifts from a mode of intercession to a rousing sequence of rhetorical questions, which rephrase the opening lines of the ode ('To what blest genius of the isle | Shall Gratitude her tribute pay [. . .]?') and finish with a quotation from *Hamlet*.

> Can *British* gratitude delay,
> To him the glory of this isle,
> To give the festive day
> The song, the statue, and devoted pile?
> To him the first of poets, best of men?
> *'We ne'er shall look upon his like again!'*
>
> (p. 15)

The change of perspective and style represents the last transition in the ode's recitative. The pentameter visions of the Warwickshire countryside give way to lines that first contract and then expand, the latter movement associated with the sublime by Webb. As for what is spoken, these verses continue to position Shakespeare as an exemplar, not just 'the first of poets' but also the 'best of men'. This is the most explicit statement of Shakespeare's eminence in the entire work, making clear an association between artistic and moral greatness already suggested in those lines praising Shakespeare's ability to bring forth 'the penitential tear'. This playwright's power over the emotions, which singles him out as a great artist (and frees him, like the dramatic spirit, from a strict attachment to dramatic imitation by action), is born from a preternatural sensitivity to those emotions and an extraordinary capacity for sympathy that guarantees his moral behaviour as the 'best of men'. The quotation from *Hamlet* – the Danish prince's praise of his dead father to his re-married mother – is an apt reference for its strength of feeling. It also, however, as so often in this ode, combines praise of Shakespeare with a reminder of Garrick's own exploits: the line is one that Garrick, as Hamlet, would often have spoken at Drury Lane, and – according to an old theatrical tradition which held that Shakespeare played the ghost of Old Hamlet to Richard Burbage's Dane – a line that also positions Garrick as Shakespeare's privileged interlocutor or even his son.[79]

This final recitative, encapsulating Shakespeare's ascendancy as dramatic spirit and the ode's use of the writer's own words in a sequence of attention-grabbing transitions, is immediately followed by a duet. Sung by a boy and a woman in Arne's setting, it consists of two questions: the first – 'Shall the hero laurels gain, | For ravag'd fields, and thousands slain?' – echoes earlier references to Alexander the Great and is sung first by Barthélemon and then echoed by Master Brown.[80] The two voices then combine to ask a second question, 'And shall his brows no laurels bind, | Who charms to virtue humankind?' Like the other sung sections of this ode, this passage offers no new material and contains little internal variation in terms of emotion.[81] It instead takes its cue from those questions spoken by Garrick both immediately before and (with respect to Alexander) elsewhere in the ode. Arne's choice of voices does create a measure of contrast, however, while also making even clearer the question of Shakespeare's legacy: to have a woman and a child pronounce these verses implies that the answer to these questions will decide the playwright's status for future generations too.

Of course, there can only be one answer, and the last eight lines of the ode, sung as a full chorus, gives it forcefully:

> We will, – his brows with laurel bind,
> Who charms to virtue human kind:
> Raise the pile, the statue raise,
> Sing immortal *Shakespeare's* praise!
> The song will cease, the stone decay,
> But his Name,
> And undiminish'd fame,
> Shall never, never pass away.   (p. 16)

No music survives for this conclusion, which is only the second chorus of the ode. The increased number of voices, from Garrick's recitative to a duet to a full ensemble piece, implies an increased volume and – to borrow Webb's way of thinking once more – an even more powerful set of vibrations with which to conjure passions. The final image of the ode, the endless endurance of Shakespeare's name, long after songs and statues (the business of the Jubilee) are over, gives one final proof that this work is not so much interested in Shakespeare as a playwright or as a poet, but rather as a unique genius, capable – through his mastery of human emotion – of charming 'to virtue humankind'. That the ode ends in such a way also reveals another side to Boswell's report: its account of how Grosvenor continued to feel the effects of the performance after its conclusion actually fulfils the prophecy of these lines. Shakespeare lives on in the emotion Garrick has aroused for him, as the musical and verbal movements of this work coincide with the movements of a refined sensibility.

My decision to methodise and apply the thought of one art critic's book to an ode composed and performed in the same year as that book's publication is necessarily to take a partial view of the subject. Yet Webb's writing about the correspondence between verse and music, about the passions understood as movement, still offers a way of understanding Garrick's ode as more than a particularly elaborate entertainment at a historically significant point in Shakespeare's ascendancy. Although I have worked closely with Webb in this chapter, his ideas do intersect with many other, perhaps better-known, thinkers of his time. His distinction between images that arouse emotion and those that merely describe it has its roots in the contrast Charles Avison (and many others) drew between 'Expression' and 'Imitation'.[82] Webb's tendency to privilege words over music has a long history, and Webb's investigation of the conflation between music and verse in the dawn of time owes much to Rousseau and Brown.[83] Last but not least, Webb's attempts to resurrect the lyric tradition of his time overlaps on one hand, with contemporary efforts, like Batteux's, to define what lyric is, and on the other, with comparisons made by Etienne Bonnot de Condillac between French and Greek verse, all while partaking (as Garrick's own ode to Shakespeare does) in a general eighteenth-century effort to raise the status of English writing so that it might rival the greatest compositions of Greece and Rome.[84] The techniques that emerge from my study of this writer include the categorisation of the transitional movements of verse and music into four primary kinds, and a particular attention to verse features, from the metrical to the lexical, that are capable of producing such movements and thus, at best, a kind of sublime hurrying of their audience even in moments of suspension.

The critical importance of Garrick's ode to Shakespeare lies in two connected areas. First, as becomes clear through the application of techniques modelled on Webb's analysis and argument, it lies in the positioning of Shakespeare as a figure that incorporates the essence of both the lyric and the dramatic modes at a time when the process leading to a division of poetry into epic, dramatic, and lyric had only just begun. Shakespeare is lyric and dramatic in that he is a master of the passions, capable of rivalling those ancient bards who, powered by emotion, made no distinction between song and speech. In making this argument, Garrick also implicitly claims a similar position for himself, something that Webb's work does not account for. The second area concerns our modern approach to odes and to those who performed them: we do these works a disservice when we subject them to analysis from the point of view of modern disciplinary priorities. These works, as newspaper accounts and the utility of Webb's treatise suggest, were transdisciplinary intermedial events, typical of a transdisciplinary eighteenth-century culture, where what mattered was not specifically the poetry, the music, the gesture, the pronunciation, but everything, all at once, caught up in a dynamic, sublime process capable of seizing audience attention and hurrying the 'imagination [. . .] through a train of glowing impressions' until it 'wonders at a splendour of her own creating' (pp. 51–52).

CHAPTER 4

King Lear

Unrivalled Excellence

When they buried David Garrick, one of those present threw a copy of *Hamlet* into the grave. As far as Thomas Davies was concerned, however, this anonymous mourner, acting 'by desire of Mrs. Garrick', consigned the wrong play to oblivion.[1] It was not the part of the Danish prince that should have ended with its greatest interpreter, but rather that of King Lear. There is no shortage of press evidence that appears to confirm Davies's point, with numerous articles measuring other actors' performance of this part against Garrick's.[2]

Francis Gentleman, writing in his *Dramatic Censor* (1770), offers an explanation for the enduring significance of Garrick's King Lear. 'To enter upon the representation of this odd and violent old monarch, is a daring flight of theatrical resolution,' writes Gentleman, noting that such an endeavour requires 'especially an imagination possessed of the same fine frenzy which first drew [Lear] into light'. Thankfully, Garrick is 'the man whom nature has happily formed to animate with unrivalled excellence her most favourite theatrical production'.[3] According to Gentleman, the reason behind Garrick's success was thus twofold: he seemed to possess a talent that not only allowed him to play such a demanding part but was also the same imaginative talent as that possessed by Shakespeare. As Garrick brought Lear to life on the stage, critics like Gentleman saw Shakespeare's own original creation of the part repeated. Such an identification (one often encouraged by Garrick himself) sometimes turned specifically on the range of roles that the Elizabethan playwright and the Georgian performer could each create: Joseph Warton paralleled Shakespeare's ability to 'pourtray characters so very different as FALSTAFF, and MACKBETH' with Garrick's capacity 'to personate so inimitably a LEAR, or an ABEL DRUGGER'.[4] Press articles from across the actor-manager's career, many but not all in periodicals where Garrick could exercise influence, also used the violent old monarch to exemplify the depths of tragedy that Garrick could plumb one evening before giving out a comedy the next.[5]

Yet while the part of King Lear defined Garrick's Shakespearean pre-eminence in the press, the actual play performed by Garrick at Drury Lane remained largely that of Nahum Tate, who had adapted the Jacobean tragedy for Carolinian audiences in 1681. In Tate's version, and in Garrick's later revisions of it, there is no Fool, Cordelia and Edgar are in love, and both Lear and Gloucester survive to see their honest children married and their evil offspring dead. This revised plot still pleased in 1786, when the *General Advertiser* mistakenly praised Garrick for the decision to have the tragedy's catastrophe fall upon an 'odious' person rather than the fragile monarch, and would hold the stage well into the nineteenth century.[6] Newspaper accounts also testify to public enjoyment of the production at all ranks of society. The *Morning Chronicle* for 15 May 1773 carried a letter bemoaning the aristocratic author's failure to secure a ticket to one of Garrick's farewell performances of Lear, while the same publication reported in 1774 on a waiter overturning a bowl of punch in an attempt to imitate Garrick's performances of madness.[7] Over a decade after this, the *Gazetteer* looked back fondly to an on-stage sentinel, hired to police audience behaviour, who broke down in tears as he watched the actor-manager play the mad king.[8]

It is the argument of this chapter that the scale of Garrick's achievement in *King Lear* depends on the extent to which the play (following Tate and Garrick's alterations) offered a remarkable sequence of contrasting emotions for the performance of transition. A key source for such emotional variation is madness, not least because, as Philip Fisher has observed, 'The passions are located in the space that a civilization leaves open between its concept of insanity and its concept of irony'.[9] It was to Garrick's capacity to play the passions of a mad king that many of his contemporary rivals and successors in the role were compared, while both Lear's raving and his recovery made for potent material for waiters to imitate and sentinels to weep over. The representation of all the nuances of Lear's insanity required a mastery of the art of transition, yet, as I will show in the first part of this chapter, Garrick's practice of such an art was not without its challenges. While both hostile and laudatory commentators on his performances explored the aesthetic, socio-logical, and psychological questions and ironies of how to perform a king's madness, performance editions and promptbook markings reveal Garrick's own efforts to perfect his rendition of the part through the use of everything from innovative make-up to minute textual editing. Garrick's edits included the reduction of Tate's romantic subplot, yet he never, despite his many claims to be restoring Shakespeare's Lear, excised it entirely. As the second part of this chapter shows, the Tate-Garrick versions of Edgar's pretend madness performed an essential service as a source of what Lord Kames called 'seasonable respite', a kind of transition (also found in Garrick's Lear) designed to moderate and so maintain spectators' emotional engagement in the tragedy.[10] Such moderation is alien to Shakespeare's play of 1608, and, while the eighteenth-century Lear can tell us much about the uses of transition to create a celebrated performance in Georgian London, it thus also serves as a critical standpoint for re-evaluating the Jacobean tragedy. Demonstrating the utility of such a standpoint for the contemporary study of Shakespeare is the task of my conclusion.

Madness

Tate dedicated his adaptation of *King Lear* to his friend Thomas Boteler, crediting him with a 'Zeal for all the Remains of *Shakespear*' that encouraged Tate in 'so bold an Undertaking'.[11] Surveying his completed efforts in this dedication, Tate highlights the play's depiction of madness, observing that '*Lear's* real and *Edgar's* pretended Madness have so much of *extravagant Nature* (I know not how to express it) as could have started, but from our *Shakespear's* Creating Fancy' (p. 3). The identification of madness as both the most salient feature of *King Lear* and Shakespeare's signature achievement was echoed almost a century later in Garrick's Shakespeare ode, when he composed and recited lines describing how 'The poet's pow'r combin'd, | *Madness* and *age*, *ingratitude* and *child*'.[12] Yet as well as repeating Tate's evaluation of *King Lear*, this passage of Garrick's poem also served to remind his audience of his own ability to portray on the stage an elderly monarch descending into madness and, at the end of the second act, cursing his child Goneril's ingratitude. Lear's madness could be as distinctively Garrickean as it was Shakespearean. A letter from 'W.N.' to the *St James's Chronicle*, one of several periodicals in which Garrick held shares, makes this very point, claiming that 'Garrick's Madness in Lear is the greatest masterpiece I ever saw'.[13] In an echo of John Milton's sonnet on Shakespeare, W.N. goes on to observe that Garrick 'has made me mad with too much conceiving'.[14]

While the writing and performing of madness became a double proof of Shakespeare's and Garrick's genius, episodes of insanity were also a significant element of stage spectacle in the long eighteenth century more generally. Near the end of Nicholas Rowe's *Jane Shore* (first performed in 1714 and much repeated afterwards), our heroine's antagonist, Alicia, spurns Jane's pleas for mercy.

> Mercy! I know it not – for I am miserable.
> I'll give thee Misery, for here She dwells;
> This is her House, where the Sun never dawns,
> This Bird of Night sits screaming on the Roof,
> Grim Spectres sweep along the horrid Gloom,
> And nought is heard but Wailings and Lamentings.
> Hark! Something Cracks above! it shakes, it totters!
> And see the nodding Ruin falls to crush me!
> 'Tis fall'n! 'tis here! I feel it on my Brain![15]

Soon after this, Alicia (first played by Mary Porter) sees visions of her decapitated beloved Lord Hastings and, like Lear evading Cordelia's gentlemen, runs raving from the stage pursued by servants. In a study of such scenes as these, Helen E. M. Brooks has shown that actresses representing the mental breakdown of women in emotional distress (a breakdown typical of so-called she-tragedies) offer a paradoxical image of femininity, one in which 'the centrality of female suffering and emotional distress' in a play became the means by which actresses such as Porter, Anne Oldfield, or Susannah Cibber were each 'enabled, in performance, to demonstrate her exceptional psycho-physical skill and control: skills which were conventionally and physiologically understood as masculine'.[16] As Brooks shows, this paradox was the source of much anxiety among (male) commentators in the period. Gentleman's annotations on *Hamlet*, not quoted by Brooks, exemplify the issue by observing how the transitions of Ophelia's madness both 'render her a very interesting object' and risk breaking decorum with 'too much extravagance'.[17]

Although Garrick, by virtue of his sex, avoided the specific paradox examined by Brooks, his highly emotional renditions of Lear's madness also raised issues of decorum. A letter signed 'Hercules Vinegar' to the printer of the *St James's Chronicle* argued that 'Mr. Garrick is the worst Actor that ever appeared upon the stage', asserting that 'His *Hamlet* wants Coolness and Propriety, his *Othello* wants Weight, and his *Lear*, *Richard*, and almost all his other Parts in Tragedy, Dignity'.[18] Even after Garrick's death, *Woodfall's Register* printed an anecdote of Garrick giggling at a wig-wearing dog in the audience when his Lear was meant to be holding Cordelia's corpse.[19] Although this anecdote is probably apocryphal (Garrick never performed a version of Lear where Cordelia dies), its survival and re-publication still speak to a lingering view of Garrick as somehow insufficiently dignified to play royalty. Unlike the gendered anxieties of 'she-tragedy', Garrick's madness raised issues of social class. An analysis of the role of King Lear (and Garrick's performance of it) by his contemporary Samuel Foote testifies to this.

In his *Treatise on the Passions* (1747), Foote begins his discussion of Lear's mental state by defining madness, like John Locke, as 'right Reasoning on wrong Principles', so that 'there is always a Consistency in the Words and Actions of a Madman'.[20] This gives rise to Foote's desire that 'it be a Direction to the Actor to employ his first Enquiry into the Cause of the Madness he is to represent, that his Deportment may be conducted suitably therewith'.[21] Such an aetiological approach, not uncommon in eighteenth-century writing about madness, provides clear results for Lear, whose mind may be 'at first, entirely possess'd with the Thoughts of his Daughters Ingratitude' but whose 'Reason forsakes him' only when his mind 'makes a farther Progress, and looks back to the remote Cause, which was a voluntary Resignation of the Regal Power', since such a process brings 'the Idea of his former Grandeur [. . .] to his View' and sets it against 'his present Misery'.[22] Thus, for Foote, 'The Desire of Royalty [. . .] is the Point that distracts *Lear*'s Judgment; and the Belief that he possesses that Royalty, the State of his Madness'. One has only to examine such lines as 'I pardon that Man's Life', 'You cannot kill me for Coining, I am | The king himself', and 'Ay, every Inch a King' (all cited by Foote) to see that Lear's 'Expressions are full of the Royal Prerogative'.

Garrick's error, as far as Foote is concerned, is to ignore the 'Royalty' in Lear's madness. Whoever plays Lear 'should express an Extravagance of State and Majesty'. 'When mad *Tom* is consulted as a learned *Theban*', Lear should not (as Garrick apparently did) 'play with his Straws, or betray the least Mark of his knowing the real Man'. Such a performance 'might be a proper Representation of a mad Taylor', Foote concedes, but it 'by no means corresponds with my Idea of King *Lear*'.[23] There is, in other words, a qualitative difference between the madness of a monarch and that of the common man, a difference which the undignified Garrick fails to render. Foote balances this criticism by devoting several pages of his treatise to praising Garrick's Lear, but other writers did not refrain from using this distinction between royal and common madness to make a more pointed, class-based critique of the actor-manager. The periodical articles deploring Garrick's lack of dignity as Lear already go one step further than Foote: they suggest that, rather than an error of interpretation, Garrick's perform-ances of Lear and others, especially when taken together, in fact betray the manager's inherent lack of dignity. The gender-based phenomenon Brooks observes in 'she-tragedies', where the actress's performance of feminine mental fragility testifies to her supposedly un-feminine self-control, finds a class-based analogue here. In the eyes of certain critics, Garrick's performances of royal or heroic madness in fact testify to a problematic lack of dignity in the actor, revealing his less than noble background as a former wine merchant and son of a Lichfield recruiting officer. No critic is more adept at exploiting this aspect of Lear's mad scenes than Theophilus Cibber.

Cibber tells, in the second of his *Two Dissertations on the Theatres* (1756), the 'not unlikely' story 'that when Mr. *Garrick* first undertook the Part of King *Lear*, he went to *Bedlam*, to learn to act a Madman'. Echoing Foote's comparison between a king and a tailor, Cibber goes on to criticise such a practice:

> One might imagine his Judgment (if he has any) might have suggested to him, a considerable Difference, in the Behaviour of a real King, by great Distress, drove to distraction, — and the Fantasque of a poor mad Taylor, who, in a Kind of frolick Delirium, imagines himself a King: — Tho' the Mockery of King *Cabbage* might cause a Smile, with our Pity; — yet, sure, the deplorable Situation of the real Monarch would rather rive the Heart, than excite Risibility.[24]

Cibber impugns Garrick's judgement by accusing him of failing to distinguish between royal and common madness. Such an accusation assumes that the state of insanity is no leveller but rather revelatory of a character's greatness. The actor's failure to capture (or even identify) such greatness not only undermines any claim Garrick might have to high-class sensibility but also threatens the generic stability of Shakespeare's tragedy itself. Drawing on Aristotle's definition of tragedy as the actions of the noble (and of comedy as the actions of the base), Cibber explains here that a performance of madness based on 'the Fantasque of a poor mad Taylor' will no longer 'rive the Heart' and produce catharsis, but instead induce comic laughter.[25] Garrick's poor judgement has resulted, for Cibber, in an inappropriate mixture of high and low genres. This is a common theme of the *Two Dissertations*, which also mocked Garrick's indecorous mixing of the art of the harlequin into even the most serious plays through his 'pantomimical Manner of acting, every Word in a Sentence'.[26] The production of improper generic instability is, however, not the only consequence of Garrick's lack of class consciousness identified by Cibber in *King Lear*. Cibber caps this critique of his rival by using Garrick's trip to Bedlam in order to separate him from Shakespeare. In

a passage that runs counter to the many poems and articles conflating
Garrick and Shakespeare in the 1760s, Cibber notes that 'no one would
think, *Shakespear* would have paid such a Visit' as Garrick did to Bedlam.
Shakespeare would not 'have learn't from the *Medley Jargon* of those
unhappy Maniacs, Matter to have furnished out his Scenes of *Lear's*
Madness!' Unlike Garrick, Shakespeare was possessed of an 'amazing
Genius', whose 'extensive Imagination took in all Nature, and, with
a Judgment adequate, arranged his Ideas'.[27]

   Cibber's account of Garrick's unshakespearean Lear as a revealing failure
of an irredeemably low-class actor-manager's judgement indicates the
extent to which this man's performance of royal madness offered as
many opportunities for comment to his detractors as to his defenders.
Whether laudatory or hostile, however, these accounts – when used in
combination – allow us to do two things: first, in the detailed critique (or
praise) of individual moments, they allow us to recover some of the speech
and action of these scenes; second, through the analysis of contrasting
descriptions of stage action, they illuminate what was at stake in the
performance of a monarch's madness at particular points in this play. In
what follows, I divide *King Lear* into three sections. The first of these is
Lear's cursing of his children and his gradual descent into madness:
contemporary accounts of how these scenes were both performed and
planned to be performed provide evidence for the complex physical
demands of rendering incipient madness as well as the range of critical
responses to such transition-heavy moments. Later in the play, as Lear raves
on the heath, fully mad, Garrick augmented the transitions of his physical
performance with make-up and other scenic devices, again to
a significantly mixed critical reception. Finally, Lear's recovery in
Cordelia's arms also relies on a mix of acting skill and special effects to
capture a different kind of transition, a redemptive shift away from
madness and towards reason, which Garrick's supporters would use to
answer Cibber and other hostile critics.

Descent

In Tate and Garrick's adaptations of Shakespeare's *King Lear*, the first act
concludes with the king calling upon 'Nature' either to render Goneril
barren or 'Defeat her joy with some distorted birth' (pp. 17–18). Due to
Tate's arrangement of Shakespeare's text, this speech acts first as
a counterpoint to the play's opening monologue from Edmund ('Thou
Nature art my Goddess' (p. 7)) and second as a mirror to the close of Act II,

when Lear, this time facing both Goneril and Reagan, begs the 'Heav'ns' to 'drop your Patience down' and, over the first rumblings of the storm, realises that he 'shall go mad' (p. 28). There are multiple sources for the text of Lear's curse, as spoken by Garrick: this chapter will draw on two, one from each end of Garrick's career. Volume 2 of *Bell's Shakespeare*, edited by Gentleman and published in 1773 (three years before the actor-manager retired), contains a version of *King Lear* supposedly 'AS PERFORMED AT THE THEATRE-ROYAL, DRURY-LANE' and 'Regulated from the PROMPT-BOOK, *With PERMISSION of the MANAGERS*, by Mr. HOPKINS, Prompter' (II, p. I). This text, however, differs markedly from that preserved in a 1756 edition of Tate's *King Lear* with heavy annotations in Garrick's hand and, according to Edward Langhans, those of both Richard Cross (Hopkins's predecessor as prompter) and Ralph Harwood (Hopkins's successor).[28] While this earlier text is too uneven to have served as the promptbook for Garrick's performances of the play in October 1756, it nevertheless allows for an insight into both his and his company's preparation for the play and how the presentation of this work evolved over Garrick's career. One key change occurs, for example, with regard to Edmund's 'Thou Nature art my Goddess': this speech opens the annotated 1756 *Lear* but not the Bell edition published seventeen years later, a fact deplored by Gentleman, whose annotation on the 1773 text records that 'We rather incline to *Tate*'s beginning with the Bastard's soliloquy' (II, p. 4). At some point in the intervening twenty years, Lear's cursing of Goneril at the end of the first act thus stopped echoing the opening words of the play. Other elements of the curse's context did, however, remain the same. Annotations in the 1756 edition of *Lear* record the elimination of lines from Goneril and Albany after the monarch's imprecation, a decision which allows the king to have the last, impressive words of the first act, and which remains the case in the version edited by Gentleman.

As for the words of the curse itself, however, they are slightly different, with Gentleman's text replacing Tate's writing with Shakespeare's. The speech's opening line reverts from Tate's 'Hear Nature! | Dear Goddess hear; and if thou dost intend | To make that Creature fruitful, change thy Purpose' (p. 18) to a version closer to how the line was printed in eighteenth-century editions of Shakespeare's tragedy: 'Hear, Nature! hear, dear goddess, hear a father!' (II, p. 20).[29] This is not the only such restorative change. By 1773, Shakespeare's 'Into her womb convey sterility' had replaced Tate's 'Pronounce upon her Womb the barren Curse', and Shakespeare's description of a 'child of spleen' to 'stamp wrinkles in her brow of youth' Tate's 'distorted birth' (with its overtones of *Richard III*). However, the words that close this speech and the play's first act in Gentleman's 1773 edition still retain Tate's phrasing to insert a mention of Goneril's 'crime' into her father's peroration:

> That she may curse her crime, too late; and feel,
> How sharper than a serpent's tooth it is,
> To have a thankless child! – Away, away.
>
>   (II, p. 20)

As well as the label of a 'crime', this adapted ending also makes the king's order to depart far weaker than Shakespeare's imperious 'Go, go, my people'. Such a variation is in line with accounts describing Garrick's rendition of the whole speech as a slow mix of vehement and tender emotions. Such slowness was not typical for Garrick and appears to have displeased some critics. 'Do not,' Cibber asked his readers, 'long Pauses damp the Fire' of the curse, which is 'hasty, rash, and uttered in the Whirlwind of his Passion'? Such slow-paced transition, Cibber once again points out, risked betraying the author's intention: Garrick's Lear, he observes, had at this point such a 'philosophic Manner' that the king's words seemed 'premeditated' and thus 'detestable and horrible', rather than able (as 'the Author designed') 'to excite Pity, and Terror' as part of a progress towards Aristotelian catharsis.[30] Later periodical accounts echo Cibber's critique. A contributor to the *Gazetteer and New Daily Advertiser* in 1765 described Garrick's pronunciation of the curse as 'more impious than rash'.[31] A retrospective article in the *General Evening Post* of 1777 compared Garrick's Lear with that of the recently deceased Spranger Barry and decided that it was Barry's speed, his ability to perform 'the quick, impassioned parts of tragedy' that made him the 'authority' in this role, ahead of the actor-manager.[32]

   Yet Garrick had his supporters too. Davies's biography defends the slowness of the curse while providing additional details about Garrick's actions. The actor's preparation 'was extremely affecting', as by 'throwing away his crutch, kneeling on one knee, clasping his hands together, and lifting his eyes towards heaven', he 'presented a picture worthy the pencil of Raphael'.[33] Recognising that 'certain critics complain' that 'Garrick was too deliberate' here, Davies counters such complaints by observing three things. First he asks his reader 'to reflect, that Lear is not agitated by one passion only [...] but by a tumultuous combination of them all together, where all claim to be heard at once, and where one naturally interrupts the progress of the other'.[34] This leads to his second point, that the complexity of 'lines [. . .] so full of rich and distinct matter' means that 'few men can roll them off with any degree of swiftness', and, even if some could (as the *Post* claimed Barry was able to), then they are departing from Shakespeare, who 'wrote them for the mouth of one who was to assume the action of an old man of fourscore [. . .] in whom the most bitter execrations are accompanied with extreme anguish, with deep sighs, and involuntary tears'. Davies's final counterargument is his report that the audience were deeply affected by the way that 'Garrick rendered the curse', seeming 'to shrink from it as from a blast of lightning', as though the words of the imprecation already brought the heath and the storm into the theatre two acts early.[35]

Whether an audience sided with Cibber or Davies, both standpoints share a strong sense of the emotional intensity of this climactic speech. Garrick himself recognised this, and the annotations to the 1756 edition of Tate's *Lear* focus audience attention on the imprecation by altering the lines that cue it. Rather than have Goneril remark, half to her husband Albany and half to the audience, 'Mark you that?', Garrick proposed that she instead speak the line 'We fear you not —' (p. 17). Such a change replaces a phrase that invites the audience to cast, with Goneril, a critical eye over Lear's speech with one that instead encourages emotional response, as (given the dash) the patriarch interrupts his daughter and seizes control of the scene.[36] Cibber describes the 'Fire' of the speech that follows and Davies its 'tumultuous combination' of passions, but it is Gentleman's annotations to the *Bell's Shakespeare* version of 1773 that best capture the key tensions of this moment, as Lear seems to hover between madness and reason. Ignoring debates over contemporary performance, Gentleman's note proposes two ways of performing the curse, with his preference being for a tripartite division, 'commencing with a burst of passion, and repressing a swell of grief, till the last two lines; then melting into a modulated shiver of utterance, watered with tears' (II, p. 20). Such a division helps explain others' divergent responses to this moment: this curse is a mix of emotions corresponding to Lear's unstable mental state. To perform the speech is to strike a balance between competing demands. As Lear descends into madness, Gentleman suggests not a slow nor a fast but rather a 'melting', transitional delivery of the first act's final lines: 'How sharper than a serpent's tooth it is, | To have a thankless child! – Away, away'.

The emotionally dense verse of Lear's curse, along with its 'melting' conclusion, reappears at the end of the second act, when the king's daughters once more 'work him up almost to Frenzy'.[37] Again, Garrick cut a line here from Tate to allow Lear's speech to conclude the act, while adding (both in the annotated 1756 edition (p. 28) and by 1773 (II, p. 36)) lines from Shakespeare's work back into Tate's adaptation. The final lines of the speech run as follows in Gentleman's edition:

> O let not women's weapons, water-drops,
> Stain my man's cheeks. No, you unnat'ral hags –
> I will have such revenges on you both,
> That all the world shall — I will do such things,
> What they are, yet I know not; but they shall be
> The terrors of the earth. You think I'll weep:
> No, I'll not weep. I have full cause of weeping:
> This heart shall break into a thousand flaws,
> Or ere I weep. O gods! I shall go mad. [*Thunder.*
> [*Exeunt.*   (II, p. 36)

Each of the two long dashes in Gentleman's printing of these lines captures a moment of transition. The first coincides with the amplification of Lear's anger, as he shifts from speaking of womanly weeping to thoughts of those women, his daughters, who have done him harm. The second dash checks that anger, breaking the monarch's train of thought so that the next lines rise to a new, more fragile crescendo, as the motif of weeping returns and comes to fix itself in the king's mouth. As in his curse on Goneril, Lear's last words here again offer what Gentleman called a 'melting' release, a moment of pathos that a correspondent calling himself 'Trim' described as 'a moment of perfection' in a letter of 1778 to the *Morning Post* on the subject of Garrick's acting.[38]

Cibber gives an unflattering account of Garrick's business at the end of this speech, which he uses to support his argument that the actor was 'not quite equal to the Character' of Lear.[39] According to Cibber, Garrick's Lear fainted after the line 'I shall go mad', a decision which ignores the fact that 'the preceding, and following Parts, point out to us that *Lear* rushes wildly from beneath the Roof, where he has been so unhospitably treated', although a defender of Garrick might – like Gentleman and Davies – point to the 'melting' conclusions of these end-of-act speeches to justify such a collapse. Yet, even were the fainting permissible, Cibber also takes exception to the execution of such action.

> His spirits being quite exhausted, he drops almost lifeless, into the Arms of his Attendants. – Do they carry him off? — Why, — No. Relaxed as we may suppose his whole Machine – (for his Head and Body are both thrown extravagantly behind, as if his Neck and Back were broke) yet his Knees (which in Nature would most likely falter first) are still so able to support

him, in that odd-bent Condition, that he walks off, with the regular Stiff-Step, of a Soldier in his Exercise, on the Parade.[40]

'Is this consistent? Is this natural? Is this Character?' Cibber pursues, with no need to give the answer to such questions. Instead, he describes the actor's acrobatic distortion of his neck and back (a trick reminiscent of the pantomime) as proof that Garrick is no better than any other actor, who 'is satisfied, if he can gain a Clap from the upper Gallery; — while the Pit, and Boxes, with a silent Shrug alone, condemn such *outré* Behaviour'.[41] Such a comment illustrates an alternate way of attacking Garrick's performance of madness, not as a short-sighted misreading of Shakespeare but rather as a deliberate, tasteless appeal to the uneducated low-class spectators of the Drury Lane galleries. Even Foote, in his more balanced analysis of Garrick's acting, also makes this point when he observes that Garrick's talent for navigating the emotional nuances of a speech, setting one extreme against another, can easily degenerate into a cheap 'Trick', since 'The Transition from one Passion to another, by the Suddenness of the Contrast, throws a stronger Light on the Execution of the Actor; and thus the Groundlings, who are caught more by the Harmony and Power of the Voice than Propriety, are easily drawn in to applaud what must grieve the Judicious'.[42] Set alongside Cibber's comments, Foote's remarks also make explicit what Cibber's rhetorical questions about naturalness and character insinuate, namely that Garrick's acting was a deliberate departure from Shakespeare's creation, a hubristic effort to interpose the actor between the author and the audience and thus to please the galleries at the expense of the boxes.

When combined, the laudatory and hostile accounts of Garrick performing Lear's descent into insanity allow us both to recover some of the speech and action of these scenes (the retention of words like 'crime' or the melting endings in Tate, the restoration of lines from Shakespeare, the kneeling, the fainting, and so on) and to map what was at stake in the performance of the transitions generated by a monarch's incipient madness. On one hand, those sympathetic to the actor-manager praised his ability to navigate the collapsing channels of Lear's thoughts to produce clear and moving (even 'melting') performances which naturally brought the character to life and so repeated Shakespeare's original creative gesture. Against this, a harsher view of the performance emerges as a spectacle, which departs from the believable performance of an elderly, unstable man through an irrationally slow delivery and awkward pantomimic movement, all of which separated actor from author, pleasing the footmen and alienating the cognoscenti. The performance of madness's transitions, whether judged well or ill, thus raised psychological, sociological, and aesthetic issues: could an actor understand madness, charting a clear path through the tumult of Lear's thoughts? Would such an understanding capture the fact that this was the madness of a monarch, and so, perhaps, qualitatively different from that in any other human being (including an actor, for all his pride)? And would that performance appeal to all the ranks of society assembled in the theatre or would it divide them, supplanting the nation's poet with Drury Lane's leading actor?

Raving

These jointly psychological, sociological, and aesthetic issues run throughout all versions of the eighteenth-century *King Lear* and are at their sharpest when Lear is seen raving on the heath. In his *Elements of Dramatic Criticism* (1775), William Cooke quoted at length from the storm scenes of the play's third act to illustrate 'sentiments dictated by a violent and perturbed passion', a kind of spectacle he believed absent from the works of his eighteenth-century contemporaries, since it required what these playwrights were not: an author capable of assuming 'different [...] and even opposite characters and passions in the quickest succession'.[43] It was, of course, on such sequences of extreme emotional variation that Garrick thrived as an actor, and, in both his annotations in the 1750s and the printed records of his later performances, we find evidence of his attempts to negotiate the challenges of representing the mental and meteorological drama at the heart of Shakespeare and Tate's tragedy by drawing on a wide range of performance techniques and materials that would augment his transitions.

As annotated and cut by Garrick, the second act of Tate's *King Lear* ends with the king's realisation that he 'shall go mad' (p. 28). The opening of the play's next section, set in *'A Desert Heath'* (p. 29), carries three manuscript notes (Figure 4.1). First, an order for 'Lamps down' (p. 29), the lowering of the stage's footlights to dim the stage, signalling the exterior, night-time setting of the scene and contrasting sharply with the interior, domestic events of earlier scenes (where lamps have been 'up' (p. 24)). The second note is an acronym, 'UDPS', indicating that the act's opening stage direction, *'Enter* Lear *and* Kent *in the Storm'*, would take place at the furthest possible point from the audience, the upper-door on the prompt side of the stage, and so requiring Garrick and Astley Bransby to then cover

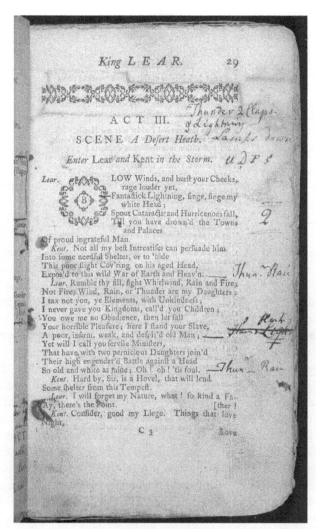

Figure 4.1 The start of Act III of Nahum Tate's *King Lear*, as annotated by members of the Drury Lane company in an edition of 1756 (p. 29). © The British Library Board (shelfmark C.119.dd.22).

some considerable distance towards the audience, while – as indicated in a third note – the storm's noises ('Thunder 2 Claps of Lightning') played around them (p. 29). The 'UDPS' marking is the only time this script marks a specific point of entry, preferring OP ('Opposite Prompt') or PS

for all other such stage directions. This suggests that a very specific effect
was desired at this point, one further heightened by Garrick's appearance as
Lear. An article from 1788, reviewing Kemble's performance of the role,
noted that both he and Garrick 'did not wear the white beard' when
playing Lear, but rather 'trusted [. . .] to the common expedient of whiten-
ing his face', on which 'Two or three black lines, well applied, would
further identify for age'.[44]

At the start of Act III, surviving evidence thus suggests that the lights
would dim and the curtain rise on an empty and deep stage, with its
open space created by having the scenery of the heath installed as far
from the audience as possible.[45] Thunder would rumble around the
auditorium, punctuated by two claps of lightning. Into this environment, Garrick as Lear, with his face painted white and Bransby's Kent at
his side, would step into view from the depths of the theatre. At such
a moment, when the pallor of his face was perhaps all that was clearly
visible in the gloom, the king might seem no more than any other fragile
old man, and so what Cibber and others would consider an inappropri-
ately undignified presentation of a monarch. Yet, as the scene pro-
gressed and as Garrick's Lear moved forward, the annotated script of
1756 records a dialogue between the king and the storm, seemingly
granting his speech the godly power that its opening lines clamour
for: 'Blow Winds, and burst your Cheeks' (p. 29). Such a dialogue
between the speech and the space, lighting, and sounds of the stage is
built around the transitions within Lear's outbursts, the fine shifts in his
mental and emotional state that Garrick, if we believe his supporters,
was so adept at finding. As recorded in the manuscript annotations on
Tate's text, Garrick's apparent delivery of Lear's second speech, this
time in full sight of the audience and in the full force of the storm,
offered a particularly clear example. A marginal note to this passage
describes 'Thunder' as a preface and adds a request for 'Rain' (p. 29).
On the heels of such effects, Lear issues another set of imperatives, their
sentimental contours marked out with handwritten suggestions for
meteorological interjections.

> _____*Thun*[&]*Rain*
> *Lear.* Rumble thy fill, fight Whirlwind, Rain and Fire;
> I tax not you, ye Elements, with Unkindness;
> I never gave you Kingdoms, call'd you Children;
> You owe me no Obedience, then let fall
> Your horrible Pleasure; here I stand your Slave,   *flash*
> A poor, infirm, weak, and despis'd old Man _____ ~~*Thun.&Light.*~~ ≠

Yet will I call you servile Ministers,
That have with two pernicious Daughters join'd
Their high engender'd Battle against a Head
So old and white as mine; Oh! Oh! 'tis foul. ___*Thun*&___*Rain*
(p. 29)

According to the annotations here, this speech is bookended by simula-
tions of thunder and rain. In Gentleman's performance edition of the play
from 1773, one finds both more lines from Shakespeare and a slightly
different placement of the final cue for thunder, now set to rumble its fill
just before Lear's final exclamation of 'Oh, oh! 'tis foul!' (II, p. 38). Such
precision means that the sound of the thunder accompanies the collapse of
the king's articulate expression, a collapse itself now familiar to an audience
from the melting endings of Lear's earlier speeches: behind 'Oh, oh! 'tis
foul!' lies the character's 'O Gods! I shall go mad' (p. 28; II, p. 36) at the end
of Act II and the weak order of 'Away, away' (p. 18; II, p. 20) at the close of
the first act.

In addition to providing a pair of sonic bookends for the speech
(preserved, apparently, into the 1770s), the manuscript notes also indicate
an attempt to key the representation of the storm to a shift in Lear's psyche
within the body of the monologue. As the hapless monarch's enraged
imprecations give way to the pathetic realisation that 'I stand your Slave,
| A poor, infirm, weak, and despis'd old Man', a long handwritten dash
marks out the moment of transition (p. 29). The suggestion of thunder to
accompany this point is cancelled but the idea of 'a flash' maintained. If the
word 'flash' indicates the use of a firecracker like those used in pantomimes
or some other sudden illumination, this use of light would have both
literalised Lear's own enlightened insight in the midst of his madness
and broken through the gloom of lowered lamps to make Garrick's
whitened face strikingly visible.[46] Those sitting close enough (including,
before 1763, those sitting on the stage) would have seen the new passions
rise in Lear as he addresses the elements as 'servile Ministers' of his 'two
pernicious Daughters' (p. 29). Gentleman's note to this speech and its
predecessor observes their 'awful solemnity', where 'What *Lear* utters in
the scene is emphatically characteristic, and teems with instructive pre-
cepts, most poetically connected' (II, p. 37). The addition of thunder, rain,
and – perhaps – flashes of light too are part of Garrick's efforts to meet the
demands of this section. A pale-faced entry at the back of a dim stage sets
the scale of the spectacle to come; the thunder underlines Lear's character-
istically melting conclusion; the flash captures a moment of insight and
emotional transition, a poetical connection around which the entirety of

the second speech pivots; and – throughout this scene – the dialogue of storm and speech captures the paradox of a mad king: one whose words might seem to have the force to raise the elements yet, as he himself comes to believe, have abdicated that also. While the testimony of Foote, Cibber, Davies, and the periodicals may encourage us to focus on Garrick's captivatingly decorous (or rebarbatively undignified) performance, the events of the heath, at the height of Lear's madness, remind us that this scene played itself out simultaneously upon a single, controversial performer's body and the fabric of Drury Lane theatre. The spectacle of transition was thus not the sole preserve of those able to afford seats from which they could see the actor's face.

Recovery

The use of theatrical arts to amplify transitions is not exclusive to the heath. It is also essential to Garrick's portrayal of Lear's recovery from madness in the arms of his daughter Cordelia, a moment which many writers of the eighteenth century and beyond considered one of the greatest beauties in his rendition of this role. At this point, however, the Drury Lane production used music rather than flashes and thunder-runs. John Burgoyne's preface to his comic opera *The Lord of the Manor* (1781) argued of this scene, as Michael Pisani has noted, that 'no person, who had a heart or taste, ever contemplated the mute groupe of Cordelia with the aged parent asleep in her lap [. . .] without an encrease of sensibility from the soft music which Mr. Garrick introduced'.[47] This music has no precedent in Tate, although it does correspond to the request of Shakespeare's doctor for 'louder the musicke there' (sig. K2r) in the 1608 quarto edition of the play. Pisani refers to Burgoyne's mention of it as part of a larger account of the rise of melodrama towards the end of the eighteenth century, but Garrick's annotated *Lear* suggests that the manager may have been considering the use of music for this scene as early as the mid-1750s.[48] A manuscript note indicates that the fifth act of the play should begin 'Curtain slow – with soft Musick' (p. 55).

In the printed text of Tate's *King Lear*, the monarch's recovery from madness is not only without music, it is also placed at the close of the fourth act. Garrick's decision to move this scene to the other side of the interval between acts, along with heavy cutting of a dialogue between Edmund and Goneril, is evident in the 1756 annotated edition (p. 57) and maintained in Gentleman's performance edition of 1773. Such alterations mean that the opening of the act both maintains a focus on Lear and serves as a happy counterpoint to the stormy beginning of the third act of the play. At that act-opening, the curtain rose on a large stage space to the noise of thunder and the sight of Lear mad and out of Kent's control; now the curtain rises on a smaller stage space, configured to represent an interior, with Lear unmoving in his daughter's arms and soft music playing.[49] After entr'acte entertainments that could include songs, a flute concerto, and even a short farce (as they did for one night's performance of this play in 1743), the audience returns to the main piece to find Lear in a strikingly different situation to that in which they left him, no longer descending deeper into madness but rising out of it.[50] Gentleman approved of such a change, praising its 'propriety' while noting that such a decorous scene nevertheless contained 'as fine strokes for a good actor to lay hold of a feeling audience by, as any in the play' (II, p. 67).

Burgoyne's description of the power of music to provide 'an increase of sensibility' in the audience was a key part of Garrick's attempts to lay hold of his public at the start of his play's final act. As music theorists of the eighteenth century knew well, different kinds of music could arouse different passions in a listener. Daniel Webb, writing in 1769, explained such an effect in terms of a correspondence between the movements of a piece of music and the vibrations of human sensibility. Garrick's call for 'soft' music, in the light of Webb's work (discussed at length in Chapter 3), thus appears completely appropriate, serving both to soften the hearts of the audience and as a way of making legible Lear's own recovery from the abrupt and violent emotional contrasts of his madness to a more calm and rational state.

Davies, in his retrospective account of Garrick's performances as Lear, does not mention the use of music, arguing instead that this actor had the ability to rationalise madness, to follow Lear through all the twists of his insanity and bring him to a new calm at the start of the fifth act, and the audience to new heights of enjoyment.

> In the preceding scenes of Lear, Garrick had displayed all the force of quick transition from one passion to another: he had, from the most violent rage, descended to sedate calmness; had seized, with unutterable sensibility, the various impressions of terror, and faithfully represented all the turbid passions of the soul; he had pursued the progress of agonizing feelings to madness in its several stages. Yet, after he had done all this, he exhibited himself in this fine scene, in such a superior taste, as to make it more interesting than any thing the audience had already enjoyed.[51]

This paragraph grants Garrick a preternatural sensitivity to the emotions of Shakespeare's creation, to the point that, no matter how complex or 'turbid' they might seem, he was able to pursue their progress, providing evidence of an aetiological understanding of Lear's madness as it grew out of 'agonizing feelings'. At the same time as offering such praise for Garrick's ability to represent madness, Davies also defends such representation from accusations of impropriety: Garrick's mastery entailed, for Davies, not just the sensitive and sympathetic performance of Lear's trauma but equally the expression of a 'superior taste' as the events of Lear's recovery allowed for it.

This assertion of 'superior taste' is an answer to the kind of accusation implicit in Cibber's sneer at accounts of the actor-manager's trips to Bedlam. Davies's description of Lear's 'progress of agonizing feelings', as distinguished by Garrick, is also part of an alternative model for understanding Lear's condition, one which stands in contradistinction to Foote's 1747 model and its accusation that Garrick had failed to capture Lear's essential kingliness. While Foote held that, at root, Lear's madness depended on the frustration of his desire for 'Royalty' and that Garrick failed wherever his Lear was insufficiently royal, Davies, perhaps even with such critique in mind, finds Lear's hamartia in his emotional constitution. A few pages before the passage quoted above, Davies argues that Shakespeare has introduced 'a character, amiable in many respects, brave, generous, frank, and benevolent; but, at the same time, wilful, rash, violent, and headstrong'. The 'unhappy resolution' to divide Britain soon leads 'from the short fury of anger' to 'unlimited resentment, furious indignation, and the most violent rage'. The 'agony and distress' of such passions lead Lear 'to the door of madness'.[52] Such a diagnosis does not emphasise Lear's regal status but rather his sensibility, and thus presents a Lear that Garrick, even for those who doubted his refinement, remained eminently qualified to portray.

Such a Lear, whose passions are more important than his royal birth, is one not so susceptible to the class-based criticism levelled by Cibber and others. Davies's detailed description of the performance of Lear's recovery insists on both its rigorous (and decorous) sensitivity to the uncertain return of the monarch's reason while also testifying to the number of moments in the scene that elicit an emotional response from all the ranks of the audience. As Garrick's Lear rose from his opening position, his head on Cordelia's lap, 'his hand closed in her's', their dialogue began with the king's statement 'I am mightily abus'd, I should even die with pity | To see another thus' (II, p. 68). Davies picks out these lines as one of those containing the transitions, the 'breaks and interruptions, of imperfect reason and recovering sense' which 'are superior to all commendation, and breathe the most affecting pathos'.[53] Another occurs a few lines later when Lear fears 'I am not in my perfect mind' (II, p. 68). Again, it is another short and largely monosyllabic phrase that, like many other lines here, does not quite cohere with the phrases around it, yet is all the more powerful for doing so, for being both a dynamic moment of change and an iconic point of realisation. The force of such lines reaches its zenith, for Davies, when Lear finally recognises Cordelia.

> The audience, which had been sighing at the former part of the scene, could not sustain this affecting climax, but broke out into loud lamentations.
>   Be your tears wet?[54]

The layout of Davies's page, with its abrupt presentation of the king's words to his daughter, adds an additional meaning to them. These four words not only remind the reader of Lear's touching observation of his child but also function as a question to that reader, asking whether they – either in the moment of reading or back when they saw this performance – cried as Susannah Cibber's Cordelia wept. Such a double meaning returns us to Gentleman's analysis of the scene as one in which 'there are some fine strokes for a good actor to lay hold of a feeling audience by', a point illustrated with a reference to the same moment identified by Davies, 'where [Lear] awakes, as it were from a trance, and discovers *Cordelia*'.

'Be your tears wet?' Davies's description of this scene in print appeared only months after the death of Garrick in 1779. The first purchasers of the volume could thus easily have been among those who had seen the actor perform this part, like Sir William Freeman who wrote in a letter (printed in 1776) that 'The Man who can view [Garrick] in Lear without Tears must have something about his heart which I have not'.[55] The writings of Cibber and Foote indicate that they were among such men, and there is as little chance of settling the controversies of Garrick's Lear now as there was in the eighteenth century. What is significant, however, is the very fact of the controversy. The performance of madness was a significant test of an actor's quality through transition: it required a masterful delivery of an extreme variety of passions, from the violent to the melting, as well as the quelling of such passions in the recovery of sanity. To perform Lear was to measure one's understanding of royal madness against Shakespeare's and to risk dividing an audience with one's interpretation of the text. Yet for all the ways in which this controversy turns on the person of Garrick, one should not lose sight of the extent to which Garrick's performance was augmented by sound effects, by make-up, by textual editing, and by music. Indeed, when we consider the play as a whole, the tears wept over Garrick's

Lear become part of an emotional pattern to which the entire production contributes, whether playing the mad, the sane, or some combination of the two.

Pretended Madness

Tate's dedication of his *King Lear* to Thomas Boteler claims that it was not just the monarch's 'real' madness but also '*Edgar's* pretended Madness' that made his subject such a play as 'could never have started, but from *Shakespear's* Creating Fancy' (p. 3). Such a phrase encourages us to read Lear's insanity alongside Edgar's feigned madness as two integral parts of Shakespeare's achievement. Despite such claims, however, Edgar's part, both as Poor Tom and as Gloucester's son, underwent far more revision in Tate's adaptation than in Lear's, with Tate's addition of a romance between Edgar and Cordelia that culminates in a recovered Lear blessing their forthcoming marriage. Tate justified such an addition in two ways: by suggesting that it 'renders *Cordelia's* Indifference, and her Father's Passion in the first Scene, probable' (p. 3), and by presenting it as a means of providing a 'Countenance to *Edgar's* Disguise', making what was, in Shakespeare, 'a poor Shift to save his life' into a 'generous Design' (pp. 3–4). The latter of these two arguments testifies to Tate's evident concern for the decorum of the young man's performance of madness: unless it were suitably framed as part of a romance plot, it risked becoming little more than a 'poor shift', degrading Edgar and providing little entertainment for a theatre audience. As before with Lear's real madness, even the pretend insanity of this play is not without risk. Some seventy years after Tate, Cibber may well have had a similar sense of Edgar's part in mind when he attacked Garrick's Lear. His mockery of the actor-manager's decision to visit Bedlam implicitly associates Garrick with Edgar's impersonation of a Bedlam beggar, and so with what could easily be a 'poor shift', a feigning, false madness rather than the true royal insanity of Lear. In such a way does the eighteenth-century Edgar shadow the eighteenth-century King Lear, giving an alternate perspective on the dangers of acting madness. Through a study of Edgar's part, a fuller understanding of this play's connection between the art of transition and the representation of mental health emerges.

Edgar narrates his transformation into Poor Tom on page twenty-two of Garrick's annotated 1756 copy of Tate's *King Lear*. This page, however, bears relatively few marks. Two pairs of concentric circles joined by a double line (◎══════◎) indicate a change of scene was expected to take place as Edgar entered to deliver his speech, a change that would have hidden the deeper recesses of the Drury Lane stage where Kent lay sleeping in the stocks (p. 22). A 'PS' at the start and an 'OP' at the end of the speech also inform us that Edgar would enter from the side of the stage nearest the prompter and exit opposite (pp. 22–23). Yet the words Edgar spoke while on stage are left unaltered in this document. Such words narrate a remarkable sequence of emotions. The opening lines of the scene register Edgar's fear; he has 'heard myself proclaim'd' and, although he has managed to 'Escape the hunt' for a moment, 'No Port is free' and 'no Place | Where Guards and most unusual Vigilance, | Do not attend to take me' (p. 22). But no sooner has he finished articulating such trepidation than the young man abstracts himself from it with a sudden melancholy contemplation of the benefits of suicide: ' – How easy now | 'Twere to defeat the malice of my Trale [trial], | And leave the Griefs on my Sword's reeking Point' (p. 22). Yet Edgar is no Hamlet, and this sombre turn is immediately checked in the next line, as he tells of how 'Love detains me': '*Cordelia*'s in Distress' and he 'must be near to wait upon her Fortune' (pp. 22–23). Such thoughts take root, and the next two lines are suffused with hope: 'Who knows but the white Minute yet may come, | When *Edgar* may do Service to *Cordelia*' (p. 23). In the space of thirteen lines, Tate's adaptation thus requires the performer playing Edgar to express first fear, then despair, then love, then hope before taking the dreadful resolution to 'submit | To th'humblest Shifts to keep that Life a-foot' (p. 23). The majority of these lines are still in place in Gentleman's edition (supposedly regulated from the Drury Lane promptbook) of 1773, where a pair of footnotes record that this brief moment 'seldom fails to gain the performer applause', offering a 'fine scope for variation and extension of acting powers' (11, p. 30): an opportunity, in other words, to execute extreme transitions between such different emotions as fear, despair, love, and hope. In this 1773 text, Shakespeare's words have replaced Edgar's final lines, so that the character's climactic resolution to play the madman now also coincides with a striking shift in language, featuring unusual verbs ('elfe all my hair in knots'), vulgar details ('Blanket my loins'), and a renewed focus on the body of the performer (11, p. 30). It is as if Shakespeare's words have become the only ones suitable for capturing the assumption of insanity.

Edgar's transformation demonstrates the extent to which feigned madness can provide a similar 'scope for variation' as the violence of real madness. When Edgar's impersonation meets the terrifying spectacle of the deranged king, however, it serves a different function. An unusual mark in the margin halfway through one of Lear's speeches in Garrick's 1756 text

(*HHl*) appears to indicate the point at which Edgar was to sneak into the hovel, making the character's first line as a madman – 'Five Fathom and a half, poor *Tom*' – surprise the audience as much as those on stage (p. 34).[56] As the supposed Bedlamite and the king enter conversation, Tate and Garrick both kept much of Shakespeare's raving, with only two small changes. The 1756 printing of Tate's play contains dashes that, typically for mad scenes, mark out the unpredictable rhythms and transitions of Edgar's ramblings ('The Foul Fiend follows me —Through the sharp Haw-thorn blows the cold Wind ———— Mum, go to the Bed and warm thee —— Ha! What do I see?' (p. 34)), while manuscript annotations mark some of Edgar's lines for deletion (p. 35). Crucially, however, Shakespeare, Tate, and Garrick all agree in having Edgar speak an aside revealing his response to Lear's mental state, his fear that 'My Tears begin to take his Part so much, | They mar my Counterfeiting' (p. 36; II, p. 45). Indeed, Tate and Garrick both add to this level of detached commentary by inserting an additional aside later in the same scene. Just after Poor Tom proclaims, 'I smell the blood of a *British* man', Edgar's rational voice re-emerges and cries '—— Oh! Torture!' (p. 38; II, p. 47). While this line asks for an especially quick transition from a giant's rage to a young man's pity, it also reveals how Edgar's part in this scene gives voice to audience sympathies. Shakespeare's Edgar does this too, but not to the extent of the eighteenth-century character, whose feigned madness not only offers 'scope for fine variation' but acts as a bridge to the even more extreme emotional transitions of his king at the heart of the tragedy.

While added lines and manuscript annotations hint at the importance Tate and Garrick accorded to Edgar's assumed madness, one eighteenth-century critic studied it directly. That critic was John Hill, a botanist, journalist, entrepreneur, and sometime friend of Garrick, whose book *The Actor* was once advertised for the price of '3s. bound in Calf' in the *London Daily Advertiser and Literary Gazette* just beneath a notice announcing that day's performance of *King Lear* at Drury Lane.[57] Hill's book, first published in 1750, was heavily based on Pierre Rémond de Sainte-Albine's *Le Comédien* (1747).[58] In addition to translating the French treatise, Hill also, however, added numerous passages of his own creation, expanding on his source material and providing examples taken from the English stage. The seventeenth chapter of Hill's work is devoted to variety in acting. He begins by criticising those actors who wrongly suppose that 'they are under no necessity of varying their play, when they perform the same kinds of parts'. Instead of this, Hill recommends that the performer 'decompose his parts, and regulate himself by the several subordinate passions, of which the grand one that makes his character is form'd'.[59] The French that Hill was translating here contained only the injunction 'qu'il analise chacun de ses rôles qui paroissent à peu près semblables' ('that he analyse each of his roles which seem quite similar'), meaning that Hill adds three things: the focus on diversity within a role (instead of just between them), the idea of 'decomposing' a part, and an attention to both the relation between 'subordinate passions' of each transition and the over-arching 'grand one' that forms the *dramatis persona* (p. 292).[60] This extended technique is, Hill claims, particularly useful in parts 'which have a general resemblance' (p. 292), something which he illustrates through a comparison of how Covent Garden's Lacy Ryan performed madness, first as Edgar in Tate's version of *King Lear* and then as Orestes in Ambrose Philips's *The Distressed Mother* (1712).

Philips's play, like Tate's, was an adaptation (of Jean Racine's *Andromaque* (1667)), but Hill offers no comment on the provenance of either text and even appears to take Tate's *Lear*, as perhaps many theatre-goers also did, for Shakespeare's version. First, Hill describes the insipid show put on by an anonymous actor, impossible now to identify, who performed both 'The raving of *Orestes* and the pretended madness of *Edgar*' (p. 292) in exactly the same way. Ryan, on the other hand, played each part so as to make visible the distinction between them.

> In the character of *Orestes*, we read in him a heart torn to pieces with anguish and with rage, and which gives room in his ravings for no other thoughts: In the other we read a settled sorrow thro' all the fancy'd wildness of his deportment, and can see that it is but put on, and that all the while some other passion wholly possesses his heart. (p. 292)

Hill identifies two different configurations of tragic passion in Ryan's Orestes and Ryan's Edgar. In Orestes, the truly mad, the character's passions are all-consuming and leave no 'room in his ravings for other thoughts'. The same might be said for King Lear on the heath. In Edgar, however, Hill discerns two levels on which the passions appear: one is the superficial level of the assumed madness and 'fancy'd wildness', the other that of his thwarted love for Cordelia, the 'settled sorrow' that 'wholly possesses his heart' and thus acts like a base note over which the explosions of feigned insanity appear. The importance of this configuration in Edgar appears when Hill first criticises those performers who 'bestow all their care and attention on the mad part' (p. 292), and then praises Ryan as one who clearly paid attention not just to Poor Tom's raving but also the scene which follows it, when Edgar, roaming the heath, saves Cordelia from a pair of ruffians and then reveals himself to her.

> There is not perhaps on the stage a more moving scene than that of *Edgar*'s discovering himself to *Cordelia. Shakespear* [*sic*] meant the mad things that precede it principally as foils to it; and 'tis in this sense that the player we are commending in the part performs it. (p. 293)

In Hill's reading, Edgar's feigned madness is part of a larger pattern and, to the discerning theatregoer, makes that pattern visible. When he rants as Poor Tom, the audience should (as Ryan's supposedly did) still perceive the powerful sorrow beneath, because this thwarted love then makes the subsequent scene of Cordelia's rescue all the more powerful. Hill describes such a pattern as one of 'foils', where Edgar's supposed madness acts to generate a pleasing variety of passions both in the moment of his raving and across the duration of the play. Hill goes even further, however, and argues that such variety, because it balances reason and madness, transforms scenes of insanity, which could all too easily appeal indecorously to the lowest members of the audiences exclusively, into something that even the most refined theatregoer should appreciate.

> These are the real beauties of the part of *Edgar*: the galleries may be affected by noise, and a series of frantick actions, which neither they nor the person who exhibits them understand; but 'tis the change to reason, the contrast of these passionate and affecting speeches alone, that charms the more judicious part of an audience; and the making the madness not the principal part of the character, but subservient to these, is the great secret of that difference for which we are applauding Mr. *Ryan* for making between the raving of *Edgar* and that of *Orestes*. (pp. 294–95)

Hill's analysis of Ryan's performance does not simply argue for the power of performed emotion to capture an audience, it also emphasises the extent to which those passions benefit from a 'change to reason' in order to touch the public. Such a 'change to reason' redeems mad scenes from accusations of bombast, and instead ties the most effective transitions to an actor's ability to combine rational and irrational behaviour. Edgar's asides in the hovel do this, producing a powerful contrast between mad anger and rational pity.

Hill's theories allow a modern reader to understand the pathos of Edgar's lines in the hovel as 'foils', both as striking instants of contrasting emotion (and reason) and as moments that remind an audience of the character's position in the wider plot. When Davies surveyed Garrick's *Lear*, he also commented on Edgar's behaviour, pointing to a similar effect of 'foils' when describing the young man's serendipitous rescue of Cordelia on the heath as 'a gleam of sunshine and a promise of fair weather in the midst of storm and tempest', one which earnt 'applause' every one of the 'twenty or thirty times' that Davies saw it. The scene, like others with Edgar, gives what Davies calls 'a pause of relief' for 'the harassed and distressed minds of the audience'.[61] Unlike Hill, however, Davies writes such a defence of Edgar's part in the wake of George Colman's efforts to perform a *King Lear* without Tate's additions. While Colman, admits Davies, had the authority of such luminaries as Samuel Richardson and Joseph Addison for his decision to excise the Edgar-Cordelia love plot, Garrick's biographer was himself not alone in preferring Tate's version.[62] Gentleman also defended Edgar's role as a foil to the darker elements of the tragedy. In his *Dramatic Censor*, Gentleman argued that the 'incident of Edgar's saving Cordelia from the Bastard's ruffians' was 'worthy of praise as a happy thought' and might even be approved by 'SHAKESPEARE, that competent and liberal judge of human nature' as 'an ornament' to his play.[63]

Gentleman's suggestion, that Edgar's romance (including the impact of that romance on his decision to feign madness) might make Shakespeare's play better, leads to the question of how successful tragedy was defined in the eighteenth century. Hill's *Actor* distinguished between comedies and tragedies by arguing that the former contained a variety of weak emotions and the latter a few contrasting and powerful passions (p. 17).[64] Cibber, when he attacked Garrick's insipid performance of Lear's curse, relied on a similar definition: a slow delivery of the imprecation jeopardised the power of tragedy by presenting differing passions of insufficient force.

Yet definitions that concentrate on the force of individual passions do not adequately explain Edgar's role as a foil, nor account for how audience engagement with such passion was maintained. For this, we can turn to Henry Home, Lord Kames, and his explanation of how we experience art in his *Elements of Criticism* (1762). In a chapter devoted to emotions in fiction, Kames distinguishes what he calls an 'ideal presence' as distinct from both 'real presence' and 'superficial or reflective remembrance': fiction produces an 'ideal presence' when it brings an absent object to our mind, which we perceive through 'an act of intuition, into which reflection enters not'.[65] Because of the way we perceive 'ideal presence', Kames suggests that it may 'properly be termed a *waking dream*', something that 'vanisheth the moment we reflect upon our present situation'.[66] When discussing drama later in his treatise, Kames reuses the term 'waking dream' to describe the 'perfection of representation', which is 'to hide itself,

to impose on the spectator, and to produce in him an impression of
reality, as if he were a spectator of a real event'.[67] Yet such a 'waking
dream' is still defined for the theatregoer by its potential collapse, for 'any
interruption annihilates that impression, by rousing him [...] and
unhappily restoring him to his senses'.[68] In order to prevent such
a collapse, Kames points to the use of 'seasonable respite' in a tragedy.
Moments of respite serve to 'relieve the mind from its fatigue; and
consequently prevent a wandering of thought' that would otherwise
occur should a play (as some might wish) maintain the same level of
emotional intensity throughout its performance.[69] Kames's theories
share much with ideas articulated by Samuel Johnson and Adam
Smith, and they serve here to illustrate how we might set the role of
Edgar, and Hill's concept of 'foils', in a new light.[70] Rather than
breaking the compelling emotional spectacle of the tragedy, Edgar's
asides, his rational madness, and his romantic scenes with Cordelia
may in fact provide the very mental space necessary for a full appreciation
of Lear's madness by an eighteenth-century audience. As Davies put it,
Edgar provides 'a pause of relief'. Hill's acting treatise, for all its emphasis
on the importance of powerful emotions for creating tragedy, also
endorses this position when he writes that a good dramatist is one who
'suspends for a few moments the rage, or the misery of his principal
characters, to relieve for a time the audience and the player, it is generally
done with design to engage them immediately afterwards in scenes yet
more affecting' (p. 20).

Edgar's feigned madness provides such suspension. So too, we might
now argue, do certain moments even in the part of King Lear, notably his
recovery, which Davies revealingly positioned as the climax of Garrick's
performance, the moment when 'he exhibited himself [...] in such
a superior taste, as to make it more interesting than any thing the audience
had already enjoyed'.[71] To borrow further from Hill, the restoration of the
king's senses is a 'change to reason', an emotional shift in a character, which
is both effective in the moment and – across the tragedy as a whole – an
important element, a moment of relief, in a larger pattern of foils.
Attention to Edgar's part, so heavily altered in the eighteenth century,
makes this pattern visible, and with it, two connected ways of understanding the art of transition as both a microscopic and a macroscopic phenomenon. Microscopic transition occurs within a specific character, whether it
is the way in which Garrick's Lear traced the contours of a curse or whether
it is Edgar's rapid progression through fear, despair, love, and hope as he
prepares to become Poor Tom. These scenes, done well, were also

understood by some, however, as part of a larger structure of aesthetic experience. This macroscopic pattern of transition appears in terms of a progression through a scene or set of scenes. This is the work of 'foils', whether it concerns Hill's identification of Edgar's contrasting scenes of madness and love or Kames's defence of an uneven theatrical experience, with moments of 'seasonable respite' harnessed to prevent a disruptive 'wandering of thought'.

Although Kames is remarkable for theorising such a phenomenon in detail, all the figures discussed in this chapter were sensitive to it. Even Tate's preface to his adaptation, published eighty years before Kames's work, also testifies to his awareness of a play's need to create coherent emotional patterning. A lack of such careful sequencing is, for example, one of the problems of Shakespeare's *Lear*, which Tate calls a 'Heap of Jewels unstrung' that are nevertheless 'dazzling in their Disorder' (p. 3). Exchanging gems for plants, Tate repeats the same point about sequencing and ordering when writing his prologue, whose lines describe the 'Heap of Flow'rs' which now 'shall chance to wear | Fresh Beauty', 'strung by this coarse Hand' into a new arrangement (p. 5). In fact, Tate's arrangement, his 're-stringing' of this play, both through the careful positioning of moments of relief between moments of tragedy and – on a miniature level – the organisation of emotional patterns within rewritten speeches, betrays no 'coarse' hand. Eighteenth-century commenters sympathetic to Garrick or, in Hill's case, to Ryan found the play, for all the risks of madness, to contain ample material for suitably decorous performance, and Edgar's feigned madness was a crucial part of this.

Shakespeare

Tate's description of the way in which he 'strung' the powerful individual emotions of Shakespeare's text into a palatable sequence of distress and relief is more than a defence of Edgar's professions of love for Cordelia and the ramifications of this for his impersonation of madness. It is also a defence of Tate's new ending for the play, where, 'in a Success to the innocent distrest Persons' (p. 4), Lear saves Cordelia and himself from execution and, with a tired but happy Gloucester at his side, blesses his daughter's marriage to Edgar. To support his claim that such a rearrangement could improve the disordered (yet impressive) beauties of Shakespeare's play, Tate cites John Dryden's just-printed preface to *The Spanish Friar*.

> Neither is it so Trivial an Undertaking to make a Tragedy end happily, for
> 'tis more difficult to save than 'tis to kill: the Dagger and the Cup of Poison
> are always in Readiness; but to bring the Action to the last Extremity, and
> then by probable Means to recover All, will require the Art and Judgment of
> a Writer, and cost him many a Pang in the Performance. (p. 4)[72]

Dryden's words provide evidence for what Blair Hoxby has defined as a distinctively pre-Romantic understanding of tragedy, one where the passions were the essential elements of tragic drama and the full expression of feeling rather than the full expression of volition mattered most. Lear's survival in Tate, rather than his death in Shakespeare's text, provides the greatest range of emotion, even if it does not offer the concluding annihilation of an individual will that German writers of the turn of the nineteenth century would soon make central to their influential definition of tragedy.[73] In Hoxby's chronology, Garrick's Lear should belong to the same world as Shakespeare's, a world now lost to most, where pathos was more important than plot trajectory. At the same time as belonging to this world, however, and as this section shall argue, Garrick's Lear, and particularly its final scene, offers us a particularly useful glimpse into the nuances of pre-Romantic tragedy. It shows us how, on one hand, Tate and Garrick together were able to find new forms of emotional variety within Shakespeare's text without necessarily altering its words (reconfiguring microscopic transition by altering macroscopic situations) and, on the other, how, when these men did alter or add lines, they did so with different aims in mind, producing different ranges of emotion. Finally, the eighteenth-century Lear allows us to look at Shakespeare's text with fresh eyes, seeing it not as a Romantic tragedy of conflict and annihilated will but as Tate and Garrick saw it: a play with such an extreme approach to the representation of powerful passion that it could not be staged without the rearrangement of its emotional beauties.

As already discussed, Garrick's fifth act departed from Tate's in order to begin with Lear's recovery from madness as a powerful emotional set-piece which drew its strength from a 'change to reason'. This was not the only change Garrick made, however. A scene in which Goneril and Edmund prepare for the upcoming conflict between their forces and those loyal to the former king is also excised in annotations on the 1756 text (pp. 57–58), and only partially restored by the time of Garrick's retirement (11, pp. 69–70). This means that a few plot details are lost, most notably an Officer's report that 'old *Gloster*' has been led through the rebel ranks and 'so enraged their rustick Spirit, that with | Th'approaching Dawn we must expect their Battle' (p. 58). Such a detail had built upon earlier hints in Tate's version at civil unrest under Lear's two daughters, but these hints are also removed by Garrick as his version of the play, even more so than that of 1681, rushes from emotional climax to emotional climax (in this case, from Lear's moving recovery to Edgar and Gloucester's experience of the battle). The same priorities are evident in Garrick's treatment of events after the failure of Kent and Cordelia's forces and the defeat of Edmund at the hands of Edgar. Here, the actor-manager of Drury Lane again cuts Goneril and Regan's lines as they first dispute each other's love for Gloucester's bastard and then reveal that each has poisoned the other. The key information, the punishment of evil by the evildoers' own hands, remains, but the play once more rushes back to King Lear and Cordelia. Rather than hearing Goneril crow her desire to 'let me see | How well that boasted Beauty will become | Congealing Blood, and Death's convulsive Pangs', she simply informs her sister 'Thou drank'st thy Bane, amidst thy rev'ling Bowls' (p. 64). Regan replies in kind, and a dying Edmund concludes the scene by asking 'Who wou'd not chuse, like me, to yield his Breath, | T'have Rival Queens contend for him in Death?' (p. 65).

What happened next is ambiguous: no exit is marked for anyone, but the annotated printing of the play suggests a discovery scene, in which the stage cleared and the flats parted to reveal 'Lear *asleep, with his Head on* Cordelia's *Lap*' (p. 65). The use of distinctive manuscript marks used elsewhere for changes of scene (◎══════◎) testify to this decision, which had the added merit of allowing the play's final moments to repeat the stage picture of the fifth act's opening, as father and daughter are once again presented to the audience.[74] What happens next is also a repetition. The entry of 'Captain *and* Officers *with Cords*' (p. 65) repeats the entry of the Bastard's Ruffians sent to seize Cordelia in the storm of the third act. This time, however, the maiden is not rescued by her lover but by her father, as Lear '*Snatches a Partisan, and strikes down two of them; the rest quit* Cordelia, *and turn upon him*' (p. 66). Only then do Edgar and Albany appear to put a stop to the Bastard's plot and assure a happy ending. In Tate's rearrangement (maintained by Garrick), Lear's defence of his daughter thus both echoes Edgar's actions on the heath and supplants them, establishing the monarch, no matter how old and fragile he might be, as – once more – a patriarchal authority. Doing so requires the actor playing Lear to make a massive effort. As the soldiers enter the prison, Lear awakes with lines that demonstrate the scope for performance of different passions available to characters suffering from mental instability. First there are the half-asleep mutterings of a bellicose dream ('Push, push the battle, and the Day's our own'), then the confusion of waking ('Who holds my Hands?'), then the despair as realisation dawns ('——O thou deceiving Sleep, | I was this very Minute on the Chace; | And now a Prisoner here' (p. 65)). Only after this does the monarch rage and act 'an old Man's Vengeance' (p. 66) in the final part of this demanding sequence. In December 1765, *The Daily Gazetteer* reported that Garrick had 'withdrawn himself in some measure from the more laborious exertion of his abilities' and names Lear among such exertions when it both praises the decision and mourns the fact that 'we are not to expect to freeze again with horror at Macbeth, Richard and Lear'.[75]

As far as the last act of *King Lear* is concerned, it is the entry of the officers with cords that constitutes the last moment at which an audience might freeze with horror. Beyond this point, Tate's play, and Garrick's version of it, both offer an extremely reassuring conclusion. The script of 1756 indicates little cutting of Tate's final scene, with only the deletion of a line in which Cordelia reacts to the death of her sisters. The loss of her words, 'O fatal period of ill-govern'd Life!' (restored in Gentleman's edition of 1773) may keep Cordelia free of association with Regan and Goneril but may also be intended to keep the focus on Garrick's Lear, whose own response thus faces no competition, and instead performs a swift transition, marked by a dash, from mourning to marriage: 'Ingrateful as they were, my Heart feels yet | A Pang of Nature for their wretched Fall ——| But, *Edgar*, I defer thy Joys too long', Lear announces, and then gives Gloucester's son his daughter's hand (p. 69). Both children express their joy, but Gloucester himself begs the gods for his 'Discharge', prompting Lear to chide him (p. 69). This speech is Lear's last in all versions of Tate's play. Circular markings (⊕) in the margins of the 1756 promptbook suggest that this speech may have been framed by music: if true, this would have added to the speech's gravity, further emphasising a return to stability.[76] In Tate, Lear's words were followed by those of Edgar, the new ruler of Britain, and while his speech remains in the 1756 promptbook, it disappears from Gentleman's performance edition of the 1770s. As before in the prison, a recovered Lear takes over from Gloucester's son.

> No, *Gloster*, thou hast business yet for life;
> Thou, *Kent*, and I, retir'd from noise and strife,
> Will calmly pass our short reserves of time,
> In cool reflections on our fortunes past,
> Cheer'd with relation of the prosp'rous reign,
> Of this celestial pair; thus our remains
> Shall in an even course of thoughts be past,

Enjoy the present hour, nor fear the last.

(II, p. 80)

If Lear's madness was characterised by extreme emotional volatility, this concluding speech stands as its antithesis. The measured pentameter of each line, the heaviness of the rhymes, and the repeated statements of tranquility ('calmly pass', 'cool reflections', 'even course') all combine to finish the tragedy at a point of restored balance, the past resolved and a 'prosp'rous' future envisaged. The sentiments expressed by Tate here, unaltered by Garrick, are reminiscent of the endings of other Restoration tragedies, including those by Dryden, whose authority Tate had cited in his dedication: *The Indian Emperor* concludes with Guyomar's vision of a new colony where 'We to our selves will all our wishes grant; | And nothing coveting, can nothing want'; *The Conquest of Granada* with Almanzor's proclamation of Ferdinand and Isabel's reign; and *Aurengzebe* with the Emperor handing Indamora and the crown to his son.[77]

Yet while Tate and Garrick's *King Lear* kept an ending reminiscent of Dryden's heroic tragedy on British stages throughout the eighteenth and into the nineteenth century, this final speech prompts another way of studying this adaptation of Shakespeare too. Lear's last speech is more than a happy tragic ending; it also appears to be reworking some of the motifs from Shakespeare's own conclusion, when an exhausted Edgar (folio) or Albany (quarto) delivers a pair of couplets as Lear and his daughters lie dead around him.

> The waight of this sad time we must obey,
> Speake what we feele, not what we ought to say,
> The oldest haue borne most; we that are yong
> Shall neuer see so much, nor liue so long.
>
> (sig. L4r)

These lines share the same temporal themes as Tate and Garrick's conclusion: the past, the present, and the future; youth and age. Yet while Shakespeare's speaker figures himself as one who must obey the 'waight of this sad time', Tate and Garrick's Lear instead presents the man as one half of a 'celestial pair', no longer a youth doomed to a short life, but rather on the brink of prosperity. As for the 'oldest' who 'haue borne most' and now lie dead, Tate's verses recognise the 'noise and strife' and difficult 'fortunes past' but turn resolutely towards the future: there are 'short reserves of time' remaining, and no need to 'fear the last'. Each line of the adaptation's conclusion thus answers Shakespeare's and suggests that one might not read forward from the eighteenth-century *Lear*, with all its celebrated transitions, its foils, and its passions, but instead look backwards and consider what we may, from such a vantage point, find in Shakespeare's play.

There are many transitions in Shakespeare's *Lear*, in both its folio (1623) and quarto (1608) printings, some of which survive in Tate's writing and many more of which were reincorporated by Garrick. In the moments following his father's attempted suicide, Edgar – in all versions of the play – urges Gloucester to 'Bear free and patient thoughts', only to be interrupted by Lear's arrival, '*mad*' (sig. I3v), '*drest madly with Flowers*' (Gentleman (II, p. 61)), or '*A Coronet of Flowers on his Head; Wreaths and Garlands about him*' (Tate (p. 51)). The surprise of the monarch's entry triggers a momentary transition in Edgar from reassurance to surprise but also serves as a macroscopic, structural shift: just as one patriarch improves, another intrudes and reminds the audience of the grim state of British affairs. The structure here is one of a fall, of a point that appears to function as a nadir only to be ruthlessly undercut by another event a moment later. Such a structure is characteristic of Shakespeare's play. As Edgar himself puts it at the start of Shakespeare's Act IV (but not in Tate or Garrick's versions), 'the worst is not. | As long as we can say, this is the worst' (sig. H2v). There are other examples of this in the Jacobean script, some of which (but not all) survive into the eighteenth century: Lear does not just banish Cordelia *but Kent too*; both Regan *and Goneril* fall for Edmund; one of Gloucester's eyes is put out and – despite the servant's intervention – *the other too*. For all this play's talk of 'nothing', there always seems to be, as Edgar tells us, something worse in reserve.

That these lines, the most explicit statement of a structural pattern whereby events progress from worse to worse, were never spoken in the eighteenth century should not surprise us. Edgar's view is of a tragedy without respite, without even the respite of knowing oneself at the lowest point. It is this relentless degeneration that is at the core of Shakespeare's play, something which becomes all the more visible when it is compared with the 'foils' of the eighteenth-century adaptation, which provide the relief so lacking in their predecessor, inserting love scenes or – on a smaller, yet connected, level – providing characters with emotional transitions that kept an audience in pathetic suspension. As one reviewer of Tate's play wrote in 1751, 'It was judicious in the Author to make the Catastrophe favourable to his virtuous Characters', but, nevertheless, 'even with this Advantage it hurts us'.[78] What hurts – but not unduly – in the conclusion of the adapted Lear are its transitions, and it is the successful renegotiation of these transitions that Tate and Garrick undertook in order to please the audiences of their day.

Cibber's hostile appraisal of Garrick also identified the transitions of this *King Lear*'s last act as a sequence of massive emotional shifts. His *Two Dissertations* praise Barry's ability to navigate the passion of the play's final scene far better than Garrick, notably when it comes to the announcement of Cordelia's marriage to Edgar, when the king's 'distressed Mind, thus suddenly relieved, by so quick a Transition to Joy, may, in that Gust of Rapture, drop a Tear, but 'twill be a Tear of Transport'.[79] Such a mix of happiness and sadness in the performer seems calculated to move the audience to a state of pleasurable pain, a judicious conclusion that nevertheless hurts us. Gentleman was also aware of this and sketches the entire rollercoaster of the adaptation's last act in his *Dramatic Censor*: 'the attempt to assassinate him alarms human apprehension' while 'the happy effect of his desperation, raises a degree of satisfactory astonishment'.[80] In his edition of the play for John Bell, Gentleman also draws attention to this specific moment of change from 'alarm' to 'satisfactory astonishment'.

> GENT. Look here, my lord, see where the generous king
> Has slain two of 'em.
> LEAR. Did I not, fellow?
> I've seen the day, with my good biting faulchion
> I cou'd have made 'em skip: I am old now,*
> And these vile crosses spoil me; out of breath!
> Fie, oh! quite out of breath, and spent.   (II, p. 77)

The asterisk here sends the reader to Gentleman's note, which observes how 'This speech affords a transition, which often furnishes, as audiences have experienced, an admirable stroke for acting merit' (II, p. 77). The monosyllabic core of this transition, 'I am old now', is Shakespeare's, used unaltered from the Jacobean text.

> CAP. Tis true my Lords, he did.
> LEAR. Did I not fellow? I haue seene the day,
> With my good biting Fauchon I would
> Haue made them skippe. I am old now,
> And these same crosses spoyle me, who are you?   (sig. L3v)

Yet while these lines are very similar, events around them could not be more different. In the eighteenth-century version, Cordelia lives, and her father, even as he realises his senescence, nevertheless speaks as a patriarch still capable of defending his daughter. In the early seventeenth century, however, Cordelia is dead and Lear's line a restatement of his own impuissance, a further deepening of the tragedy in the play's last scene. Garrick and Tate could preserve Shakespeare's words while altering their emotional content, both on a microscopic and a macroscopic level. In this way, they break from a descending pattern that runs throughout Shakespeare's conclusion, a pattern (particularly visible from an eighteenth-century point of view) in which the characters of this play bear a relentless and draining kind of transition.

Shakespeare's lines narrate such exhaustion through transition throughout his play's last scene. In the final moments of the drama, every person on the stage except Lear reaches a point where they can no longer respond to events: Kent's question in response to Lear's entry with Cordelia dead in his arms, 'Is this the promist end?' (sig. L3v), wishes for relief, wishes that this was 'the worst'. Yet it is not the end, and as Lear begins to mourn his daughter, Kent, Albany, and Edgar find themselves no longer able to summon up fresh passion, and must instead, as Albany says, 'Fall, and cease'. As their monarch himself soon observes, they become 'men of stones' (sig. L3v). Yet Shakespeare's Lear, however, goes on, and continues to swing between a whole variety of passions, becoming the cynosure of the theatre. From screaming 'A plague upon you murderous traytors all' to whispering '*Cordelia, Cordelia,* stay a little'; from the repetition of 'neuer' to the polite request to 'vndo this button' and the final order, 'Breake hart, I prethe breake'; at every point in these last few minutes, Lear is moving between emotions (sigs L3v–L4r). But, as Garrick and Tate suspected, the audience, like Kent, Edgar, and Albany, have been left behind at this point: they too feel painfully how the play would stretch Lear out longer. The theatregoers, having been moved again and again by all the awful events of the last three hours, now share in the overwhelming emotional exhaustion that covers those around the king and leaves Lear to speak his final words alone. While this was undoubtedly effective in Shakespeare's time, and remains so in our own, such an improper pressure on the theatregoer was not possible for Garrick or Tate. Indeed, Johnson famously notes that he even had difficulty *reading* Shakespeare's conclusion, let alone watching it.[81]

Davies, in his defence of Garrick's Lear, repeats Johnson's observation about the unbearable trauma of Lear's Shakespearean ending. He does so to vindicate Garrick's choice of text over Colman's attempts to stage a version of the play without Tate's alterations. Yet whether we examine the Tate-Garrick drama or Shakespeare's, this chapter has demonstrated that an attention to transition, to emotional sequence, is a valuable method for doing so. When applied to Garrick's Lear, considered by many to be his greatest achievement as an actor, the part emerges as one which offers both extraordinary opportunities for the expression of emotion and significant risks. In the actor-manager's performances, hostile critics found ample material to demonstrate an inability to capture royal madness, which simultaneously damned Garrick as a bad actor and as a tasteless social climber. Friendlier writers, like Davies, offered alternate frameworks for understanding Lear's insanity, rooted in emotional instability (and not in the consciousness of royalty), which showed the actor in a better light, as one who could not only encompass the extremes of the role but even somehow rationalise them so as to appeal as much to the pit and the boxes as to the gallery. As for Garrick himself, what may be gleaned from his annotated script and its various modifications over the decades, not to mention a range of other sources, records a willingness to use all the affordances of the Drury Lane stage to express the passions of the king, whether through pale make-up, dimmed lights, and crashing thunder or through the introduction of soft music as he made a thrilling 'change to reason'.

The combination of reason and insanity in this play, and its expression through transition, is as visible in Edgar as it is in Lear. Garrick's emendations limited the part of Gloucester's son, yet he still served throughout the eighteenth century as a source of needful relief. In a role that also demands many swift changes of the passions, Edgar articulates the audience's shock at the king's behaviour in the hovel, and, in his scenes with Cordelia, he serves as what Hill called a 'foil' to the play's darkest moments. Through Edgar, the structure of the eighteenth-century drama appears clearly as one designed to keep alive a Kamesian 'waking dream': not through intense engagement but instead by allowing for moments of suspension, not least at the play's conclusion. At the same time, it is Edgar's vision, in Shakespeare's play, of a world where 'the worst is not. | As long as we can say, this is the worst' that most clearly captures my reconstituted eighteenth-century reading of the Jacobean text. The adaptations and the criticism of the long eighteenth century, sensitive to the need for transition, show us how to respond to Shakespeare's work as a piece of relentlessly extreme sequential emotion. Tate and Garrick recoiled from this; they broke the cruel pattern of bad to worse at the heart of

Shakespeare's play and made transition the herald of salvation. The last moments of their plays offer a newly rational cadence to contentment and justify Gentleman's claim that 'the transitions of Lear are beautiful'.[82] Shakespeare's conclusion, on the other hand, exhausts his characters and audience, leaving Lear alone, still torn between a range of emotions, still in transition when all others have ceased, and, even now, all the more terrible for it.

CHAPTER 5

Dramatic Character

For Elizabeth Montagu, the soliloquies of Macbeth were proof of Shakespeare's genius.

> [...] He exhibits the movement of the human mind, and renders audible the silent march of thought: traces its modes of operation in the course of deliberating, the pauses of hesitation, and the small acts of decision: shews how reason checks, and how the passions impel; and displays to us the trepidations that precede, and the horrors that pursue acts of blood.[1]

This analysis indicates Montagu's sensitivity to the transitions in the speeches of the Scottish king. Shakespeare's Macbeth offers a powerful, fluctuating spectacle: the 'march of thought' has its 'pauses', each decision is one of many 'small acts', the mind is held in tension between 'reason' and the 'passions', and the whole process operates between points of fear and horror. Montagu's comments appeared in her *Essay on the Writings and Genius of Shakespeare, Compared with the Greek and French Dramatic Poets, With Some Remarks Upon the Misrepresentations of Mons. de Voltaire* (1769), as part of a chapter devoted to the Scottish play. She continues her observations with the claim that, while the 'Greek and French writers represent' characters who 'narrate' or 'declaim in the solitude of the closet', Macbeth's speeches demonstrate how Shakespeare adds 'to the drama an imitation of the most difficult and delicate kind, that of representing the internal process of the mind in reasoning and reflecting' (p. 184). Such an imitation is a 'very useful art', because, by vividly expressing the 'anguish of remorse', it also serves a moral purpose *'to amaze the guilty and appal the free'* (p. 184).[2]

This passage provides an example of how a critic of the later eighteenth century made use of the transitions of a text to support her broader argument against Voltaire's disparaging assessment of Shakespeare's tragedies as 'monstrous farces'.[3] Such literary critical uses of transition are the subject of this chapter, which focuses on writing about Shakespeare for two reasons. First, there is the strong connection between an interest in dramatic transition and Shakespeare's writing: the frequency of plays by Shakespeare on stages in the wake of the Licensing Act of 1737 meant that the points and transitions of his plays acquired a certain notoriety, as indicated by their frequent appearance in acting manuals, prints, letters, and other sources.[4] In particular, David Garrick's cultivation of a connection between himself and Shakespeare, through his performances of plays and programming of seasons at Drury Lane and through his ode and Shakespeare Jubilee, helped associate Shakespeare's dramas with his own highly transitional performance style.[5]

In addition to the connection between Shakespeare and (Garrick's) dramatic transitions, my second reason for focusing on writing about Shakespeare in this chapter is the prominence that this figure had acquired by the later decades of the eighteenth century. Such prominence (partly due to Garrick's efforts) meant that writing about Shakespeare had a particularly significant cultural impact, both in Great Britain and abroad. In 1760s Britain, Shakespeare's status was such that the publication of Samuel Johnson's edition of his plays in 1766 constituted, in the words of Antonia Forster, a 'monumental event' for reviewers, with articles devoted to it in *The Gentleman's Magazine* (ten pages), *The Critical Review* (forty-two pages), and *The Monthly Review* (thirty-one).[6] As for Shakespeare's influence abroad, Montagu's *Essay* itself provides us with an example: it went through five editions in the first eleven years after its appearance in Britain and was read throughout Europe, with translations into German (1771), French (1777), and Italian (1803). To write on Shakespeare was, as Montagu herself recognised, to take up a position on one of the most important – and contested – battlegrounds of eighteenth-century Anglophone culture.[7]

Montagu's successful entry into this arena inspired many, including the professor of humanity at Glasgow University, William Richardson, who both praises the *Essay* and carefully distinguishes his own work from it in the first of four volumes he published on Shakespeare's characters. Considering Montagu's and Richardson's writing alongside each other allows for a larger argument to be made about the development of the concept of transition in literary critical writing of the later eighteenth century. Both writers evoke transitions as proof of Shakespeare's exceptional ability to imitate human experience, to the point that his creations have a distinct moral value. Their attention to these two things – Shakespeare's artistic skill and moral impact – contribute, however, to an evolution in the way in which the phenomenon of transition is understood,

particularly when we compare Montagu and Richardson to early eighteenth-century figures like John Dennis and Aaron Hill. Dennis and Hill
emphasised the moment of change, what Dennis called 'the admirable
gradation of Thought' in a Horatian ode or *Paradise Lost*, and what Hill
paradoxically described as a performer's rendition of 'the very *Instant* of the
changing Passion'.[8] Montagu and Richardson, as they demonstrate
Shakespeare's ability to create natural human behaviour with a moral
charge, do not emphasise the moment of change so much as the way in
which the patterns of transition contribute to the depiction of what one of
their contemporaries called 'the *whole* character'.[9] In Montagu's writing
about Macbeth, while she certainly has specific instances in mind (as she
details them later), her praise of Shakespeare's writing actually focuses on
collections of moments, on transitions in the plural: 'pauses of hesitation',
'small acts of decision', and the ongoing psychological processes whereby
'reason checks' and 'the passions impel'.

To inscribe striking moments within a systemic view of character is
a significant change in emphasis, as an appreciation of the iconic and
dynamic power that transition brings to the artistic expression of emotion
becomes the starting point for further enquiry. Philip Fisher regrets that
'pathology', a word 'which would exactly suit the study of the passions',
now 'serves instead [...] for the study of abnormality, the study of
diseases'.[10] As I return to the material that I have so far only evoked, this
chapter will attempt to bridge this word's customary and etymological
meanings by showing how attention to the transitional expression of
emotion for pathos (a 'pathos-ology', if you will) gives way, in literary
criticism of the eighteenth century, to an attempt to explain emotion, to
diagnose, rationalise, and pathologise it. I begin by charting the existence
of an attention to transition as a key element in some prominent literary
critical writing of the later eighteenth century. I then argue that, within
such writing, the understanding of transition evolves. Borrowing a term
that Montagu, Richardson, and their contemporaries make frequent use
of, one might describe this evolution as a shift from dramatic transition to
'dramatic character'. Montagu does this as she argues for the moral impact
of Shakespeare's dramatic characters (as opposed to the impact of a specific
transition) and Richardson as he suggests that Shakespeare's dramatic
characters are such perfect imitations of life that their transitions might
serve as the subjects of philosophical enquiry into human nature. In both
cases, moments of transition become symptomatic expressions of an
underlying character. In the third part of this chapter, I use Maurice
Morgann's *Essay on the Dramatic Character of Falstaff* (1777) to illuminate

the tensions inherent in such a critical standpoint, as efforts to pathologise pathos, to explain moments of transitional spectacle in terms of a character's fundamental traits and qualities, risk minimising the very spectacle that invited such explanation in the first place.

The Powerful Agency of Living Words Joined to Moving Things

As befits a text whose author wished to 'labour' the 'peculiar excellencies of Shakespeare as a dramatic poet',[11] the first chapter of Montagu's *Essay* considers 'the offices and ends of the drama' (p. 25). Montagu provides an Aristotelian definition of the dramatic poem as 'an imitation of the actions of men, by the means of action itself' (mimesis), distinguishing it from the epic, which is 'an imitation of the actions of men [...] by narration' (diegesis) (p. 25). Regardless of its epic or dramatic form or the country in which it was practised, the 'general object of poetry' has always been 'the instruction of mankind' (p. 26). Yet the efficacy with which poetry achieves such an object is connected to its form, and Montagu – again citing Aristotle – argues that the dramatic form is a superior vehicle of instruction. Aristotle, she argues, placed 'the invention of the dramatic imitation' at the head 'of all the eminent perfections' of Homer, because he realised 'the powerful agency of living words, joined to moving things, when narration yields the place to animated action' (p. 28).

The language of life and movement here is Montagu's own and should remind us of her praise of Shakespeare's ability to show 'the movements of the human mind'. Such language is one of three interrelated aspects of her critical approach. The others are her elevation of Shakespeare and her emphasis on the capacity of tragedy to fascinate and transport an audience and thereby provide moral education. This last idea emerges clearly in her definition of a tragedy:

> A tragedy is a fable exhibited to the view, and rendered palpable to the senses; and every decoration of the stage is contrived to impose the delusion on the spectator by conspiring with the imagination. It is addressed to the imagination, through which it opens to itself a communication to the heart, where it is to excite certain passions and affections: each character being personated, and each event exhibited, the attention of the audience is greatly captivated, and the imagination so far aids in the delusion, as to sympathize with the representation. (pp. 29–30)

Montagu caps her definition with two quotations from Pope's 1713 prologue to Joseph Addison's *Cato*. The first defines tragedy's task as 'To make mankind in conscious virtue bold, | Live o'er each scene, and be what they behold', while the second succinctly captures the process of sympathetic audience engagement in the question 'When Cato groans who does not wish to bleed?' (p. 30).

The decorous invocation of such authorities as Pope and Aristotle in this opening section masks the polemic dimensions of Montagu's description of 'the offices and ends of the drama'. Her belief that drama, specifically tragic drama, provides moral instruction by mimetically joining living words to moving things and so inspiring a state of sympathetic 'delusion' in its audience takes direct (but undeclared) aim at the position outlined by Johnson in the preface to his edition of Shakespeare's plays. Johnson had both used the word 'delusion' as part of a dismissive summary of the idea that audiences could be enthralled by a performance and belittled the specific power of 'dramatic exhibition' as, simply, 'a book recited with concomitants that encrease or diminish its effect'.[12] A comedy like *The Taming of the Shrew* might benefit from performance, but Johnson openly wondered 'what voice or what gesture can hope to add dignity or force to the soliloquy of Cato'?[13]

Montagu, on the other hand, cites Pope to suggest – *contra* Johnson – that the extra-textual, concomitant groans of Cato are in fact crucial to the sympathetic process she calls 'delusion'. Her audience members are susceptible to the spectacle of 'each character being personated [. . .] each event exhibited': their imaginations are fired by the experience of seeing actions unfold (rather than hearing them narrated), and they thus enter into a non-reflective state where their hearts are open for moral instruction. Consider the following example from much later in her *Essay*, when she returns to the idea of delusion in a description of Shakespeare's depiction of Rome in *Julius Caesar*.

> To the very scene, to the very time, therefore, does our poet transport us: at Rome, we become Romans; we are affected by their manners; we are caught by their enthusiasm. But what a variety of imitations were there to be made by the artist to effect this! and who but Shakespear was capable of such a task! (p. 248)

As before with Cato, so too does this passage have a Johnsonian precedent. When demonstrating the follies of accepting 'delusion' as a model of audience experience, Johnson scoffs that 'if the spectator can be once persuaded that his old acquaintance are Alexander and Caesar [. . .] he is in a state of elevation above the reach of reason, or of truth'.[14] Montagu's chapter on *Julius Caesar* is ostensibly a rebuttal of Voltaire's unflattering comparison of Shakespeare's play to Corneille's *Cinna*, but it also serves to distinguish her work from her predecessor, as she once again argues for emotional audience engagement rather than a more rational, contemplative response. Montagu attributes such engagement to the 'variety of imitations' in Shakespeare's work. As the examples given in her *Essay* indicate, points and transitions are a key part of this variety.

When Lucius tells Brutus of the arrival of the other conspirators 'muffled up at midnight', Brutus, observes Montagu, 'cannot help breaking out' with 'O Conspiracy! | Sham'st thou to shew thy dang'rous brow by night [. . .] ?', and so expresses his disgust far better than any narration of it would (p. 259). When Constance rebukes Cardinal Pandulph in *King John* – 'He speaks to me that never had a son' – the spectators, struck by the forceful expression of 'the peculiar tenderness of maternal love', no longer find the legate's 'arguments of consolation' reasonable (p. 36). When Lear wishes Goneril might feel how 'sharper than a serpent's tooth it is, | To have a thankless child', the monarch reveals his wounded 'paternal tenderness', and such a moment is all the more potent for leaving out 'whatever of this enormity is equally sensible to the spectator' while instead exposing the king's 'internal feelings' to the audience (p. 35). These direct expressions of the passions that Lear, Constance, and Brutus suffer are used by Montagu to illustrate the moral force of the theatre. They are also all recognisably moments of transition. Brutus breaks out into anger, Constance scorns the cleric and the king, and Lear collapses from anger to self-pity. Indeed, the last two of these transitional moments were also celebrated points of theatrical performance: Garrick's Lear was considered one of his greatest roles, while Constance was a star vehicle for actresses from Elizabeth Barry to Sarah Siddons.[15]

Yet Montagu's *Essay* is not especially interested in contemporary practice, and she instead concludes this part of her chapter on dramatic poetry with a portrait of the man who wrote these scenes, whose 'expressions open to us the internal state of the persons interested, and never fail to command our sympathy' (p. 37).

> Shakespear seems to have had the art of the Dervise, in the Arabian tales, who could throw his soul into the body of another man, and be at once possessed of all his sentiments, adopt his passions, and rise to all the functions and feelings of his situation. (p. 37)

This celebrated passage, an early version of which survives in a letter from Montagu to Lord Lyttelton, draws on the language of the supernatural to express the extraordinary sympathetic powers of Shakespeare that, in

Montagu's model, enable the sympathetic engagement of the audiences in his plays.[16] An audience sympathises because they experience the delusion that the characters are real, yet this is only possible because the creator of those characters (and not, notably, the performer of them) has made such perfect imitations that they bear comparison to the disguises of the magical creature who repeatedly deceives Aladdin in *The Arabian Nights*. That creature, as Montagu explains, did not just imitate a moment from the life of another man, but rather possessed him totally. We are thus to understand here that Shakespeare's sympathetic powers are similarly absolute: his plays may contain striking moments, singular transitions like those of Constance, Lear, and Brutus, but they are simply one element among 'all the functions and feelings' of Shakespeare's complete creation.

Nowhere is this shift of focus from momentary effect to totality of character more visible than in Montagu's lengthy analysis of Macbeth. The praise given here to Shakespeare's ability to trace 'the movement of the human mind', quoted above, is itself preceded by a compliment on his 'attention to consistency of character' (p. 183), and such consistency emerges clearly in the course of the chapter, even as Montagu marks out moments of transition. Macbeth's soliloquy on the 'supernatural soliciting' of the witches expresses, for instance, his 'abhorrence [. . .] at the suggestion of assassinating his king', bringing him to the determination that he will wait till 'chance may crown me, | Without my stir' (pp. 185–86). Yet in the 'pause' made by Banquo's interjection, Montagu argues for a transition in the thane's thoughts, such that 'we may suppose the ambitious desire of a crown to return' (p. 186). Rather than point this as a single moment of change, however, these lines are presented instead as evidence of 'The conflicts in the bosom of Macbeth' (p. 185), conflicts which Montagu plays out for us repeatedly: first, as Macbeth reflects on all the reasons why he should not kill his king ('He's here in double trust') and then again as Macbeth 'summons up the resolutions needed to perform' (p. 189) the murder. Such conflicts are proof of Macbeth's inherent nobility, and even after Duncan's death, Montagu continues to paint the character favourably: he does not undertake to eliminate Banquo 'like a man, who, impenitent in crimes, and wanton in success, gaily goes forward' but rather 'seems impelled on' while desiring to 'keep Lady Macbeth innocent of this intended murder' (pp. 191–92). A little later, Montagu again encourages us to see Macbeth's 'abhorrence' (p. 193) of the witches in his address of them, a feeling that is consistent with a righteous loathing at what they have helped him to become. Ultimately, 'The man of honour pierces through the traitor and the assassin' (p. 195): such a conclusion reconfigures points and transitions as moments of conflict in a complex character suffering under extraordinary circumstances. As Montagu puts it, Shakespeare preserves in Macbeth a 'consistency of character', which is both 'naturally susceptible of those desires which were communicated to it' and 'interesting to the spectator by some amiable qualities' (p. 196). In the course of the play, this figure exemplifies 'the dangers of ambition, and the terrors of remorse', thus providing 'all that could be required of the tragedian and the moralist' (p. 196).

Montagu thus considers Macbeth as a complete creation, whose striking transitions are evidence of a consistent character in that they are symptoms of a general situation, that of a noble man susceptible to the suggestion of others. In Montagu's analysis of Brutus, she reaches a similar conclusion. The Roman's angry outburst against conspiracy is simply proof of the fundamental constitution of his character: 'Disguise and concealment are so abhorrent to the open ingenuity of his nature' (p. 259), or, later, 'A peculiar gentleness of manners, and delicacy of mind, distinguish him from all the other conspirators' (p. 262). Montagu hypothesises that Shakespeare characterises Brutus in such a way 'to interest the spectator' in him as one to whom 'Clemency and humanity [. . .] determine the whole character, and the colour of his deed' (p. 274). The audience may be struck by sudden emotional sequences, but their interest and sympathetic engagement also depend on the nature of the character as a whole. Although she does not state it clearly, one potential reason for Montagu's arrival at such a position is her opposition to Voltaire, who, in addition to describing Shakespeare's plays as 'monstrous farces', had also offered some praise of their ability, amidst all their barbarity, to 'dart such resplendent flashes [. . .] as amaze and astonish'.[17] Rather than accept Voltaire's implication that these dramas are best appreciated for their successful vignettes, Montagu seeks to reintegrate these moments into Shakespeare's plays as proof of the value of the entire work. However, and as so often in this *Essay*, what might be a response to the French philosopher also provides a cloak and shield for Montagu to challenge her English predecessors obliquely, since she also broadly accuses them of an attention to parts and not the whole. 'Modern criticism', she writes, 'dwells on minute articles' (p. 274) and ignores the principle object of the drama: totally engaging the spectator so as to offer moral instruction.

In the final pages of her *Essay*, Montagu returns to this theme, claiming that 'the dramatic requires a different species of criticism from any other poetry' (p. 287). Drawing once more on the language of 'living things', she sketches what this criticism might attend to:

A drama is to be considered in the light of a living body; regularity of features, grace of limbs, smoothness and delicacy of complexion, cannot render it perfect, if it is not properly organized within, as well as beautiful in its external structure. Many a character in a play, like a handsome person paralytic, is inert, feeble, and totally unfit for its duties and offices, so that its necessary exertions must be supplied by some substitute. The action is carried on much after the manner it is done in epic poetry, by the help of description and narration, and a series of detached parts. (p. 287)

Montagu's emphasis here is on a distinction between the internal and the external. Shakespeare's characters succeed because he captures (with dervish-like sympathy) and expresses (with suitable attention to context) the interior life of his creations. The relationship between transition, the compelling performance of changes in emotion, and criticism thus evolves: transition in Shakespeare cannot be the phenomenon of a moment because that would entail a critical failure, the superficial treatment of his drama as a lifeless creation where action is either carried on by 'a series of detached parts' or reliant on the 'exertions of some substitute', like an actor. Instead, transition, in a great playwright, becomes the expression of the internal consistency of the drama, the first step in a process of understanding a larger whole. It is the showing of emotion that allows drama to make a moral impact on Shakespeare's enraptured spectators, but that moral impact depends on accepting that these moments of strong emotion derive from an imitation of a character in its entirety, and so depends on accepting an understanding of Shakespeare's character as beings who are as deep and complex as you or I.

Poetry Subservient to Philosophy

William Richardson opened his *Philosophical Analysis and Illustration of Some of Shakespeare's Remarkable Characters* (1774) with a list of what he considered to constitute a 'genuine and original Poet'.[18] Such a figure 'displays the working of every affection, detects the origin of every passion, traceth its progress, and delineates its character' (p. 1). In so doing, 'he teaches us to know ourselves, inspires us with magnanimous sentiments, animates our love of virtue, and confirms our hatred of vice' (p. 1). The moral outcome of the poet's imitation depends on our emotional engagement with that work:

> Moved by his striking pictures of the instability of human enjoyments, we moderate the vehemence of our desires, fortify our minds, and are enabled to sustain adversity. (pp. 1–2)

Richardson's opening statements sketch an understanding of poetry that is similar to Montagu's approach to tragedy. Both critics recognise the beneficial moral impact of an artwork that engages our emotions with convincing imitations of human behaviour. Richardson's suggestion that the 'genuine and original Poet' is one that 'displays' all the intricate 'working' of a figure's 'affections' is close to Montagu's emphasis on showing rather than telling and the unrivalled impact of 'living words joined to moving things'. As well as sharing a similar approach to the morality of poetry with Montagu, Richardson's writing also contains the same sensitivity to moments of transition – what he calls at the start of his book 'striking pictures', although, as in Montagu's *Essay*, Richardson's *Analysis* tends to consider such moments in the plural, so as parts of a larger whole. In the passage quoted above, it is when 'striking pictures' are considered as a group that they carry a moral charge by serving to represent 'the instability of human enjoyments'.

In the final sentences of his introduction, Richardson implicitly recognises that his readers may be tempted to note certain similarities between his writing and Montagu's when he argues that 'my design by no means coincides with that of the ingenious author of the Essay on the Writings and Genius of Shakespeare' (p. 40). Praising Montagu as one engaged in 'rescuing' Shakespeare from 'partial criticism' and 'drawing the attention of the public to various excellencies in his works', Richardson both minimises the intellectual scope of his predecessor's publication and makes his own intention sound all the more radical: 'to make poetry subservient to philosophy, and to employ it in tracing the principles of human conduct' (pp. 40–41). What Richardson means by this is relatively simple. Recognising that Shakespeare 'unites the two essential powers of dramatic invention, that of forming characters [. . .] and imitating [. . .] the passions and affections of which they are composed', he vows to analyse the 'component parts' of Shakespeare's creation in order to 'improve the heart' and 'inform the understanding' (p. 40). Indeed, as Richardson also argues, Shakespeare's writing is a better subject for such moral analysis than one's own interaction with reality.

At the heart of the *Analysis* lies an intellectual problem. Isaac Newton had shown that, despite the apparent chaos all around us, 'On a more accurate inspection' we find 'that harmony and design pervade the universe; that the motions of the stars are regular; and that laws are prescribed to the tempest' (p. 12). The same thing, Richardson holds, should be true for the human mind: although we may not have defined them yet, 'every accurate and sedate observer is sensible' of 'The laws that regulate the intellectual system' (p. 14). In particular, there must be laws governing the passions, yet two factors made the study of this object especially difficult. First, there was the problem that 'the passions are swift and evanescent', with no way to 'arrest their celerity, nor suspend them in the mind during pleasure' (p. 17); as anyone attentive to transition would know, they are 'combined, blended, or opposed [...] they are suddenly extinguished, in a moment renewed, and again extinguished' (p. 18). Second, the passions are not only impossible to seize in the moment of one's experience of them but also because they can even 'elude the most dextrous and active memory' (p. 19). Richardson's solution to the intellectual problem of discovering those rules that must, in a Newtonian universe, govern the passions was to turn to Shakespeare's writing and treat it as a source of specimens of human nature.[19]

This solution requires a recognition of Shakespeare's ability to inhabit and express a vast variety of emotional states. For Montagu, this made Shakespeare like the dervish; Richardson prefers the name of Proteus, long used to describe theatrical excellence.[20]

> Possessing extreme sensibility, and uncommonly susceptible, he is the Proteus of the drama; he changes himself into every character, and enters easily into every condition of human nature. (p. 38)

Because Shakespeare does this, his writing lays out on the page or the stage imitations of a 'passion in all its aspects, by pursuing it through all its windings and labyrinths [...] combining it in a judicious manner with other passions and propensities' (p. 40). In short, Shakespeare provides the necessary specimens for a Newtonian study of the passions. Here lies the difference between Montagu and Richardson. Montagu aimed to forge a style of criticism that captured Shakespeare's dramatic genius, his unrivalled capacity for imitation that makes his characters morally instructive (unarticulated by Johnson and misrepresented by Voltaire). Richardson's introduction makes clear that he accepts Montagu's definition of Shakespeare's genius for imitation, but he then uses it to justify a transformation of Shakespeare's writing into a superior source for the study of the passions than either oneself or other humans. Such an approach results in an even more pronounced shift in the uses of transition than Montagu: Richardson not only enters even more deeply than Montagu into the minutiae of Shakespeare's lines of speech but also, as he uncovers in them symptomatic shifts in feeling, claims to use them as the basis for statements about both the entirety of a character *and* the fundamental principles of all human behaviour. He pathologises pathos.

Macbeth and Hamlet provide the first two examples of this method. The second section of Richardson's analysis of the Scotsman begins by briefly recognising the dramatic effectiveness of performing a variety of emotions, when he notes that 'Every variation of character and passion is accompanied with corresponding changes in the sentiments of the spectator' (p. 55). Yet such 'variation' is soon encapsulated within a statement that focuses on the entire system of Macbeth's character: he is one who displays 'the distraction which ensues from the conflict between vicious and virtuous principles', and it is the display of this conflict in general rather than the momentary changes of the passions which captures audience attention by making this character 'the object of compassion mixed with disapprobation' (p. 55). This is a significant distinction. Lisa Freeman has demonstrated how theatre performance exploited an understanding of identity as 'the unstable produce of staged contests between interpretable surfaces' to produce meaning.[21] Richardson turns against this, claiming that, while variations of character and passion may cause changes of emotion in the spectator, in the case of Macbeth it is the way in which these changes are symptomatic of the overall state of the character as one torn between virtuous and vicious principles that render him such an affecting object. The emphasis thus moves from the moment of variation, of conflicting surfaces, to the system that underlies that variation, the whole character of Shakespeare's creation. This shift of emphasis resembles that performed by Montagu, but Richardson's analyses also go further than his predecessor's by then taking the experience of Macbeth as a model for understanding human behaviour in general. We can trace the steps of such analysis – from moment to whole character to human nature – in Richardson's writing about the early scenes of Shakespeare's Scottish play.

Focusing on a pair of asides in the third scene of the play's first act, Richardson describes a series of abrupt transitions in Macbeth's mental state. When the thane observes that 'If chance will have me King, why, chance may crown me', we see, according to Richardson's analysis, that, 'in agony, and distracted with contending principles', Macbeth has 'abandoned the design of murdering Duncan', a decision which allows him to achieve some measure of tranquil resignation, as expressed in the character's second aside, 'Come what come may, | Time and the hour runs thro' the roughest day' (p. 57). Yet this calm does not last long: Duncan's decision to name Malcolm as his heir, taken in the play's next scene, 'rouzes and alarms' Macbeth, who then speaks the following words apart, as 'The surprize, and the uneasy sensation excited by the perception

of difficulty' agitate his mind, 'their emotions coinciding with his ambition' to 'renew and increase its violence' (pp. 57–58).

> The Prince of Cumberland! – That is a step,
> On which I must fall down, or else o'erleap,
> For in my way it lies. (p. 58)

Richardson breaks off his quotation halfway through the third line of this
aside, noting another sharp transition at this point, which occurs when
Macbeth's 'conscience and his humanity are again alarmed, again interfere
and shew him the horror of his designs' (p. 58). This new emotional state
runs through the next line and a half.

> Stars, hide your fires,
> Let not light see my black and deep desires.
>
> (p. 58)

From Macbeth's 'If chance will have me King' to his 'Stars, hide your fires',
the thane has moved from an 'agony' of indecision, to calm, to surprise, to
violent anger, and then to horror. Richardson has identified a show-
stopping sequence of transitions between different extremes of emotions,
using the layout of his book's page to accentuate them. Yet the identification of such moments is only the first step in Richardson's analysis, for even
as he marks out such a progress, his choice of language presents it as
symptomatic of the whole character of Macbeth. First, he notes the crucial
role played by 'ambition' in this sequence, which acts like a catalyst (always
present and unchanging) to 'renew and increase' the violence of Macbeth's
reactions (p. 58). Second, he not only identifies the constant presence of
ambition but notes how the emotions of Shakespeare's Scotsman follow
a discernible pattern. The 'conscience and humanity' of Macbeth are 'again
alarmed', by his words, and 'again interfere' and force him to feel the
'horror of his designs' (p. 58). The repetition of 'again' here places each
individual moment within a larger, seemingly predictable, sequence, indi-
cative of Macbeth's conflicted character as a whole.

In the course of its next few pages, Richardson's chapter continues to
exhibit moments of transition in Macbeth. From the horror of 'Stars, hide
your fires', Macbeth's muted response to his wife's suggestion that Duncan
'never | Shall sun that morrow see' indicates a renewed acceptance of his
plan to commit regicide (p. 59). Yet the thane panics once again when he
wishes 'If it were *done*, when 'tis done, then 'twere well | It were done
quickly', before recovering his resolution in the face of Lady Macbeth's

chiding of him (pp. 61–63). Each of these transitions is again explained as part of a larger system of character, as Macbeth continues to vacillate. Yet from such vacillations Richardson draws more than a portrait of Macbeth's psyche: he also claims that the constitution of Shakespeare's character effectively models principles of human nature. The relative calm of the thane upon his return to Glamis indicates the way in which 'Habituated passions possess superior advantages over those opposite principles which operate by a violent and sudden impulse' (p. 58). Macbeth's 'habituated passion' is his ambition, and the 'violent and sudden impulses' – while great for spectacular transitions – spend their strength without overcoming it. Richardson repeats the point several times and adds a moral admonition.

> The lively feelings, opposed to ambition, unable, by the vivacity of their first impression, to extirpate the habit, languish, and are so enfeebled. The irregular passion, like the persevering Fabius, gathers strength by delay: the virtuous principle, like the gallant, but unsupported Hannibal, suffers diminution, even by success. Thus, it is manifest, that the contest between the obstinacy of an habituated passion, and the vehemence of an animated feeling, is unequal; and that there is infinite danger even in the apparently innocent and imaginary indulgence of a selfish passion. (pp. 63–64)

Richardson's use of Roman history seems to anticipate Macbeth's own fall from power, even as he explains the process by which the Scotsman came to act on his ambitions. Such an explanation, with an admonitory conclusion on the dangers of indulging 'a selfish passion', completes the progress of Richardson's analysis. From the observation of points and their transitions as Macbeth moves between surprise, anger, and horror, through the inscription of such turns within the whole character's constitutive systemic conflict between ambition and virtue, to the moral insight and attendant lesson of this conflict: that habituated passions eventually triumph over even our most strongly felt impulses against them, and that, for this reason, one should avoid reinforcing such a perilous thing as ambition.

The example of Macbeth is followed by that of Hamlet, where Richardson's method is even clearer. He begins with the declaration that 'In analyzing the mind of Hamlet, I shall accompany him in different situations [. . .] observe the various principles of action that govern him [. . .] and sum up the whole with a general view of his character' (p. 82). This summary demonstrates one of the ways in which Richardson, in his study of a 'mind', emphasises the entirety of a character over striking moments of emotion: he externalises sources of variety as 'different situations' or stimuli and figures the internal workings of a character as both stable and potentially universal, composed of 'principles' and susceptible to a 'general' rather than a particular view. In the case of Hamlet, the constant of the prince's character appears at the very start of the play, as his behaviour provides proof of a person 'Exquisitely sensible of moral beauty and deformity' (p. 94). Hamlet's soliloquy, 'O, that this too too solid flesh would melt', is a 'vent' (p. 96) to those passions such a sensitive person would typically feel when 'he discerns turpitude in a parent' (p. 94). Yet while many 'find relief' in such an outburst, Hamlet does not (p. 96). 'In cases of this nature,' Richardson then clinically observes, 'the mind passes from general reflections to minute and particular circumstances' (p. 96). He traces such a progress in Hamlet's soliloquy, noting how 'Hamlet's indignation is augmented gradually, by admiration of his father' ('so excellent a king'), 'by abhorrence of Claudius' ('That was to this, | Hyperion to a Satyr'), and, finally, by 'a stinging reflection on the Queen's inconstancy' (pp. 97–98).

> Why, she would hang on him,
> As if increase of appetite had grown
> By what it fed on: and yet, within a month –
> (p. 98)

Richardson breaks off his quotation at the dash-marked moment of transition. He then introduces Hamlet's next words as evidence that what has just been said 'affects him so severely, that he strives to obliterate the idea', saying 'Let me not think on't –' (p. 98). These words are themselves cited by Richardson on a new line so that his page layout corresponds to the emotional turns of the moment (from admiration to abhorrence, anger, and repulsion), with another paragraph of analysis intervening to introduce the next twist in Hamlet's thought, as the prince's effort to 'obliterate the idea' is only half successful and he ends up expressing it 'by a general reflection':

> Frailty, thy name is woman!   (p. 98)

By spreading a line and a half of playtext over half a page, Richardson both emphasises a rapid sequence of transitions between emotional states and at the same time slows that sequence in order to anatomise it and, ultimately, generalise it too (Figure 5.1). This last outburst is 'too refined and artificial for a mind strongly agitated' yet nevertheless can serve as a model, since it 'agrees entirely with just such a degree of emotion as disposes us to moralize' (p. 98). In this sentence, Richardson's choice of pronoun captures the scope of his attempts to make poetry subservient to philosophy. On one level, 'us' means the audience or readers, prompted by Hamlet's outburst to moralise on his situation; on another, this 'us' describes us as

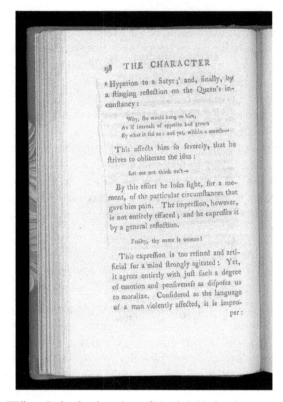

Figure 5.1 William Richardson's analysis of Hamlet's 'O that this too too solid flesh would melt' soliloquy (p. 98). By permission of Newcastle University Library, GB186 (shelfmark 822.33 SHA(5), 18th C. Coll.).

sympathetically in the same situation as Hamlet: every one of us with sufficient sensitivity would moralise like Hamlet under these circumstances. Such an ambiguous pronoun is the result of Richardson's belief that the study of Shakespeare's characters is equivalent to the study of human nature itself, so that Hamlet is both an object of our attention and a mirror of our inner lives.

In Richardson's claim that Hamlet's words contain 'such a degree of emotion as disposes us to moralize' lies an echo of the kind of argument Montagu had made in her defence of Shakespeare as moralist and tragedian, one who joins the powerful agency of living words to moving things to make his audiences better people. Also like Montagu, and in this chapter's sole explicit mention of performance, Richardson transfers responsibility for the success of the scene in which the prince confronts his mother to Shakespeare, claiming that 'The scene [. . .] has been highly celebrated, and cannot fail, even though less advantageously represented than by a Garrick and a Pritchard, to agitate every audience' (pp. 129–30). This is a rare comment, but its aesthetic judgement is of a piece with contemporary writing about the stage. Francis Gentleman's annotations on this scene for the Bell's Shakespeare edition of the play draw attention to the way in which Hamlet's 'reasoning and remonstrances [. . .] are truly pathetic and persuasive'.[22] Richardson himself comments on the 'striking effect' achieved by the prince's 'counterfeit presentment of two brothers' and on the fact that Hamlet's speech to his mother contains 'a transition from admiration to abhorrence', which, 'in a remarkable degree, heightens the latter' (pp. 132–33).

Yet Richardson's interest in this passage is never simply aesthetic. Even as he articulates the power of the 'transition' between Hamlet's admiration for his father and abhorrence for Claudius, he notes that this contrast is in fact 'co-operating with other causes', and so, once again, part of a larger, more systemic than sequential view of the Danish prince. That view becomes clear at the conclusion of Richardson's chapter, which arrives soon after he has completed his analysis of Gertrude's meeting with her son, since 'excepting the madness of Ophelia, and the scene of the grave-diggers', the rest of Shakespeare's play provides Richardson with 'nothing new in the characters' (p. 136). Asking permission to use 'the language of an eminent philosopher without professing myself of his sect' (David Hume), Richardson rephrases his opening assessment of Hamlet when he concludes that 'a sense of virtue [. . .] seems to be [his] ruling principle' (pp. 136–37). This general principle runs throughout the play and ties together all the transitions of a moment in the same way Macbeth's ambition also did. Richardson demonstrates this cohesion with a series of observations about Hamlet's 'sense of virtue'. It 'rivets his attachment to his friends', 'sharpens his penetration', 'inclines him to think more deeply' of any person's 'transgression', it 'excites uncommon pain and abhorrence on the appearance of perfidious and inhuman actions', and so on. This list is effectively a plot summary of Shakespeare's play, but, stripped of reference to specific moments of the drama, it serves to lift the particular events of Hamlet's life to the status of a model for the behaviour of those who also possess a 'strong sense of virtue'. Hamlet becomes a pathology, a set of typical behaviours associated with a single condition, now made available for study and application by Richardson.

While it is particularly striking with Hamlet, Richardson's consistent interest in uncovering general principles of human behaviour results in the consistent selection of a specific set of Shakespeare's characters for all of his essays on dramatic character: figures whose many lines and complex sequences of emotion provide the detailed evidence required for his Newtonian experiments. Indeed, one might go further and argue that Richardson's choice of subject in his later works, all of which bear the title of *Essays on Shakespeare's Dramatic Characters*, are presented in such a way as to flatten differences between them and accentuate those shared characteristics of highly developed sensibility and intelligence that are necessary to their status as philosophical specimens. Pathology overwrites the particularity of pathos. Thus Richard III is a character in whom we see 'great intellectual ability, employed for inhuman and perfidious purposes', and Falstaff, similarly, offers an example of 'the effect produced on the mind by the display of considerable ability, directed by sensual appetites and mean desires'.[23] In another vein, the character of King Lear is read by Richardson as a kind of elderly Hamlet, whose derangement 'illustrates, that mere sensibility uninfluenced by any sense of propriety leads men to an extravagant expression both of social and unsocial feelings'.[24]

The Less We See, the Better We Conceive

There is another way of presenting Richardson's work. Before beginning his detailed analysis of Macbeth's violent sequences of contrasting emotions, this critic first notes a problem with his material: the witches. When Shakespeare wrote this play, Richardson explains, he adopted the same strategy as the historians of his 'ignorant age' who were 'little accustomed to explain uncommon events by simple causes, and strongly addicted to a superstitious belief in sorcery, ascribed them to praeternatural agency' (p. 46). In order to study Macbeth's character as symptomatic of general principles of human nature (and not as some fantasy of sorcerous mind control), Richardson admits that it is necessary to 'hazard a conjecture, supported by some facts and observations, concerning the power of fancy, aided by partial gratification, to invigorate and inflame our passions' (pp. 46–47). This phrase offers a justification for the use of *Macbeth* in the *Analysis* by emphasising the point of view of the play's protagonist: it does not matter whether the witches are real or not, since it is the capacity of our 'fancy' to 'inflame our passions' that is really modelled in the thane of Glamis, regardless of how that fancy was encouraged. In the course of the next few pages, Richardson thus lays out the workings of this process, starting from the general rule that 'we embrace in imagination the happiness that is to come' (p. 47).[25] The kind of happiness we imagine for ourselves, Richardson continues, depends on both 'the probability of success' and 'moral considerations' (p. 48). He refers the reader to the writings of Francis Hutcheson for the latter, before noting that 'by this imaginary indulgence [. . .] our passions become immoderate': too many attempts to imagine potential dangers makes the fearful, for example, paranoid as they 'figure [. . .] dangers that have no reality' (p. 49). Such a situation is the result of a feedback loop, whereby what our passions drive us to imagine in turn nourishes those passions. If what we imagine looks like it might become reality, such proximity 'quickens and promotes the passion' (p. 53). Richardson cites Hume's account of James VI's increased desire for the English throne in the final years of Elizabeth I's life as an example of this. He then announces that achieving the happiness we imagine, particularly in the case of the ambitious, 'produces vanity' and 'invigorates our ambition' (p. 54). Richardson's example of this is Alexander the Great's behaviour after his conquest of Persia.

'In this manner,' concludes Richardson, 'by joy, by the prospect, and proximity of a more splendid object, and by vanity, all depending on partial gratification, the passion is swelled and becomes excessive' (p. 54). His next sentence returns us to Macbeth, whose success in battle at the opening of Shakespeare's play results in a situation where 'His ambition, fostered by imagination, and confirmed by success, becomes immoderate: and his soul, elevated above measure, aspires to sovereignty' (pp. 54–55). In other words, Macbeth corresponds exactly to the general principle that Richardson has just been detailing and exemplifying. Even though there are witches in Shakespeare's play, its protagonist nevertheless operates as other human beings have done and will do, and so is a fit subject in which to trace the principles of human conduct. And yet there is an issue here: Richardson is no longer using Shakespeare's characters as the raw materials for an investigation into the Newtonian principles that must govern human behaviour; instead he is using them to exemplify principles that he brings from elsewhere. The *Analysis* fluctuates, in other words, between imposing principles *a priori* and allowing them to emerge *a posteriori*. The results of the latter kind, like Richardson's claim that 'the contest between the obstinacy of an habituated passion, and the vehemence of an animated feeling, is unequal' (p. 63), have already been considered. I turn my attention here to the former.

The logic of such an *a priori* approach is simple. Richardson's belief in Shakespeare's unrivalled talent for 'forming characters [. . .] and

imitating [...] the passions and affections of which they are composed'
leads to two conclusions. The first is that the passions and affections of
these characters can be studied as part of an effort to discover new
general principles of human nature; the second is that such characters
are the source of material to substantiate existing general principles.
Yet one might go even further; if Shakespeare's characters adhere to
general principles of human nature, then one should be able to use such
principles to conjecture things about these characters that Shakespeare's
text does not make explicit. This is what Richardson means to do when
he asks the reader to accept 'conjecture': he is using external models of
human behaviour (Hume, Hutcheson, and others) to make explicit what
Shakespeare leaves implicit, responding to the attention-drawing
qualities of a character's transitions and points with an attempt to
rationalise them. Richardson ultimately reads transition as a question
to be answered, and his answer either takes the form of an existing
principle of human nature (applied *a priori*) or his own formulation of
one (given *a posteriori*).[26]

The epistemological practices of Richardson's writing share much with
another literary critical text of the later eighteenth century: Maurice
Morgann's *An Essay on the Dramatic Character of Sir John Falstaff* (1777).
Indeed, as the titular use of 'Dramatic Character' might indicate,
Morgann's work places itself in the same tradition as both Montagu and
Richardson, although his position on what might be considered 'dramatic'
is more openly hostile to contemporary stage practice than either of his
predecessors'. Morgann also dismisses Montagu's writing on Falstaff as
'involved in a Popular error' of finding 'Cowardice' in this character, an
error he attributes, in Montagu's case, to the fact that the fat knight 'was
too gross, too infirm' for her ladylike 'inspection' (pp. 111–12). To correct
this error and prove that Falstaff is in fact no coward, Morgann makes
several claims about Shakespeare's practice, claims which help to explain
the connection between transition and conjecture found in Richardson.
Rather than focus on Morgann's 'vindication of FALSTAFF's Courage', an
exercise he himself describes as 'no otherwise the object than some old
fantastic Oak, or grotesque Rock may be the object of a morning's ride
[...] yet being proposed may serve to limit the distance, and shape the
course' (pp. 4–5), I examine here what Morgann calls the 'heavier parts' of
his essay (p. 6). In these sections, Morgann explains his approach to
Shakespeare's writing and, in doing so, provides a clear example of how
striking stage effects, transitions and points, invite a kind of literary
criticism that ironically diminishes their importance as it looks beyond

them in an attempt to apply general principles of human nature in order to make the implicit explicit.

One of the heaviest parts of Morgann's essay is his explanation of how Shakespeare creates a character, which takes the form of a five-page footnote. He begins by observing that Shakespeare's characters distinguish themselves through 'a certain roundness and integrity', so that 'we often meet with passages, which tho' perfectly felt, cannot be sufficiently explained in words, without unfolding the whole character of the speaker' (p. 58). This phrase encapsulates much of Montagu and Richardson's work, as they seek to explain striking moments composed of transitions through reference to Macbeth's ambition-riven soul or Hamlet's sense of virtue. Morgann continues, however, with a 'conjecture' of his own, stating his belief that Shakespeare's characters were 'Not [...] the effect [...] so much of a minute and laborious attention, as of a certain comprehensive energy of mind, involving within itself all the effects of system and labour' (p. 58). Shakespeare's genius was thus analogous to the working of nature itself: just as 'Bodies of all kinds, whether of metals, plants, or animals, are supposed to possesses certain first principles of *being*' which then combine with 'those things only, which are proper to its own distinct nature' to create an individual, so too do the playwright's characters (p. 59). 'There are certain qualities and capacities, which he seems to have considered as first principles' (like 'courage and activity') (p. 59), and these combine with other material 'drawn in from the atmosphere of surrounding things' to produce a unique person (p. 60). Morgann's racist example of this process is Othello, whose line '*Be thus when thou art dead, and I will kill thee and love thee after*' is 'a sentiment characteristic of, and fit only to be uttered by a *Moor*' (p. 60).

Having described a process capable of producing a character with 'a certain roundness and integrity' through the combination of 'first principles' and context, Morgann continues his footnote by observing that 'it was not enough for *Shakespeare* to have formed his characters with the most perfect truth and coherence' (p. 61). These characters had to be made compelling, or, in Morgann's words, 'it was further necessary that [Shakespeare] should possess a wonderful facility of compressing, as it were, his own spirit into these images, and of giving alternate animation to the forms' (p. 61). What Morgann describes here, the compression of an author's spirit into a striking, iconic image that nevertheless possesses a dynamic quality (an 'alternate animation'), is recognisable as the same paradoxical aesthetic effect of movement in stillness that runs throughout this book: 'the very *Instant* of the *changing Passion*' described by Hill, the motion Webb identifies in Raphael's statues, and the breathtaking suspension of speech that Garrick's acolytes found in his pauses. It is the art of transition. For his part, Morgann argues that Shakespeare achieved such an effect of 'alternate animation' from within, presenting the playwright in the same way as Montagu and Richardson as a paragon of sympathy who 'must have *felt* every varied situation, and have spoken thro' the organ he had formed' (p. 61). The end product of this two-step process of natural, quasi-ecological accretion around first principles and sympathetic compression through the infusion of the writer's spirit is the striking moment, what Morgann calls 'the point of action or sentiment [. . .] held out for special notice' (p. 61).

Yet when we come across such striking moments, 'who does not perceive', Morgann asks, 'that there is a peculiarity about it, which conveys a relish of the whole?' (p. 61). Such a perception is central to the writings of Montagu and Richardson and their tendency to treat transitional spectacle as symptom, but Morgann makes explicit the way in which these characters invite conjecture by describing how Shakespeare occasionally 'boldly makes a character act and speak from those parts of the composition, which are *inferred* only, and not distinctly shewn' (p. 62). This kind of rhetorical trick (a variety of *ennoia* or *circumlocutio*) is 'in reality that art in *Shakespeare*, which being withdrawn from our notice, we more emphatically call *nature*' (p. 62). This is how Hamlet, Macbeth, Othello, and Falstaff all achieve that 'roundness and integrity': it is the creation of 'a felt propriety and truth from causes unseen', made possible by Shakespeare's decision to hide his workings behind moments 'held out for special notice'. Morgann thus reads Shakespeare as a master of ellipsis and suggests that such ellipsis produces the appearance of nature.

Ellipsis, often marked on the page by dashes or on the stage by pauses, is a necessary condition of transition, the gap between two distinct objects in which the phenomenon operates. But impelled by his belief in the wholeness of Shakespeare's characters, Morgann builds upon his observation of Shakespeare's elliptical art in such a way as to remove such gaps. He thus proposes, in the final sentence of his footnote, a kind of criticism that is ultimately hostile to the operations of transition.

> If the characters of *Shakespeare* are thus *whole*, and as it were original, while those of almost all others writers are mere imitation, it may be fit to consider them rather as Historic than Dramatic beings; and, when occasion requires, to account for their conduct from the *whole* of character, from general principles, from latent motives, and from policies not avowed. (p. 62)

Morgann's suggestion here points to the same kind of criticism as that practised by Richardson, who, in making 'poetry subservient to philosophy', frequently turns to historical examples (Alexander, Hannibal, James VI) in order to substantiate his analyses of Shakespeare's characters and the principles of general nature they embody. Morgann distinguishes himself from Richardson, however, through the clarity of his statement and his decision to frame this position in terms of 'Historic' and 'Dramatic beings' rather than as the subordination of 'poetry' to 'philosophy'. Michèle Willems has taken the terms of this footnote and used them to characterise Morgann's practice throughout his essay, describing its analysis as one in which 'dramatic time, the only one which concerns the dramatist, is transformed into historic time'.[27] Willems's point is that, rather than deal with the actions of Falstaff as they are presented to us in the course of *Henry IV part I*, *Henry IV part II*, *The Merry Wives*, and *Henry V*, Morgann deliberately reorders things. In some cases, this is no more than a rhetorical device, as, for example, when he delays discussion of the humiliation of the fat knight at Gadshill until after he has amassed evidence for Falstaff's bravery. More significantly, however, Willems shows Morgann to be interested in reconstructing Falstaff's biography in a linear fashion, to the extent that he offers a sketch of Falstaff's early years based on 'the leading quality' of his character: his 'high degree of wit and humour, accompanied with great natural vigour and alacrity of mind' (pp. 17–18). Running over three pages, Morgann's account of Falstaff's progress from witty youth to an old man who is both 'a humourist and a man of humour' is a work of Willems's 'historic time' (pp. 18–20). Rather than focusing on the striking moment brought about by ellipsis, an explanation of which (as I have shown) still often constitutes the first stage in both Richardson's and Montagu's criticism, Morgann instead lays out a linear and continuous narrative, tracing the steps whereby Falstaff becomes the Falstaff we meet in Shakespeare's writing. Such conjecture operates by announcing the 'principles' of this character and then examining how those principles interact with a hypothetical environment. It is no coincidence, of course, that this is the very way that Morgann claimed that both Shakespeare's genius and nature itself created individuals, yet the peculiarity of this method lies in its rational sequence: every point of Morgann's story seems to follow logically from that which proceeds it; there is no abrupt transition, no spectacular rupture, no dramatic character whom we first meet *in medias res* and asking Prince Hal 'what time of day is it, lad?'[28] Unlike Shakespeare's Falstaff, Morgann's version of the character is precisely located in time and space, with all his actions laid out before us and not just a few for our 'special notice'.

In addition to his imposition of 'historic time' to match Shakespeare's 'Historic' beings, Morgann's method also departs from that of Richardson and Montagu in the kind of attention it brings to Shakespeare's text. Whereas Richardson and Montagu both seize upon the way Shakespeare's writing exhibits, as Montagu wrote of his Macbeth, 'the movement of the human mind', Morgann instead parses the play for evidence to support his essay's argument that Falstaff was no coward. Textual evidence is there to offer direct support for an understanding of the central principle of the fat knight's character in general, rather than – as is the case for the other writers discussed in this chapter – to be the relics of a dynamic process which must then be explained as rooted in some overarching principle. For this reason, many of Morgann's quotations are not in fact from lines spoken by Falstaff himself: he draws our attention instead to how other characters speak of or interact with him. Over the course of a dozen or so pages, Morgann thus points first to the behaviour of low-class characters around Falstaff (Mistress Quickly employs two officers to arrest him; Pistol yields to him), then to praise from nobles (Bardolph's compliments; Hal's decision to give his friend 'a charge of foot'), and finally to signs of respect from military men (Coleville yielding to Falstaff and the fact that 'a dozen Captains stay at door for him' when he is recalled to court) (pp. 29–42). Morgann admits that Shakespeare 'has thrown the most advantageous of these circumstances into the *background* as it were, and brought nothing *out of the canvass* but [Falstaff's] follies and buffoon-ery' (p. 44), yet this is not to say that such things are unimportant. Indeed, Morgann's belief that Shakespeare operates through a kind of rhetorical *ennoia*, whereby what is 'held out for special notice' should lead us to look beyond it, perfectly supports such an approach: we are struck by 'follies and buffoonery', but the critic should not linger there at all before looking beyond such moments to those things in the 'background', which help us to conceive of the whole of Falstaff's character, overcoming the ellipsis used to generate impressive spectacle. As Morgann himself puts it, 'if Shakespeare meant sometimes rather to *impress* than explain, no circum-stances calculated to this end [. . .] are too minute for notice' (p. 47).

Morgann's reading of Shakespeare's characters thus operates by dwelling least on what is striking and obvious, preferring instead to highlight the less remarkable yet (for Morgann) far more revelatory details hidden around such moments. In the case of Falstaff, such an approach presents him as an essentially ironic figure, one who appears, in his most spectacular moments, an obvious coward but who is in fact, when we pay attention to these details, courageous. Morgann's reading, with all its efforts to unearth the whole character and not just what is most obvious about a person, presumes a disjunction between points and 'true' character traits: a striking moment is not (as Montagu and Richardson assume) always straightforwardly symptomatic of human nature. This potential for a more complex relationship between a powerful scene and the 'historic' being Shakespeare has created at its heart leads us to one final consequence of Morgann's approach to drama. In addition to the reordering of dramatic time into historic linear sequence and the minute attention to what is said but not emphasised, Morgann also offers highly derogatory analyses of contemporary performances of *Henry IV part I*. This is his description of a rendition of the Gadshill episode:

> The very Players who are, I think, the very worst judges of *Shakespeare*, have been made sensible, I suppose from long experience, that there is nothing in this transaction to excite any extraordinary laughter; [... and ...] hold themselves obliged to supply the vacancy, and fill it up with some low buffoonery of their own. Instead of the dispatch necessary on this occasion, they bring *Falstaff, stuffing and all*, to the very front of the stage; where with much mummery and grimace, he seats himself down, with a canvas money-bag in his hand, to divide the spoil. In this situation, he is attacked by the *Prince* and *Poins* [...] till the *Player Falstaff*, who seems more troubled with flatulence than fear, is able to rise [...] with the assistance of one of the thieves [...]; after which, without any resistance on his part, he is goaded off the stage like a fat ox for slaughter by these *stony-hearted* drivers in *buckram*. I think he does not *roar*, – perhaps the player had never perfected himself in the tones of a bull-calf. (pp. 127–28)

Morgann's central criticism of 'the players' is that their staging has augmented what Shakespeare held out for special notice (the ambush of Falstaff by Poins and Hal) to such an extent that there is now no way to glimpse the whole of Falstaff's character: the '*Player Falstaff*' is simply and obviously a coward, and anything that might suggest otherwise is unavailable in the theatre. The actors are thus bad readers, who have missed the kind of background hints that let a sensitive critic into the whole of Falstaff's character. Morgann makes those hints visible to his reader through the use of italics: Poins comments on how Falstaff 'roar'd' at the conclusion of the ambush, yet the players appear to have ignored this, allowing the fat knight to exit meekly, helped by figures he will subsequently describe as 'stony-hearted'. In the wake of such criticism, some advice for a better version of the scene is given: first, the actors should follow the details of the text rather than a desire to excite 'extraordinary laughter'; second, the scene should be performed with 'the dispatch necessary on this occasion'; and, third, as Morgann goes on to suggest, 'This whole scene should be shewn between the interstices of a back scene', since 'The less we see in such cases, the better we conceive' (p. 128).

With this advice to hide the action of the drama in order to facilitate a more precise reading of Shakespeare's characters we reach the limit of what Morgann himself describes as the 'heavy' parts of his essay. Elsewhere in this text, he retreats from such a position and recognises the value of Shakespeare's ellipses and transitions for the production of compelling drama. In a panegyric to the experience of watching Shakespeare's plays, Morgann emphasises how the transformations of *Macbeth* produce the kind of transport Montagu describes in her *Essay* as 'delusion'.

> *Macbeth* changes under our eye, *the milk of human kindness is converted to gall; he has supped full of horrors*, and his *May of life is fallen into the sear, the yellow leaf;* whilst we, the fools of amazement, are insensible to the shifting of place and the lapse of time, and till the curtain drops, never once wake to the truth of things, or recognize the laws of existence. – On such an occasion, a fellow, like *Rymer*, waking from his trance, shall lift up his Constable's staff, and charge this great Magician, this daring *practicer of arts inhibited*, in the name of *Aristotle*, to surrender; whilst *Aristotle* himself, disowning his wretched Officer, would fall prostrate at his feet and acknowledge his supremacy. (pp. 69–70)

Morgann's listing of lines from the play might mark out some of the work's most striking moments: Lady Macbeth's persuasion of her husband and her wish for spirits to 'unsex me here' and Macbeth's reflections on his state as the English army brings Birnam Wood to Dunsinane. Yet Morgann's key point is that, as we follow the arc of Macbeth's story, we neither, as Thomas Rymer claimed to do, note any violence done to the unities, nor, as a careful philosophical approach might endeavour to achieve, 'recognize the laws of existence'.[29] It is only later, in the quiet of the study, that we can do what Richardson and Morgann both attempt, in their efforts to use Shakespeare's writing as evidence for or the illustration of principles of human behaviour. Indeed, Morgann's panegyric continues with his imagining what Aristotle would say had he known Shakespeare's writing. Abandoning the idea that 'relations of place, or continuity of time, are always essential', Morgann's Aristotle proclaims a new creed:

> Nature, condescending to the faculties and apprehensions of man, has drawn through human life a regular chain of visible causes and effects:

But Poetry delights in surprize, conceals her steps, seizes at once upon the heart, and obtains the Sublime of things without betraying the rounds of her ascent: True Poesy is *magic*, not *nature*; an effect from causes hidden or unknown. (pp. 70–71)

Aristotle's words, as imagined by Morgann, expose the contradiction at the heart of this critic's essay. On one hand, his belief in a Newtonian 'regular chain of visible causes and effects' is central to his defence of Falstaff as courageous and not cowardly, which aims to make that chain visible through close textual analysis and the anti-transitional reordering of dramatic into historic time; it is equally central to the writings of Richardson and his attempts to make Shakespeare's poetry subservient to philosophy. On the other, Morgann shows himself here to be sharply aware of the kind of spectacle that depends for its effect on 'causes hidden or unknown'. Dennis, a lifetime before Morgann, had described enthusiastic passions in such a way and demonstrated how the gradations of a poem, the transitions between its emotions, could compel audience attention and – as Morgann puts it – seize 'at once upon the heart'.[30]

Morgann's Aristotle thus presents a quandary to the critic. Simply put, to study the causes of surprise, of those transitions which seize the heart and obtain the sublime, is to expose something that – in terms of aesthetic experience – is better left hidden. By wanting to explain theatrical effect, to answer the question of a transition by filling in the ellipses it operates within and draw from it a moral teaching, one jeopardises the very object that first attracted attention. Right at the end of his essay on Falstaff, Morgann admits as much, when he observes that the '*Falstaff* of Nature' that he has uncovered is no more than 'a disagreeable draught' out of which, 'by a proper disposition of light and shade, and from the influence and compression of external things' one can produce the poetic Falstaff of the stage, '*plump Jack*, the life of humour, the spirit of pleasantry, and the soul of mirth' (p. 172).

The Mind Is Like a Theatre, the Theatre Like a Mind

Montagu praises Shakespeare's dervish-like ability to imitate 'the internal process of the mind in reasoning and reflecting' and create totally consistent, 'living' characters; Richardson is engaged in 'analysing the mind of Hamlet' in search of fundamental principles of human nature; and Morgann considers Falstaff as a 'Historic' being whose intentions are never as cowardly as they sometimes seem. All three writers thus combine an attention to the thoughts of a character with a presumption of that character's unity. That unity ultimately favours the page rather than the stage: Morgann criticises actors for missing minute textual clues about Falstaff's 'whole character', Richardson takes the principles of Hamlet and Macbeth and applies them to us all, and Montagu accords Shakespeare the status of the supreme imitator.

All three writers considered here use Shakespeare's drama to think about the mind, and – minimising spectacular transition – thus ascribe a consistent identity to a character's mind. This practice bears a remarkable similarity to a process David Hume, nearly half a century earlier, had examined in a chapter of his *Treatise of Human Nature* devoted to our belief in 'personal identity'.[31] Hume exposes this belief to sceptical doubt, and his analysis offers us a standpoint from which, by way of conclusion, we might cast both late eighteenth-century literary criticism and transition itself in a new light. Hume even begins his critique with the theatre. Having argued that humans are nothing but a 'bundle or collection of different perceptions, which succeed each other with an inconceivable rapidity, and are in perpetual flux and movement', he continues with the claim that 'The mind is a kind of theatre, where several perceptions successively make their appearance; pass, re-pass, glide away and mingle in an infinite variety of postures and situations' (pp. 252–53). Such a comparison emphasises one aspect of the eighteenth-century stage – its constitution as a set of striking moments, sometimes called hits, points, or turns, all understood as powered by transition and all appearing in this chapter in the form of those passages analysed by Montagu and Richardson and the kind of magical 'Poesy' evoked by Morgann.

Yet no sooner has Hume made the comparison between the flux of bundled perceptions in our minds and the variety of moments depicted on the stage than he retreats from it, warning us that 'The comparison of the theatre must not mislead us' (p. 253). Any sense we might have of his position here is then further complicated by the fact that, two years after the publication of the *Treatise*, he added an appendix to inform the reader that the entirety of the section on personal identity in which this theatrical metaphor appears is 'defective' (p. 635). Exactly what Hume considered 'defective', however, is not immediately obvious. The theatre metaphor serves to introduce Hume's aim in this section, namely to demonstrate why – even though our mind is nothing but a succession of perceptions – we nevertheless 'ascribe an identity to these successive perceptions' when we think about 'personal identity as it regards our thought or imagination' (p. 253). Donald Ainslie suggests that the issue here is that Hume is unable to explain why we believe that the perceptions by means of which we observe our minds are themselves part of our minds. This issue is hidden by the theatre metaphor which leads Hume to explain our beliefs about the mind 'from the perspective of the observer of the mind, or, analogously, the spectator of the play' while disregarding that this spectator is nevertheless within our minds as well.[32] Throughout this section there is indeed a strange tension between third- and first-person viewpoints on the mind. Hume even asks us to 'suppose we could see into the breast of another' (p. 260) when demonstrating how the transitions we make between ideas about our minds give rise to our belief in personal identity.

Much has been written on Hume's use of the theatre metaphor and the difficulties it creates in *The Treatise*.[33] Yet, for all its flaws, it does offer a standpoint for drawing together the literary critical work of this chapter, for all three of my authors claim that Shakespeare – directly or indirectly – offers what Hume wanted us to imagine: a chance to 'see into the breast of another'. Hume may have made an abortive attempt to compare the mind to a theatre, but Richardson, Montagu, and Morgann all claim that Shakespeare's theatre is extraordinarily like a mind. This means that Hume's defective section of the treatise, with its critique of how we come to ascribe personal identity to the theatre-like flux of our minds, can still offer a framework for understanding how Morgann, Montagu, and Richardson come to find 'dramatic character' in what they consider to be the mind-like flux of Shakespeare's theatre.

Hume explains that we come to believe that something has a distinct existence as a single object (it has 'simplicity') through time (it has 'identity') because of the easy transitions we make between our perceptions of that thing. This is the case whether we are thinking about perceptions of 'plants and animals' or 'the identity of a self or person' (p. 253). You or I will think that the perceptions we have of a tree are all of the same identifiable tree because our perceptions of it so resemble each other that we move between them with ease. The same is true when we think about the identity of ourselves or someone else: that identity is in fact only a quality we attribute to our perceptions because we have come to unite those perceptions in our mind. That union, explains Hume, comes about through the same three uniting principles he discusses throughout the *Treatise*: contiguity, resemblance, and causation. The last two of these principles in particular produce 'an easy transition of ideas' such that 'our notions of personal identity, proceed entirely from the smooth and uninterrupted progress of the thought along a train of connected ideas' (p. 260).[34] The belief I have in your or my thoughts as the product of a single, unified self is in fact the result of smooth transitions, which hide the fact that I have only a bundle of different perceptions about such things.

As noted in this book's introduction, we must distinguish between Hume's use of the word 'transition' here and the spectacular transitions that have been my principle subject. Both kinds are at work in this chapter. There is the theatrical transition of those spectacular moments that Montagu, Richardson, and Morgann perceive, and then there are the Humean transitions these critics make as part of their discursive response to these perceptions. It is these latter transitions that give rise to the critics' belief in the 'consistency' of dramatic characters. And these transitions are facilitated by the same principles Hume identified in his *Treatise*. Resemblance is particularly important: Montagu, Richardson, and Morgann all note the similarities between different moments in the depiction of Shakespeare's characters, such that these moments appear to be repetitions of each other. Macbeth, for example, is repeatedly ambitious and then remorseful; Hamlet, for Richardson, repeatedly shifts between polarised emotional states, like admiration and abhorrence. The repetition of each of these perceptions of a character's thought processes allows, in Humean terms, for an easy transition to an idea about that character's identity: Macbeth is noble, Hamlet is sensitive, and so forth. Hume's principle of causation is similarly illuminating. Montagu calls for us to study drama as though it were an organic 'living body' where every element is bound to a larger whole and purpose. Morgann's argument about Falstaff, on the other hand, builds a biography out of Shakespeare's text (and his own conjectures) based on a chain of cause and effect, one capable of holding all his ideas together with the aim of proving that Falstaff is not a cowardly character.

The argument of Hume's *Treatise* thus allows us to anatomise further some of the mechanisms by which a few later eighteenth-century critics, when they treat Shakespeare's plays as extraordinary imitations of human minds, come to treat their spectacular moments, the flux of drama, as the foundation of coherent, unified ideas about a character's identity and simplicity. Hume's theatre metaphor also offers one final thing. The fact that Hume's original argument in the *Treatise* evokes the theatre to illustrate the flux of bundled perceptions in the human mind and then warns us not to be misled by the comparison indicates that, even in the late 1730s, theatre was not only about flux. This should remind us that, as I have argued throughout this book, stage transitions are simultaneously dynamic and iconic. This union fixates attention and even plays into what Hume called 'our natural propension [...] to imagine [...] simplicity and identity' (p. 253): we want to make sense of it, and so we make our own transitions in response to (and away from) the spectacle of transition. Few critics of the eighteenth century went as far as Montagu, Morgann, and Richardson in their imaginings of simplicity and identity, but – as Hume recognised in his metaphor – the potential was always already there, and the theatrical transition thus could always provoke an analytical, unifying, explanatory response that, as it elevated the author and the text, became hostile to the spectacle at the root of such provocation in the first place.

Coda

Two visits to Westminster Abbey frame the material covered in this book and delimit the period when works of art, especially but not exclusively tragic dramas, were appreciated as expressions of what I have called the art of transition. The first visit to the Abbey is that of Richard Steele, who walked there for the funeral of the actor Thomas Betterton and recounted his thoughts on this occasion in an issue of *The Tatler* published at the start of May 1710. The second visit occurs a century later and is that of Charles Lamb. He opens an essay for *The Reflector* with an account of how he caught a glimpse of David Garrick's monument while 'Taking a turn the other day in the Abbey'.[1] Both Lamb and Steele use the memorialisation of an actor to reflect on the power of the stage, but each comes to a sharply different conclusion. Steele's writing anticipates the kind of attention to transition that this book has been interested in recovering, while Lamb's essay seeks to inter such phenomena as something without critical value, a common denominator in all performance and a useless tool for the making of critical distinctions.

Steele claims that he has 'received more strong Impressions of what is great in Human Nature' from Betterton's performances than 'from the Arguments of the most solid Philosophers, or the Descriptions of the most charming Poets'.[2] He goes on to describe such impressions in a version of the same language that contemporaries like John Dennis were already using and future writers, like Aaron Hill, Francis Gentleman, or even David Hume, in his writing about the 'lively impression' of certain perceptions, would employ.[3] Steele's first example is 'The wonderful Agony' of Betterton 'when he examined the Circumstance of the Handkerchief of *Othello*':

> The Mixture of Love that intruded upon his Mind upon the innocent Answers *Desdemona* makes, betrayed in his Gesture such a Variety and Vicissitude of Passions, as would admonish a Man to be afraid of his own

Heart, and perfectly convince him, that it is to stab it, to admit that worst of Daggers, Jealousy.

Should a person study 'in his Closet this admirable Scene', Steele continues, that reader 'will find that he cannot except he has as warm an Imagination as *Shakespear* himself find any but dry, incoherent, and broken Sentences' here (p. 1). But Betterton's performance combines such fragments into something iconic and dynamic, to the point that another person who has seen Betterton act this point would observe 'that longer Speech had been unnatural, nay impossible, to be uttered in *Othello*'s Circumstances' (p. 1). Betterton's navigation of the transitions of this point make it comprehensible as an expression of Shakespeare's genius for capturing nature's own emotional vicissitudes.

In his *Dramatic Miscellanies*, Thomas Davies would give the same kind of praise to Garrick's rendition of the transitions in Lear's madness, claiming that these transitions made visible Shakespeare's scripting of the monarch's 'progress of agonizing feelings to madness in its several stages'.[4] It is against such a tradition of praising a performer's transitions as a source of critical insight into the author's creation that Lamb takes aim. Originally published as 'On Garrick and Acting' but now better known under its title of 'On the Tragedies of Shakespeare Considered with Reference to their Fitness for Stage Representation', Lamb's essay opens by calling the verses on Garrick's monument a 'farrago of false thoughts and nonsense' (p. 299). These verses were written by Samuel Jackson Pratt: they rewrite Ben Jonson's praise of Shakespeare as the '*starre of* Poets' by instead proclaiming that 'Shakespeare and Garrick like twin stars shall shine'.[5]

Lamb refutes Garrick's elevation to such a state with a celebrated argument on the limited power of the stage. In Roy Park's summary of its contents, Lamb's essay argues that 'Acting is intrinsically incapable of producing, in a medium not entirely linguistic, the fusion of real and imaginative, which constitutes the aesthetic ideal'.[6] This précis is carefully phrased, and Park notes that many have misread Lamb's text as a statement of the writer's anti-theatrical prejudice. In fact, Lamb, as he writes himself in this piece, is 'not arguing that Hamlet should not be acted, but how much Hamlet is made another thing by being acted' (p. 302). Developing this point, Lamb returns to Garrick, recalling how he has heard much 'of the magic of his eye', 'of his commanding presence', recognising that such things are 'vastly desirable in an actor', but then asking what such things 'have [. . .] to do with Hamlet?' (p. 302). The actor's talents are designed to 'arrest the spectator's eye [. . .] and so to gain a more favourable hearing to what is spoken' (p. 302). This is a superficial process, interested not by 'what the character is, but how he looks; not what he says, but how he speaks it', and so as equally applicable to the creation of a 'Banks or Lillo' as to Shakespeare's (pp. 302–03). After all, even these lesser writers, were they to rewrite *Hamlet*, could maintain sufficient scope for 'all the power the actor has, to display itself' (p. 303) because they would maintain the emotional sequence, the transitions, and the rendition of such things on the stage would mask the intellectual shallowness of the drama.

> All the passions and changes of passion might remain: for those are much less difficult to write or act than is thought, it is a trick easy to be attained, it is but rising or falling a note or two in the voice, a whisper with a significant foreboding look to announce its approach, and so contagious the counterfeit appearance of any emotion is, that let the words be what they will, the look and tone shall carry it off and make it pass for deep skill in the passions. (p. 303)

This, for the purposes of my argument here, is the core of Lamb's position: a belief that a skilled performer, benefiting from the contagiousness of staged emotion, can make their acting of emotional sequences 'pass for deep skill in the passions' rather than actually achieve the critical illumination Steele and his successors claimed for the performer. Indeed, as far as Lamb is concerned, 'ninety-nine out of a hundred' spectators in a theatre would cry as much at the fate of George Lillo's Barnwell as at that of Shakespeare's Othello, focusing on the superficial aspects of performance and so ignoring 'the texture of Othello's mind, the inward construction marvellously laid open with all its strengths and weaknesses' (p. 304). Ultimately, therefore, 'the sort of pleasure which Shakespeare's plays give in the acting seems to me not at all to differ from that which the audience receive from those of other writers', even though such plays are '*in themselves essentially so different from all others*' (p. 305). There must, as Lamb puts it, thus be 'something in the nature of acting which levels all distinctions' (p. 305). That something is the performer's transitional emphasis on emotion, the 'trick easy to be attained'.

Yet more than simply denigrating the performer's execution of transition, as many critics were already happy to do during the eighteenth century, Lamb is also denigrating transition itself.[7] A work's 'passions and changes of passion' are no particularly special beauty and are 'much easier to write or act than is thought'. What matters instead is 'the inward construction' of Othello's mind, the kind of object that later eighteenth-century critics like Elizabeth Montagu and especially William Richardson endeavoured to recover. But Lamb goes beyond even the writings discussed in Chapter 5. Richardson and Montagu took the iconic and dynamic points of a drama, and the transitions that created them, as a starting point for their inquiry. To Lamb, these things are dead ends, perhaps because he finds something unique, 'essentially different', in the pattern of Othello's strengths and weaknesses and not, as Richardson had hoped to find, a model for understanding general laws of human behaviour.

Lamb was not alone in arguing for the limited capacity of theatrical performance or the limits of a critical interest in striking moments of transition. As Simon Hull has demonstrated, Lamb shared what Hull calls the 'ideology of the unspectacular' with his friend the essayist William Hazlitt, whose review of Edmund Kean's performance of Richard II lamented that it is only the '*pantomime* part of tragedy [. . .] which is sure to tell, and tell completely on the stage'.[8] In describing Kean's expression of sudden extremes of emotion, 'the exhibition of immediate and physical distress', as the '*pantomime* part', Hazlitt reconnects this phenomenon with the artform from which Aaron Hill had sought to separate it when he encouraged actors of the 1730s to become the 'True FAUSTUS', rather than the then-popular Harlequin version, employing to better ends the execution of '*Transitions* (as the Meanings *vary*) into *Jealousy, Scorn, Fury, Penitence, Revenge, or Tenderness!'*[9]

Hill's advice to actors provides one of the clearest examples of attention to transition in the period between Steele's visit to Westminster Abbey and Lamb's. His description of the performer acting 'the very *Instant* of the *changing Passion*' encapsulates the constitutive tension of transition as simultaneously a passage between two states and an object of appreciation in its own right, a tension which allows it to imbue a performance, play, or other artwork with a combination of iconic and dynamic qualities capable of arresting attention. In the course of this book, I have shown how writers of the eighteenth century observed transitions and used them to understand the power of everything from the points of a tragedy to the verses of a poem and from the development of a piece of music to the fallibility of human cognition. Garrick has been central to almost all of these examples, and it is only fitting that I conclude this book as I begun it, with a painting of this much-painted man, now serving as an emblem of all I have argued and all that Lamb disregards in his essay on Garrick and acting.

William Hogarth's depiction of Garrick as Richard III commemorated the actor's London debut in the role while also helping the painter make the case for a specifically English style of history painting.[10] Like Johan Zoffany's image of Cibber and Garrick in *Venice Preserv'd* (discussed in the introduction), we cannot treat Hogarth's work as a record of performance but rather as a testament to a critical framework shared between the canvas and the theatre, an inheritance which included not just the history paintings that aspiring actors and artists were encouraged to imitate but also the appreciation of the union of iconic and dynamic qualities that I have called the art of transition.

At first glance, this painting appears to capture a single iconic instant, the moment when Richard III wakes from dreams presaging his defeat at the Battle of Bosworth. This was a famous point on the stage, yet, like all points, it was analysed as dynamically containing far more than a single frozen attitude. Arthur Murphy's biography of Garrick records how, in this scene, the passions of Richard 'rose in rapid succession, and, before he uttered a word, were legible in every feature of that various face'.[11] As for what Murphy calls 'a most excellent picture' of this moment, Stuart Sillars has argued that Hogarth's work also combines the iconic and the dynamic, compressing the events of the play to offer an exploration of 'a significant moment redolent of all that has been and pregnant with all to follow'.[12] Specifically, Sillars shows how 'The static commentary provided by [. . .] iconographic allusion' in this work balances 'the painting's enactment of the play's dynamic currency through careful elision of elements temporally separate in the action'.[13] The 'iconographical allusion' includes Hogarth's ironical quotation of Charles Le Brun's 1661 *Tent of Darius*, which depicts a moment of moral strength free from the pangs of tyrant conscience. It also includes the positioning of Richard's garter (to show only the word 'mal') and a composition where Richard literally turns his back on Christ. As for Hogarth's temporal elisions, the soldiers gathered round a fire in the top left of the canvas refer to a preceding scene – borrowed from *Henry V* for the duration of the eighteenth century – in which Richard walks incognito through his army to judge their mood, and the note (based on the Folio and Quarto texts) protruding from the armour at Richard's feet is that which he will soon find and read before choosing to ignore its warning about Stanley's imminent defection.[14] Sillars's detailed reading represents one of the best analyses of Hogarth's painting to date, but his conclusion is less convincing. He finishes his examination of Hogarth's picture with the claim that 'Playfully, the image paradoxically exchanges the temporal natures of theatre and painting', for 'the play's only moment of inactivity is selected for visual treatment, and the apparently static nature of an easel painting is used to foretell the future, so that the usual functions of drama and painting as respectively dynamic and static are reversed'.[15] I would suggest instead that Hogarth's image is of a piece with the other traces we have of Garrick's performance, as both endeavour to bring the iconic stasis and dynamic temporality together, a process visible to us when we think in terms of transition.

I have insisted on this word in these pages and avoided excessive repetition of another, similar and certainly more familiar, term from eighteenth-century aesthetics: variety. This is the phenomenon Hogarth places on the cover of his *Analysis of Beauty* (1753) and names as having a 'great [...] share [...] in producing beauty'.[16] It is also often used in writing about the stage, as Steele's praise of Betterton's 'Variety and Vicissitude of Passions' and many other examples quoted throughout this book demonstrate. Yet, despite all this evidence, transition is preferable to variety because it emphasises the connections between and sequencing of distinct objects. Rather than simply examining the similarities and differences between performed passions that produce a pleasing variety, transition invites us to study how the writer or performer moves from one passion to another in time and space and how the memory and anticipation of that dynamic movement results in an iconic product. This emphasis, summarised by Wye J. Allanbrook as a combination of *enargia* (vivid description) and *energeia* (lively action), is clearly present within eighteenth-century uses of the word variety: Hogarth himself describes how the varying lines of beauty and grace can *'lead the eye a wanton kind of chase'* through an image.[17] However, it is one meaning among many, especially when we read the writings of this period at such a historical distance, and a distance made all the greater by the impact of Romantic ideas about performance such as those articulated by Hazlitt and Lamb.

Two visits to Westminster Abbey frame this book. Both concern interments. Steele buries Betterton but uses the occasion to argue for the moral power of a performance that brings together the 'Variety and Vicissitude' of human passions within a single point. His writing is an early example of the critical approach I have traced in these pages, a sensitivity not just to what is expressed but also to how those emotions and sentiments are navigated by writers and performers through a series of transitions. This includes Hill's praise of 'the very *Instant* of the *changing Passion'*, Dennis's attention to the gradations of thought that mark the progress to sublimity, Webb's anatomisation of musical transition and movement, accounts of Garrick's Lear as the pinnacle of his transitional style, and, finally, the critics who begin their analysis of Shakespeare's dramatic characters with these figures' dramatic transitions. Lamb comes to Westminster Abbey to bury this idea and strip transition of its critical utility. I hope to have begun its restoration.

Notes

Introduction

1. One of the most prominent uses of the concept of 'transition' today occurs as a term for describing 'the steps a trans person may take to live in the gender with which they identify'. See 'Glossary of Terms', *Stonewall*, www.stonewall.org.uk/help-advice/faqs-and-glossary/glossary-terms [accessed 2 June 2020]. Google search trends for the UK and USA testify to such prominence: 'Google Trends', *Google*, https://trends.google.com/trends/explore?geo=GB&q=transiti on [accessed 28 February 2020].

2. See Lisa A. Freeman, *Character's Theater: Genre and Identity on the Eighteenth-Century English Stage* (Philadelphia: University of Pennsylvania Press, 2002), pp. 31–32; William B. Worthen, *The Idea of the Actor: Drama and the Ethics of Performance* (Princeton: Princeton University Press, 1984), p. 72.

3. James Boswell, 'On the Profession of a Player – Essay III', in *The London Magazine, or Gentleman's Monthly Intelligencer for the Year 1770* (London: Baldwin, 1770), XXXIX, pp. 513–17 (p. 513).

4. Francis Gentleman, *The Dramatic Censor; or, Critical Companion*, 2 vols (London: Bell and Etherington, 1770), I, pp. 334–35.

5. Gentleman, *Censor*, I, p. 334.

6. Gentleman, *Censor*, I, p. 335.

7. Abigail Williams, *The Social Life of Books: Reading Together in the Eighteenth-Century Home* (New Haven: Yale University Press, 2017), p. 2; see also Elspeth Jajdelska, '"The Very Defective and Erroneous Method": Reading Instruction and Social Identity in Elite Eighteenth-Century Learners', *Oxford Review of Education*, 36.2 (2010), 141–56. My focus on the critical function of transition distinguishes my research from the work of Williams and Jajdelska.

8. Tiffany Stern, *Rehearsal from Shakespeare to Sheridan* (Oxford: Oxford University Press, 2000), p. 258.

9. Stern, *Rehearsal*, p. 258. A claptrap is a piece of action designed to elicit applause.

10. Theophilus Cibber, 'The First Dissertation', in *Cibber's Two Dissertations on the Theatres* (London: Griffiths, 1756), pp. 1–76 (p. 69). Also quoted in Stern, *Rehearsal*, p. 258.

11. Theophilus Cibber, *The Lives and Characters of the Most Eminent Actors and Actresses of Great-Britain and Ireland: From Shakespear to the Present Time. Interspersed with a General History of the Stage* (London: Griffiths, 1753), p. 51.

12. Joseph Roach, *The Player's Passion: Studies in the Science of Acting* (Ann Arbor: University of Michigan Press, 1993), pp. 68–70.

13. Glen McGillivray, 'Rant, Cant and Tone: The Voice of the Eighteenth-Century Actor and Sarah Siddons', *Theatre Notebook*, 71.1 (2017), 2–20 (p. 16).

14. Thomas Sheridan, *A Course of Lectures on Elocution: Together with Two Dissertations on Language and Some Other Tracts Relative to Those Subjects* (London: Strahan, 1762), p. 10.

15. Richard Cumberland, *Memoirs of Richard Cumberland, Written by Himself, Containing An Account of His Life and Writings, Interspersed with Characters of Several of the Most Distinguished Persons of His Time with Whom He Has Had Intercourse and Connection* (Philadelphia: Bradford, 1806), pp. 80–82.

16. Thomas Davies, *Dramatic Miscellanies, Consisting of Critical Observations on Several Plays of Shakespeare, with a Review of His Principal Characters, and Those of Various Eminent Writers, as Represented by Mr Garrick and Other Celebrated Comedians*, 3 vols (London: Davies, 1783), I, p. 222.

17. Cibber, *Lives and Characters*, p. 51.

18. Bertram Joseph, *The Tragic Actor* (London: Routledge, 1959), pp. 59–60.

19. To pick an illustrative and somewhat random sample, the index to *The Oxford Handbook of the Georgian Theatre* contains no entry for 'transition', nor do those of Kalman Burnim's *David Garrick: Director* and Felicity Nussbaum's *Rival Queens*. Helen Brooks makes two references to transition in her book on eighteenth-century actresses; it appears twice in Peter Holland and Michael Cordner's edited collection of essays on players, playwrights, and playhouses and four times in Vanessa Cunningham's book-length study of Garrick and Shakespeare. William Worthen describes points without explicit reference to transition. See *The Oxford Handbook of the Georgian Theatre 1737–1832*, ed. by Julia Swindells and David Francis Taylor (Oxford: Oxford University Press, 2014); Kalman A. Burnim, *David Garrick, Director* (Pittsburgh: University of Pittsburgh, 1961); Felicity Nussbaum, *Rival Queens: Actresses, Performance, and the Eighteenth-Century British Theater* (Philadelphia: University of Pennsylvania Press, 2011); Helen E. M. Brooks, *Actresses, Gender, and the Eighteenth-Century Stage: Playing Women* (Basingstoke: Palgrave Macmillan, 2015); *Players, Playwrights, Playhouses: Investigating Performance, 1660–1800*, ed. by Michael Cordner and Peter Holland (Basingstoke: Palgrave

Macmillan, 2007); Vanessa Cunningham, *Shakespeare and Garrick* (Cambridge: Cambridge University Press, 2008); Worthen, *Idea of the Actor*.

20. Ray Sutton complains of how many writers of the period 'skirt round a discussion' of how actors kept up 'a continual shifting from one passion to another'. Ray Sutton, 'Re-Playing Macbeth: A View of Eighteenth-Century Acting', *Studies in Theatre and Performance*, 30.2 (2010), 145–56 (p. 147).

21. Charles Newton, *Studies in the Science and Practice of Public Speaking, Reading, and Recitation* (Norwich: Burke and Kinnebrook, 1800), p. xxxv.

22. Newton, *Studies*, p. xxxv.

23. Newton, *Studies*, pp. xxxv and xxxviii.

24. Samuel Johnson, 'TRANSI'TION, n.s.', *A Dictionary of the English Language* (London: Knapton, 1775).

25. John Hill, *The Actor; or, a Treatise on the Art of Playing* (London: Griffiths, 1755), p. 22.

26. Gentleman, *Censor*, I, p. 357.

27. Aaron Hill, *The Prompter*, 27 June 1735.

28. Nearly seventy years after Garrick's death, a print was produced representing William Hogarth's inability to depict the actor's face. Evan Sly, *Garrick and Hogarth, or the Artist Puzzled*, 1845, lithograph print, 25 × 26.7 cm, Victoria and Albert Museum, London.

29. Thomas Otway, 'Venice Preserv'd', in *The Works of Thomas Otway*, ed. by J. C. Ghosh, 2 vols (Oxford: Oxford University Press, 1968), II, pp. 197–290 (IV, p. 473). Further references to this volume in this section are given in the body of the text.

30. Williams describes Burgh's manual as 'typical of many of the home guides on reading'. Williams, *Social Life of Books*, p. 26.

31. James Burgh, *The Art of Speaking* (London: Longman, 1761), pp. 23 and 21.

32. Nick Moseley, *Actioning and How to Do It* (London: Nick Hern, 2016), pp. vii–viii.

33. Burgh, *Art of Speaking*, pp. 213–14.

34. Burgh, *Art of Speaking*, pp. 188–90; on Garrick and Macklin, see Ian McIntyre, *Garrick*, 2nd ed. (Harmondsworth: Penguin, 2000), p. 37. Stern and Palfrey describe this process as 'to passionate' in Simon Palfrey and Tiffany Stern, *Shakespeare in Parts* (Oxford: Oxford University Press, 2007), p. 86.

35. Blair Hoxby, *What Was Tragedy? Theory and the Early Modern Canon* (Oxford: Oxford University Press, 2015), p. 48.

36. For an overview of philosophical approaches, see Philip Fisher, *The Vehement Passions* (Princeton: Princeton University Press, 2002). For more information on the elocutionist movement, see Williams, *Social Life of Books*, p. 15.

37. René Descartes, 'Les Passions de l'âme', in *Œuvres de Descartes*, 12 vols (Paris: Léopold Cerf, 1909), IX, pp. 288–498 (sec. 69).

38. Descartes, 'Les Passions', sec. 29.

39. Roach, *Player's Passion*, pp. 66–68.

40. Charles Gildon, *The Life of Mr. Thomas Betterton, the Late Eminent Tragedian* (London: Gosling, 1710), p. 63.

41. Roach, *Player's Passion*, p. 66.

42. Shearer West, *The Image of the Actor: Verbal and Visual Representation in the Age of Garrick and Kemble* (New York: St Martin's, 1991), p. 2; for a similar point about engravings, see J. Gavin Paul, *Shakespeare and the Imprints of Performance* (New York: Palgrave Macmillan, 2014), p. 89.

43. Johan Zoffany, *David Garrick as Jaffeir and Susannah Cibber as Belvidera in 'Venice Preserv'd' by Thomas Otway*, c. 1763, 101.5 × 127 cm, oil on canvas, Holburne Museum, Bath.

44. William Worthen makes a similar point about William Hogarth's painting of Garrick as Richard III. See Worthen, *Idea of the Actor*, p. 93.

45. Isaac Newton, *Opticks: Or, A Treatise of the Reflections, Refractions, Inflexions and Colours of Light* (London: Innys, 1718), III, p. 322.

46. Roach, *Player's Passion*, p. 105.

47. Roach, *Player's Passion*, pp. 104–05.

48. Roach, *Player's Passion*, p. 105.

49. David Hume, *A Treatise of Human Nature*, ed. by L. A. Selby-Bigge and P. H. Nidditch (Oxford: Oxford University Press, 1978), pp. 440–41. Further references to this volume in this section are given in the body of the text.

50. Daniel Webb, *Observations on the Correspondence between Poetry and Music* (London: Dodsley, 1769), p. 52.

51. Sarah Tindal Kareem, *Eighteenth-Century Fiction and the Reinvention of Wonder* (Oxford: Oxford University Press, 2014), p. 63.

52. Adam Smith, *Essays on Philosophical Subjects* (London: Cadell and Davies, 1795), p. 16. Quoted, without mention of the opera, in Kareem, *Reinvention of Wonder*, p. 55. I discuss Hume's description of the mind as a theatre at the conclusion of Chapter 5.

53. Kareem, *Reinvention of Wonder*, p. 63.

54. Smith, *Essays*, p. 93. Quoted in Kareem, *Reinvention of Wonder*, pp. 63–64.

55. Davies, *Miscellanies*, II, p. 320.

56. William Richardson, *A Philosophical Analysis and Illustration of Some of Shakespeare's Remarkable Characters* (London: Murray, 1774), p. 14.

57. I take the distinction between arts of time and space from Gotthold Ephraim Lessing's much-refuted distinction between poetry and painting in his *Laokoon* (1766). For recent work on the temporal dimension of print, see

Christina Lupton, *Reading and the Making of Time in the Eighteenth Century* (Baltimore: Johns Hopkins University Press, 2018).

58. Aaron Hill, *The Works of the Late Aaron Hill, Esq.; In Four Volumes, Consisting of Letters on Various Subjects, and of Original Poems, Moral and Facetious, with an Essay on the Art of Acting*, 4 vols (London, 1753), II, p. 35.

59. Henry Home (Lord Kames), *Elements of Criticism*, ed. by Peter Jones, 2 vols (Indianapolis: Liberty Fund, 2005), I, p. 91.

60. I borrow the connection of these two words from Fisher. See Fisher, *Vehement Passions*, p. 4.

1 Dramatic Transition

1. 'The Preface', in *An Exact Description of the Two Fam'd Entertainments of Harlequin Doctor Faustus* (London: Payne, 1724). Further references to this volume in this section will be given in the text.

2. This scene was also published in John Thurmond, *Harlequin Doctor Faustus: With the Masque of the Deities* (London: Chetwood, 1724).

3. John Weaver, *The Loves of Mars and Venus* (London: Mears and Browne, 1717), p. 20.

4. Darryl P. Domingo, *The Rhetoric of Diversion in English Literature and Culture, 1690–1760* (Cambridge: Cambridge University Press, 2016), p. 83.

5. Lewis Theobald and John Rich, *The Vocal Parts of an Entertainment Call'd The Necromancer: Or, Harlequin Doctor Faustus* (London: Dodd, 1723); John O'Brien, *Harlequin Britain: Pantomime and Entertainment, 1690–1760* (Baltimore: Johns Hopkins University Press, 2004), p. 96.

6. For more information on such variation, see Richard Semmens, *Studies in the English Pantomime, 1712–1733* (Hillsdale: Pendragon, 2016).

7. For the success of the Faustus pantomimes, see O'Brien, *Harlequin*, chapter 4.

8. Aaron Hill, *The Plain Dealer*, 14 December 1724.

9. Hill, 14 December 1724.

10. For a detailed account of Hill's early theatrical career, see Christine Gerrard, *Aaron Hill: The Muses' Projector 1685–1750* (Oxford: Oxford University Press, 2003).

11. William Popple, *The Prompter*, 27 December 1734.

12. Aaron Hill, *The Prompter*, 13 December 1734.

13. Aaron Hill, *The Works of the Late Aaron Hill, Esq.; In Four Volumes* (London: 1753), I, p. 148. Further references to this publication in this section will be given in the text.

14. Ned Ward, *The Dancing Devils, or the Roaring Dragon* (London: Bettesworth, Bately, and Brotherton, 1724), p. 15.

15. For more on John Dennis, see Chapter 2.

16. Gerrard, *Aaron Hill*, p. 2; Brean S. Hammond, *Professional Imaginative Writing in England, 1670–1740: Hackney for Bread* (Oxford: Clarendon, 1997), pp. 286–90.

17. Aaron Hill, *The Prompter*, 12 November 1734.

18. The first observation of Hill's interest in 'pantomimic reactions' by modern scholars occurs in Lise-Lone Marker and Frederick J. Marker, 'Aaron Hill and Eighteenth-Century Acting Theory', *Quarterly Journal of Speech*, 61.4 (1975), 416–27 (p. 420).

19. Hill, 27 June 1735.

20. Hill, 27 June 1735.

21. Joseph Roach, *The Player's Passion: Studies in the Science of Acting* (Ann Arbor: University of Michigan Press, 1993), p. 80. See my introduction for a fuller discussion of Cartesianism.

22. Aaron Hill, *The Prompter*, 26 December 1735; Hill, 27 June 1735.

23. Roach, *Player's Passion*, p. 59.

24. O'Brien, *Harlequin*, p. 214.

25. Quoted in John O'Brien, 'Pantomime', in *The Cambridge Companion to British Theatre, 1730–1830*, ed. by Jane Moody and Daniel O'Quinn (Cambridge: Cambridge University Press, 2007), pp. 103–15 (p. 104).

26. Samuel Johnson, 'PLA'STICK, n.s.', *A Dictionary of the English Language* (London: Knapton, 1775).

27. Hill, 27 June 1735.

28. Hill, 27 June 1735.

29. Aaron Hill, *The Prompter*, 19 November 1734.

30. Hill, 19 November 1734.

31. Aaron Hill, *The Prompter*, 4 November 1735.

32. Hill, 4 November 1735.

33. Anne Toner, *Ellipsis in English Literature: Signs of Omission* (Cambridge: Cambridge University Press, 2015), p. 1.

34. Toner, *Ellipsis*, p. 20.

35. Toner, *Ellipsis*, p. 68.

36. Hill, 4 November 1735.

37. Hill, 4 November 1735.

38. Hill, 26 December 1735.

39. Hill, 26 December 1735.

40. For a discussion of the intersection of such dramatic passions and eighteenth-century social codes, see William B. Worthen, *The Idea of the Actor: Drama and the Ethics of Performance* (Princeton: Princeton University Press, 1984), pp. 80–81.

41. I have consulted the following editions, all published by members of the Tonson family, of John Dryden's *The Spanish Friar* to establish this point: 1681 (p. 21), 1686 (p. 20), 1690 (pp. 16–17), 1695 (pp. 16–17), 1733 (p. 34).

42. This suggestion anticipates acting theories based on the James-Lange hypothesis. See Roach, *Player's Passion*, p. 84.

43. Hill, 27 June 1735.

44. 'Pensive', *OED Online*, www.oed.com/view/Entry/140265 [accessed 12 June 2020].

45. I am grateful to Adam Mearns for the following information about the pronunciation of 'power' in 1733. The word was, as now, pronounced as a diphthong in the 1730s, although the starting point may have been more of a short 'a', formed at the back of the throat. The length of the word could also have been slightly modified by the fact that a minority of English speakers at this time would have pronounced the terminal 'r' too.

46. As when Hill argues that, in a suitably varied delivery of Chamont's anger, 'the voice seems to preserve a kind of musical modulation, even in madness' (IV, p. 373).

47. Other candidates for the addressee of this letter are a Mr Stephens, 'a citizen of London who never appeared on any stage before', who performed Othello at Covent Garden in 1734, and an unnamed actor who did the same at the Little Haymarket. Quin's age and reputation as a slow speaker make him the most likely recipient. Data obtained from London Stage Database, https://london stagedatabase.usu.edu [accessed 12 February 2020].

48. Gerrard, *Aaron Hill*, pp. 194–98.

49. David Garrick, 'Epilogue to the Clandestine Marriage', in *The Poetical Works of David Garrick, Esq.*, 2 vols (London: Kearsley, 1785), I, pp. 205–12 (p. 209).

50. Quoted in McIntyre, *Garrick*, p. 218.

51. Arthur Murphy, *The Life of David Garrick, Esq.*, 2 vols (London: Wright, 1801), I, pp. 248–49.

52. David Garrick, *The Letters of David Garrick*, ed. by David M. Little and George M. Kahrl, 3 vols (London: Oxford University Press, 1963), II, p. 635.

53. Roach, *Player's Passion*, pp. 95–96.

54. Georg Christoph Lichtenberg, 'Briefe aus England', in *Vermischte Schriften*, 9 vols (Goettigen: Dieterich, 1801), III, pp. 239–372 (pp. 270–73).

55. I am grateful to David Wiles for the observation that the French actor François-Joseph Talma describes using the exact same breathing technique as Garrick in a long note on how to perform a speech from Voltaire's *Zaïre*. François-Joseph Talma, *Réflexions sur Lekain et sur l'art dramatique* (Paris: Tenré, 1825), p. 57.

56. Joshua Steele, *An Essay towards Establishing the Melody and Measure of Speech to Be Expressed and Perpetuated by Peculiar Symbols* (London: Almon, 1775), p. 47. Further references to this publication in this section will be given in the text.

57. Peter Holland, 'Hearing the Dead: The Sound of David Garrick', in *Players, Playwrights, Playhouses: Investigating Performance, 1660–1800* (Basingstoke: Palgrave Macmillan, 2007), pp. 248–70 (pp. 258–59).

58. Holland, 'Hearing the Dead', p. 259.

59. Thaddeus Fitzpatrick, *An Enquiry into the Real Merit of a Certain Popular Performer in a Series of Letters, First Published in the Craftsman or Gray's-Inn Journal; with an Introduction to D–D G——K, Esq.* (London: Thrush, 1760), pp. 21–22.

60. Johnson, 'CATCH, n.s.'.

61. Theophilus Cibber, 'The First Dissertation', in *Cibber's Two Dissertations on the Theatres* (London: Griffiths, 1756), p. 56.

62. *Letters of David Garrick*, I, p. 34.

63. O'Brien, *Harlequin*, p. 211.

64. Samuel Foote, *A Treatise on the Passions so Far as They Regard the Stage; with a Critical Enquiry into the Theatrical Merit of Mr. G-k, Mr. Q-n, and Mr. B-y* (London: Corbet, 1747), p. 18.

65. Foote, *Treatise*, p. 18.

66. Foote, *Treatise*, p. 23.

67. See James Harriman-Smith, '*Comédien*-Actor-*Paradoxe*: The Anglo-French Sources of Diderot's *Paradoxe sur le comédien*', *Theatre Journal*, 67.1 (2015), 83–96.

68. John Hill, *The Actor: A Treatise on the Art of Playing* (London: Griffiths, 1750), p. 6.

69. John Hill, *The Actor* (1750), pp. 6–7.

70. John Hill, *The Actor* (1755), p. 265.

71. See, for example, the first chapter of Norman S. Poser, *The Birth of Modern Theatre: Rivalry, Riots, and Romance in the Age of Garrick* (New York: Routledge, 2019).

72. For more on Macklin's Shylock, see chapter 5 of Jean I. Marsden, *Theatres of Feeling: Affect, Performance, and the Eighteenth-Century Stage* (Cambridge: Cambridge University Press, 2019).

73. Quoted in Michael Caines, *Shakespeare and the Eighteenth Century*, Oxford Shakespeare Topics (Oxford: Oxford University Press, 2013), p. 75.

74. Quoted in Caines, *Shakespeare and the Eighteenth Century*, p. 75.

75. James Burgh, *The Art of Speaking* (London: Longman, 1761), p. 190.

76. Francis Gentleman, *The Dramatic Censor; or, Critical Companion*, 2 vols (London: Bell and Etherington, 1770), I, p. 283.

77. Abigail Williams, *The Social Life of Books: Reading Together in the Eighteenth-Century Home* (New Haven: Yale University Press, 2017), p. 26.

78. William Shakespeare, *Bell's Edition of Shakespeare's Plays*, ed. by Francis Gentleman, 9 vols (London: Bell and Etherington, 1773–74), II, p. 194. Further references to this edition in this section will be given in the text.

79. For more on the 'beauties-and-faults' style of editing, see Simon Jarvis, *Scholars and Gentlemen: Shakespearean Textual Criticism and Representations of Scholarly Labour, 1725–1765* (Oxford: Clarendon, 1995), pp. 49–51.

80. Catherine Alexander calls the cast lists 'the most tangible link to performance' in 'Province of Pirates: The Editing and Publication of Shakespeare's Poems in the Eighteenth Century', in *Reading Readings: Essays on Shakespeare Editing in the Eighteenth Century*, ed. by Joanna Gondris (London: Associated University Presses, 1998), pp. 345–65 (p. 358).

81. On bowdlerisation, see Colin Franklin, *Shakespeare Domesticated: The Eighteenth-Century Editions* (Aldershot: Scholar, 1991), p. 137; Noel Perrin, *Dr. Bowdler's Legacy: A History of Expurgated Books in England and America* (London: MacMillan, 1970), p. 92.

82. Data obtained from the London Stage Database, https://londonstagedatabase .usu.edu [accessed 12 February 2020].

2 *Zara*

1. Hill, 27 June 1735.

2. Aaron Hill, *The Tragedy of Zara, As It Is Acted at the Theatre Royal in Drury-Lane* (London: Watts, 1736), p. ii. Further references to this publication in this section will be given in the text.

3. Christine Gerrard, *Aaron Hill: The Muses' Projector 1685–1750* (Oxford: Oxford University Press, 2003), p. 174.

4. Aaron Hill, *The Works of the Late Aaron Hill, Esq.: In Four Volumes*, 4 vols (London: 1753), I, p. 123. Further reference to this publication in this section will be given in the text.

5. Gerrard, *Aaron Hill*, p. 176.

6. *The Prompter* began publication on 12 November 1734. Hill's article describing the imagination as 'a FAUSTUS for the *Theatres*' (discussed in Chapter 1) appears in June 1735.

7. Fredrick Louis Bergmann, 'Garrick's Zara', *PMLA*, 74.3 (1959), 225–32 (p. 226).

8. Thomas Davies, *Memoirs of the Life of David Garrick*, 2 vols (London: Davies, 1780), I, p. 112

9. Gerrard, *Aaron Hill*, p. 178.

10. Aaron Hill, *The Prompter*, 3 February 1736.

11. Bergmann, 'Garrick's Zara', p. 227.

12. Bergmann, 'Garrick's Zara', p. 227.

13. Bergmann, 'Garrick's Zara', p. 225.

14. Bergmann, 'Garrick's Zara', p. 228.

15. *Bell's British Theatre, Consisting of the Most Esteemed English Plays*, ed. by Francis Gentleman, 20 vols (London: Bell and Etherington, 1776), 1.

16. Although not discussed here, these interval entertainments correspond to Hill's belief that contemporary audiences needed periodic relief in order to appreciate serious drama. Hill wrote to Barton Booth (then manager of Drury Lane) on this topic, urging him 'to prepare, in that interval, little *significant* interludes of singing, dancing, and harlequinades, consisting of as many Acts, as the Play's, and succeeding them (the Acts) regularly, in short, apt sallies' (Hill, *Works*, 1, p. 118).

17. See the following for all the material covered in this paragraph: Gerrard, *Aaron Hill*, pp. 174–75.

18. Hill, 27 June 1735.

19. Aaron Hill, *The Prompter*, 13 June 1735.

20. For recent re-evaluation of Dennis, see Shaun Irlam, *Elations: The Poetics of Enthusiasm in Eighteenth-Century Britain* (Stanford: Stanford University Press, 1999); Anne T. Delehanty, 'Mapping the Aesthetic Mind: John Dennis and Nicolas Boileau', *Journal of the History of Ideas*, 68.2 (2007), 233–53; Phillip J. Donnelly, 'Enthusiastic Poetry and Rationalized Christianity: The Poetic Theory of John Dennis', *Christianity and Literature*, 54.2 (2005), 235–64; John Morillo, 'John Dennis: Enthusiastic Passions, Cultural Memory and Literary Theory', *Eighteenth-Century Studies*, 34.1 (2000), 21–41.

21. Gerrard, *Aaron Hill*, p. 3.

22. For a detailed account of Hill's relationship with Dennis, see Gerrard, *Aaron Hill*, pp. 106–10.

23. John Dennis, *The Advancement and Reformation of Modern Poetry* (London: Parker, 1701), p. 23. Further references to this publication in this section will be given in the text.

24. Aaron Hill, *The Prompter*, 14 May 1736.

25. Margaret Koehler, *Poetry of Attention in the Eighteenth Century* (New York: Palgrave Macmillan, 2012), p. 53.

26. Dennis repeats this argument in a later critical work: John Dennis, *The Grounds of Criticism in Poetry* (London: Strahan and Lintot, 1704), pp. 16–17.

27. See, for example, the texts reproduced here: Dennis, *Grounds*, pp. 93, 101, 108, and 140.

28. Sara Landreth, '"Set His Image in Motion": John Dennis and Early Eighteenth-Century Motion Imagery', *Eighteenth-Century Life*, 40.1 (2016), 59–83 (pp. 68–69).

29. Hill, 26 December 1735.

30. Aaron Hill, *The Fatal Vision: Or, The Fall of Siam. A Tragedy: As It Is Acted at the New Theatre in Lincoln's-Inn-Fields* (London: Nutt, 1716), p. vi.

31. Voltaire, 'Zaïre', in *Zaïre – Le Fanatisme ou Mahomet Le Prophète – Nanine ou l'Homme sans préjugé – Le Café ou l'Ecossaise*, ed. by Jean Goldzink (Paris: G. F. Flammarion, 2004), pp. 47–132 (I. 103–04).

32. The following, for example, silently alters the punctuation and removes dashes, italics, and capital letters: David Garrick, 'Aaron Hill, Zara, *A Tragedy*, 1754', in *The Plays of David Garrick*, ed. by Harry William Pedicord and Fredrick Louis Bergmann, 6 vols (Carbondale: Southern Illinois University Press, 1982), VI, pp. 135–200. Further references to this publication will be given in the text.

33. Anne Toner, *Ellipsis in English Literature: Signs of Omission* (Cambridge: Cambridge University Press, 2015), p. 68.

34. See *Plays of David Garrick*, VI, p. 151; Aaron Hill and David Garrick, *The Tragedy of Zara*, ed. by Richard Cumberland (London: Cooke, 1817), p. 3.

35. Note also that the 1736 edition has an additional dash before 'She's gone!' (p. 39), and all its dashes are single bars rather than the three concatenated short bars used in the *Essay*.

36. Claudine van Hensbergen remarks on the notable use of frequent dashes in Bernard Lintot's 1714 edition of *Jane Shore*, and so provides evidence for a printer's involvement in such typographical marking of pauses. Claudine van Hensbergen, 'Publication History and Textual Note to *The Tragedy of Jane Shore* and *The Tragedy of the Lady Jane Gray*', in *The Plays and Poems of Nicholas Rowe: The Late Plays*, ed. by Stephen Bernard and Claudine van Hensbergen, 5 vols (London: Routledge, 2016), III, 25–31 (pp. 27–29).

37. 'Je demeure immobile, et ma langue glacée | Se refuse aux transports de mon âme si offensée. | Est-ce à moi que l'on parle ? Ai-je bien entendu ? | Est-ce moi qu'elle fuit ? ô ciel ! et qu'ai-je vu ? | Corasmin, quel est donc ce changement extrême ? | Je la laisse échapper ! Je m'ignore moi-même'. Voltaire, 'Zaïre', III. 975–80.

38. René Descartes, 'Les Passions de l'âme', in *Œuvres de Descartes*, 12 vols (Paris: Léopold Cerf, 1909), sec. 73; Hill might also have Milton's description of Adam 'Astonied and Blank, while horror chill | Ran through his veins' in mind here also. See John Milton, *Paradise Lost*, ed. by Stephen Orgel and Jonathan Goldberg (Oxford: Oxford University Press, 2004), p. 231 (IX. 890ff.).

39. Respectively: Voltaire, 'Zaïre', I. 301 and V. 1510.

40. Dene Barnett and Jeanette Massy-Westropp, *The Art of Gesture: The Practices and Principles of 18th Century Acting* (Heidelberg: Carl Winter, 1987), p. 18.

41. Angelina Del Balzo, 'The Sultan's Tears in *Zara, an Oriental Tragedy*', *Studies in English Literature, 1500–1900*, 55.3 (2015), 501–21 (pp. 514–15). Another recent work is Bridget Orr, *British Enlightenment Theatre: Dramatizing Difference* (Cambridge: Cambridge University Press, 2019), pp. 78–86.

42. See David Hume, 'Of Tragedy', in *Essays, Moral, Political and Literary*, ed. by Eugene F. Miller (Indianapolis: Liberty Fund, 1987), pp. 216–25.

43. Compare the following, where there is no corresponding line: Voltaire, 'Zaïre', I. 145–52.

44. Compare 'C'est vous, digne Français, à qui je viens parler': Voltaire, 'Zaïre', II. 475.

45. Davies, *Memoirs*, II, pp. 347–48.

46. Aaron Hill, *The Prompter*, 6 June 1735.

47. Bergmann, 'Garrick's Zara', p. 228.

48. Bergmann, 'Garrick's Zara', pp. 229–30.

49. For example: 'Je la viens honorer, Seigneur, je viens vous rendre | Le dernier de ce sang, votre amour, votre espoir : | Oui, Lusignan est libre, et vous l'allez revoir'. Voltaire, 'Zaïre', II. 506–08.

50. Voltaire, 'Zaïre', II. 518.

51. This transition resembles that in *King Lear* when the monarch declares 'I am old'. See my analysis of this in Chapter 4.

52. Aaron Hill, *The Plain Dealer*, 18 January 1725.

53. An engraving of this moment is reproduced in *Plays of David Garrick*, VI, p. 166.

54. I return to this idea of structural transition in my chapter on *King Lear*.

55. Bergmann writes of the play's popularity but provides no evidence for it beyond Isaac Reed's attendance at a performance in 1784. See Bergmann, 'Garrick's Zara', p. 232.

56. Hill and Garrick, *The Tragedy of Zara*, p. viii.

57. Hill and Garrick, *The Tragedy of Zara*, p. viii.

58. 'Zara, a captive in the seraglio of Osman, discovers in the aged and imprisoned Lusignan a father, and in the gallant Nerestan a brother. They of course urge her to escape from her infidel lover; she reluctantly consents to embrace Christianity. Osman mistakes her conviction for inconstancy, and an intercepted letter confirms his suspicions. He thinks he has discovered the favoured lover in Nerestan, and is fired with jealous rage, which causes him to stab the faithless Zara, and on discovering his mistake, he destroys himself'. Hill and Garrick, *The Tragedy of Zara*, pp. viii–ix.

59. Hill and Garrick, *The Tragedy of Zara*, p. xi.

60. Blair Hoxby, *What Was Tragedy? Theory and the Early Modern Canon* (Oxford: Oxford University Press, 2015), p. 58.

61. Hoxby, *What Was Tragedy?*, p. 48.

62. One might point to Charles Lamb or George Steiner; see also Hoxby's analysis of August Wilhelm Schlegel: Hoxby, *What Was Tragedy?*, p. 108.

3 Odes

1. David Garrick, *An Ode upon Dedicating a Building, and Erecting a Statue, to Shakespeare* (London: Becket and de Hondt, 1769), p. 2. Further references to this publication in this section will be given in the text.

2. For a detailed description of how actors were taught to express wonder, see Dene Barnett and Jeanette Massy-Westropp, *The Art of Gesture: The Practices and Principles of 18th Century Acting* (Heidelberg: Carl Winter, 1987), p. 47.

3. James Boswell, 'To the Printer of the Public Advertiser', *The Public Advertiser* (16 September 1769), 1–2 (p. 2).

4. Vanessa Cunningham, *Shakespeare and Garrick* (Cambridge: Cambridge University Press, 2008), p. 107.

5. See Michael Dobson, *The Making of the National Poet: Shakespeare, Adaptation and Authorship, 1660–1769* (Oxford: Oxford University Press, 1992), p. 185; Kate Rumbold, 'Shakespeare and the Stratford Jubilee', in *Shakespeare in the Eighteenth Century*, ed. by Fiona Ritchie and Peter Sabor (Cambridge: Cambridge University Press, 2012), pp. 254–76; Ian McIntyre, *Garrick*, 2nd ed. (Harmondsworth: Penguin, 2000), pp. 412–32.

6. Cunningham, *Shakespeare and Garrick*, p. 106.

7. *A Collection of Illustrations, Portraits, Newspaper Cuttings, Extracts from Books and Sale Catalogues, Advertisements, Manuscripts and Playbills, Relating Principally to the Shakespeare Jubilee of 1769, and in Particular to David Garrick's Part Therein*, ed. by George Daniel, British Library General Reference Collection, C.61.e.2, p. 2. There is no evidence to support Daniel's claim.

8. Daniel, *Collection*, p. 13.

9. Virginia Jackson and Yopie Prins, 'General Introduction', in *The Lyric Theory Reader: A Critical Anthology*, ed. by Virginia Jackson and Yopie Prins (Baltimore: Johns Hopkins University Press, 2014), pp. 1–10 (p. 1); Johnson, 'LYR'ICAL / LY'RICK, Adj.', *A Dictionary of the English Language* (London: Knapton, 1775).

10. Even this recovery is not without controversy. See Jonathan Culler, *Theory of the Lyric* (Cambridge, MA: Harvard University Press, 2015).

11. Gérard Genette, 'The Architext (1979; Trans. 1992)', in *The Lyric Theory Reader: A Critical Anthology*, ed. by Virginia Jackson and Yopie Prins (Baltimore: Johns Hopkins University Press, 2014), pp. 17–29 (pp. 17–19).

12. Genette, 'Architext', p. 21.

13. My translation of 'De même donc que dans la Poësie épique & dramatique on imite les actions & les mœurs ; dans le lyrique, on chante les sentimens, ou les passions imitées'. Charles Batteux, *Les Beaux Arts réduits à un même principe*, revised ed. (Paris: Durand, 1747), pp. 254–55.

14. James Burgh, *The Art of Speaking* (London: Longman, 1761); Gilbert Austin, *Chironomia, or A Treatise on Rhetorical Delivery* (London: Cadell and Davies, 1806).

15. See Johann Wolfgang von Goethe, 'Noten und Abhandlungen zu besserem Verstandnis des West-Ostichen Diwans', in *Goethes Werke*, 15 vols (Munich: Beck, 1981), 11, pp. 187–89.

16. *Quintilian with an English Translation*, trans. by Harold Edgeworth Butler (London: Heinemann, 1922), x, sec. 1, chapter 61.

17. George Shuster, *The English Ode from Milton to Keats* (New York: Columbia University Press, 1940).

18. Shuster, *English Ode*, p. 179.

19. Margaret Koehler, *Poetry of Attention in the Eighteenth Century* (New York: Palgrave McMillan, 2012), p. 89; see also her 'Odes of Absorption in the Restoration and Early Eighteenth Century', *SEL: Studies in English Literature, 1500–1900*, 47.3 (2007), 659–78.

20. Shuster, *English Ode*, pp. 149–51.

21. Daniel Webb, *Observations on the Correspondence between Poetry and Music* (London: Dodsley, 1769). Further references to this publication in this section will be given in the text.

22. Daniel Webb, *Remarks on the Beauties of Poetry* (London: Dodsley, 1762), pp. 43–44.

23. David Hume, *A Treatise of Human Nature*, ed. by L. A. Selby-Bigge and P. H. Nidditch (Oxford: Oxford University Press, 1978), pp. 440–41. See my introduction for a full discussion of this point.

24. Webb advertises his debt to Cicero in a footnote (*Observations*, p. 5).

25. Webb, *Remarks*, pp. 88–89. For more on this topic, see James Kennaway, 'Stimulating Music: The Pleasures and Dangers of "Electric Music," 1750–1900', *Configurations*, 19.2 (2011), 191–211 (p. 195).

26. Citing examples from Dinouart (1754), Lessing (1755), and Jelgerhuis (1827), Barnett notes the importance of distinguishing between abrupt and smooth movements of the hands. Barnett and Massy-Westropp, *Art of Gesture*, p. 57.

27. Geminiani was Webb's teacher.

28. James Harris, 'Three Treatises Concerning Art (1744)', in *Musical Aesthetics: A Historical Reader*, ed. by Edward Lippman, 4 vols (New York: Pendragon, 1986), 1, pp. 177–84 (p. 183).

29. James Beattie, *Essays: On Poetry and Music, as They Affect the Mind*, 3rd ed. (Edinburgh: Dilly and Creech, 1779), pp. 119–20; Jean-Baptiste Dubos, 'Réflexions critiques sur la poësie et sur la peinture (1719)', in *Music and Aesthetics in the Eighteenth and Early-Nineteenth Centuries*, ed. by Peter le Huray and James Day, Cambridge Readings in the Literature of Music (Cambridge: Cambridge University Press, 1981), pp. 17–22 (p. 19).

30. Harris, 'Three Treatises', p. 184.

31. For a more detailed history of the relationship between words and music in eighteenth-century composition, see Wye J. Allanbrook, *The Secular Commedia: Comic Mimesis in Late Eighteenth-Century Music*, ed. Richard Taruskin and Mary Ann Smart (Oakland: University of California Press, 2014), pp. 93–94.

32. Todd Gilman, *The Theatre Career of Thomas Arne* (Newark: University of Delaware Press, 2013), p. 473.

33. David Garrick and Thomas Arne, *Ode upon Dedicating a Building to Shakespeare* (London: Johnston, 1769), pp. 2–7.

34. James Malek, 'Physiology and Art: Daniel Webb's Aesthetics', *Neuphilologische Mitteilungen*, 71.4 (1970), 691–99 (p. 695).

35. John Dennis, *The Advancement and Reformation of Modern Poetry* (London: Parker, 1701), p. 37.

36. Dale E. Monson, Jack Westrup, and Julian Budden, 'Recitative', *Grove Music Online* (Oxford: Oxford University Press, 2001), www.oxfordmusiconline.com/grovemusic/view/10.1093/gmo/9781561592630.001.0001/omo-9781561592630-e-0000023019 [accessed 14 February 2019].

37. John Milton, *Paradise Lost*, ed. by Stephen Orgel and Jonathan Goldberg (Oxford: Oxford University Press, 2004), x, l.889.

38. Milton, *Paradise Lost*, x, ll. 896–901.

39. See Joseph Roach, *The Player's Passion: Studies in the Science of Acting* (Ann Arbor: University of Michigan Press, 1993), pp. 68–70.

40. Hill, 27 June 1735; Barnett and Massy-Westropp, *Art of Gesture*, p. 42.

41. Dennis, *Advancement*, p. 36; See also Sara Landreth, '"Set His Image in Motion": John Dennis and Early Eighteenth-Century Motion Imagery', *Eighteenth-Century Life*, 40.1 (2016), 59–83.

42. Edmund Burke, *A Philosophical Enquiry into the Origin of Our Ideas of the Sublime and Beautiful* (London: Dodsley, 1757), p. 42.

43. John Dryden, 'Alexander's Feast', in *John Dryden: The Major Works*, ed. by Keith Walker (Oxford: Oxford University Press, 2003), pp. 545–50 (ll. 1–2).

44. Dryden, 'Alexander's Feast', ll. 66–72.

45. Dryden, 'Alexander's Feast', l. 84.

46. George Steevens, 'Shakespeare's Feast', *The Public Advertiser* (5 August 1769), p. 2.

47. Thomas Davies, *Memoirs of the Life of David Garrick*, 2 vols (London: Davies: 1780), II, p. 222.

48. Tom Mason and Adam Rounce, '*Alexander's Feast; or The Power of Musique*: The Poem and Its Readers', in *John Dryden: Tercentenary Essays*, ed. by David Hopkins and Paul Hammond (Oxford: Oxford University Press, 2000), pp. 140–73 (pp. 143–44).

49. Mason and Rounce, '*Alexander's Feast*', pp. 142–43.

50. Quoted in Mason and Rounce, '*Alexander's Feast*', p. 146.

51. Mason and Rounce, '*Alexander's Feast*', p. 148.

52. Quoted in Mason and Rounce, '*Alexander's Feast*', p. 150.

53. Mason and Rounce, '*Alexander's Feast*', p. 150.

54. Jean-Jacques Rousseau, 'Musique', *Dictionnaire de Musique* (Paris: Duchesne, 1768), pp. 308–19.

55. Hume, *Treatise*, p. 144.

56. William Collins, 'The Passions. An Ode for Music', in *Odes on Several Descriptive and Allegoric Subjects* (London: Millar, 1746), pp. 46–52 (p. 46).

57. Collins, 'The Passions', p. 46.

58. Collins, 'The Passions', p. 47.

59. The Homeric Hymns, for instance, also depict a similar scene. See David Fairer, '"Love Was in the Next Degree": Lyric, Satire, and Inventive Modulation', *Journal for Eighteenth-Century Studies*, 34.2 (2011), 147–66.

60. William Havard, 'Ode to the Memory of Shakespeare', in *William Shakespeare: The Critical Heritage 1753–1765*, ed. by Brian Vickers (London: Routledge, 2000), pp. 289–91 (p. 290).

61. Havard, 'Ode to the Memory of Shakespeare', p. 290.

62. Charles Dibdin, *Queen Mab, or the Fairies' Jubilee* (London: Johnston, 1769), p. 2.

63. Cunningham, *Shakespeare and Garrick*, p. 110.

64. William Shakespeare, 'The Tempest', in *The Arden Shakespeare Complete Works*, ed. by Virginia Mason Vaughan and Alden T. Vaughan, revised ed. (London: Thomson Learning, 2007), pp. 1071–96 (v. I. 42–44).

65. Quoted in Cunningham, *Shakespeare and Garrick*, p. 60.

66. *Letters of David Garrick*, I, p. 670.

67. See Peter Holland, 'David Garrick', in *Garrick – Kemble – Siddons – Kean*, ed. by Peter Holland, Great Shakespeareans, 18 vols (London: Pickering & Chatto, 2010), II, pp. 8–54.

68. *A Poetical Epistle from Shakespear in Elysium to David Garrick at Drury Lane, to Which Is Added a View from Heymon Hill near Shrewsbury, A Solitudinarian Ode* (London: Newberry and Owen, 1752), pp. 10–11.

69. This distinguishes Garrick's ode from what Sarah Eron describes as the 'more dialogical methods of modern apostrophe and address' found in eighteenth-century reformulations of the inspiration. See Sarah Eron, *Inspiration in the Age of Enlightenment* (Newark: University of Delaware Press, 2014), p. 1.

70. Koehler, *Poetry*, p. 99.

71. 'The Stratford Jubilee', *The Scots Magazine*, September 1769.

72. Joshua Reynolds, *Garrick between Tragedy and Comedy*, 1761, oil on canvas, 148 × 183 cm, Waddesdon Manor, Buckinghamshire.

73. *Pursuit after Happiness: A Poem. To Which is Added, An Ode to Mr Garrick, On his Quitting the Stage. Also an Elegy on the Death of Mr Barry* (London: Kearsley, 1777), pp. 30–31.
74. Cunningham, *Shakespeare and Garrick*, p. 120.
75. William Shakespeare, *Bell's Edition of Shakespeare's Plays*, ed. by Francis Gentleman, 9 vols (London: Bell and Etherington, 1773–74), II, p. 20.
76. Data obtained from the London Stage Database, https://londonstagedatabase .usu.edu [accessed 01 July 2020]; Charles Dickens, *Great Expectations*, ed. by Angus Calder (London: Penguin, 1985), p. 74.
77. George Knox, 'Remarks on Collins's Ode on the Passions', *The Edinburgh Magazine; or Literary Miscellany* (March 1801), 206–10 (p. 208).
78. Knox, 'Remarks', p. 208.
79. Nicholas Rowe, 'Some Account of the Life, &c. of Mr. William Shakespear', in *The Works of Mr. William Shakespear*, ed. by Nicholas Rowe, 6 vols (London: Tonson, 1709), I, pp. i–xl (p. vi).
80. Garrick and Arne, *Ode upon Dedicating a Building to Shakespeare*, p. 24.
81. Garrick and Arne, *Ode upon Dedicating a Building to Shakespeare*, pp. 26–27.
82. Charles Avison, 'An Essay on Musical Expression (1752)', in *Musical Aesthetics: A Historical Reader*, ed. by Edward Lippman, 4 vols (New York: Pendragon, 1986), I, pp. 185–99 (p. 190).
83. John Brown, *A Dissertation on the Rise, Union, and Power, the Progressions, Separations, and Corruptions, of Poetry and Music* (London: Davis and Reymers, 1763).
84. See chapter 3 of Etienne Bonnot de Condillac, *Essai sur l'origine des connaissances humaines*, 2 vols (Amsterdam: Mortier, 1746), II.

4 *King Lear*

1. Thomas Davies, *Dramatic Miscellanies*, 3 vols (London: Davies, 1783), II, p. 328.
2. Such comparisons can be found both during Garrick's career and after his death. See, for example, the following publications: *London Daily Post and General Advertiser*, 27 December 1743 (Garrick's Lear v. James Quin's); *St James's Chronicle*, 15 May 1764 (David Ross); *Morning Chronicle*, 26 November 1774 (Spranger Barry); *General Evening Post*, 16 January 1777 (Barry again); *Public Advertiser*, 17 September 1778 (West Digges); *Public Advertiser*, 16 October 1783 (John Henderson); *Morning Post and Daily Advertiser*, 31 July 1786 ('Mr Waldron', a theatre manager from Hammersmith); *St James's Chronicle or the British Evening Post*, 22 January 1788 (John Philip Kemble); and *St James's Chronicle or the British Evening Post*, 20 September 1800 (James Brunton). Bertram Joseph notes that

Garrick's performance was also compared to that of his predecessor, Barton Booth: Bertram Joseph, *The Tragic Actor* (London: Routledge, 1959), p. 59.

3. Francis Gentleman, *The Dramatic Censor; or, Critical Companion*, 2 vols (London: Bell and Etherington, 1770), I, p. 369.

4. Joseph Warton, *An Essay on the Writings and Genius of Pope*, 2 vols (London: Cooper, 1756), I, p. 123.

5. For example: *Entertainer*, 12 November 1754; *Morning Chronicle*, 23 July 1774. Garrick's extensive involvement with the periodical press has been analysed by Leslie Ritchie. See Leslie Ritchie, *David Garrick and the Mediation of Celebrity* (Cambridge: Cambridge University Press, 2019).

6. *General Advertiser*, 13 October 1786. For the afterlife of Tate's *King Lear*, see Lynne Bradley, *Adapting King Lear for the Stage* (London: Routledge, 2016).

7. *Morning Chronicle*, 15 May 1773; *Morning Chronicle and London Advertiser*, 5 August 1774.

8. *Gazetteer and New Daily Advertiser*, 25 August 1787.

9. Philip Fisher, *The Vehement Passions* (Princeton: Princeton University Press, 2002), p. 47.

10. Henry Home, Lord Kames, *Elements of Criticism*, ed. by Peter Jones, 2 vols (Indianapolis: Liberty Fund, 2005), II, p. 679.

11. Nahum Tate with David Garrick, *The History of King Lear, A Tragedy; As It Is Now Acted at the King's Theatres* (London: Hitch, Hawes, Brindley, Hodges, Longman, Corbett, King, Reeve, Cooper, Noble, 1756), p. 3. This annotated copy can be found in the British Library (shelfmark C.119.dd.22). Further references to this publication in this section will be given in the text.

12. David Garrick, *An Ode upon Dedicating a Building, and Erecting a Statue, to Shakespeare* (London: Becket and de Hondt, 1769), p. 6.

13. *St James's Chronicle*, 15 May 1764. On Garrick's influence as a shareholder in this publication, see Ritchie, *Mediation of Celebrity*, pp. 50–51.

14. Milton's sonnet contains the line 'Then thou our fancy of itself bereaving, | Dost make us marble with too much conceiving'. John Milton, 'On Shakespeare', in *John Milton: The Major Works*, ed. by Stephen Orgel and Jonathan Goldberg, revised ed. (Oxford: Oxford University Press, 2003), p. 20. Other publications make a similar point to 'W.N.'; see *Public Advertiser*, 5 July 1763 and *London Evening Post*, 19 January 1762.

15. Nicholas Rowe, *The Tragedy of Jane Shore* (London: Lintot, 1714), p. 56.

16. Helen E. M. Brooks, *Actresses, Gender, and the Eighteenth-Century Stage: Playing Women* (Basingstoke: Palgrave Macmillan, 2015), p. 55.

17. William Shakespeare, *Bell's Edition of Shakespeare's Plays*, ed. by Francis Gentleman, 9 vols (London: Bell and Etherington, 1773–74), III, p. 61. Further references to this publication in this section will be given in the text.

18. *St James's Chronicle*, 15 September 1761.

19. *Diary or Woodfall's Register*, 13 January 1792.
20. Samuel Foote, A *Treatise on the Passions so Far as They Regard the Stage; with a Critical Enquiry into the Theatrical Merit of Mr. G-k, Mr. Q-n, and Mr. B-y* (London: Corbet, 1747), p. 19; John Locke defined madmen as those who 'put wrong Ideas together, and so make wrong Propositions, but argue and reason right from them'. See John Locke, *An Essay Concerning Human Understanding in Four Books* (London: Dring and Manship, 1694), p. 71.
21. Foote, *Treatise*, p. 20.
22. Foote, *Treatise*, p. 20; Roy Porter observes that Locke's ideas would 'decisively [. . .] shape British thinking about madness in the second half of the eighteenth century'. Roy Porter, *Flesh in the Age of Reason* (Harmondsworth: Penguin, 2004), p. 311.
23. Foote, *Treatise*, p. 21.
24. Theophilus Cibber, 'The Second Dissertation', in *Cibber's Two Dissertations on the Theatres* (London: Griffiths, 1756), pp. 1–47 (pp. 36–37).
25. See *Aristotle's Ars Poetica*, ed. by Rudolph Kassel (Oxford: Clarendon, 1966), sec. 1448b.
26. Cibber, 'The First Dissertation', in *Cibber's Two Dissertations on the Theatres* (London: Griffiths, 1756), pp. 1–76 (p. 56).
27. Cibber, 'The Second Dissertation', p. 37.
28. Edward A. Langhans, *Eighteenth Century British and Irish Promptbooks: A Descriptive Bibliography* (New York: Greenwood, 1987), pp. 164–65.
29. For example, in Johnson's edition: 'Hear, Nature, hear; dear Goddess, hear! | Suspend thy purpose, if thou didst intend | To make this creature fruitful'. *The Plays of William Shakespeare in Eight Volumes*, ed. by Samuel Johnson, 8 vols (London: Tonson, 1765), VI, p. 41.
30. Cibber, 'The Second Dissertation', pp. 32–33.
31. *Gazetteer and New Daily Advertiser*, 26 November 1765.
32. *General Evening Post*, 16 January 1777.
33. Davies, *Miscellanies*, II, p. 280.
34. Davies, *Miscellanies*, II, pp. 279–80.
35. Davies, *Miscellanies*, II, p. 280.
36. In Shakespeare's quarto of 1608, Albany cues Lear at this point by professing his ignorance. William Shakespeare, *True Chronicle History of the Life and Death of King Lear and His Three Daughters* (London: Butter, 1608), sig. D2r. Further references to this publication in this section will be given in the text.
37. Cibber, 'The Second Dissertation', p. 34.
38. *Morning Post and Daily Advertiser*, 2 October 1778. The pseudonym probably refers to Laurence Sterne's Corporal Trim, whose public speaking style is described at length in *Tristram Shandy*.
39. Cibber, 'The Second Dissertation', p. 33.

40. Cibber, 'The Second Dissertation', pp. 34–35.

41. Cibber, 'The Second Dissertation', p. 35.

42. Foote, *Treatise*, p. 18.

43. William Cooke, *The Elements of Dramatic Criticism* (London: Kearsly and Robinson, 1775), p. 57.

44. *World and Fashionable Advertiser*, 25 January 1788; for other cases of actors using make-up, see Dene Barnett and Jeanette Massy-Westropp, *The Art of Gesture: The Practices and Principles of 18th Century Acting* (Heidelberg: Carl Winter), p. 42.

45. The subsequent scene, located in 'Gloster's Palace', carries prompt markings to this effect (p. 30). The stage then re-opens for the return to the heath (p. 33).

46. Prior to the eighteenth century, lightning was represented through bursts of sound only, and the 'claps' at the start of this scene suggests that this is what occurred there. The use of 'flash' in the promptbook, the *Exact Description*'s account of firecrackers being used in John Rich and Lewis Theobald's *Necromancer* pantomime (1724), and the late eighteenth-century experiments of Philippe de Loutherbourg for his *Eidophusikon* (1781) suggest to me, however, that rudimentary light effects could have been used for some performances of Garrick's Lear.

47. John Burgoyne, *The Lord of the Manor* (London: Evans, 1781), p. viii.

48. Michael V. Pisani, *Music for the Melodramatic Theatre in Nineteenth-Century London and New York*, Studies in Theatre History and Culture (Iowa City: University of Iowa Press, 2014), pp. 3–4.

49. In addition to the locator's mention of '*A Chamber*', promptmarks indicate new scenery at this point too (p. 55).

50. *London Daily Post and General Advertiser*, 15 January 1743.

51. Davies, *Miscellanies*, II, pp. 319–20.

52. Davies, *Miscellanies*, II, p. 315–16.

53. Davies, *Miscellanies*, II, p. 317.

54. Davies, *Miscellanies*, II, p. 318.

55. *Public Advertiser*, 25 September 1776. Another account of a spectator weeping at Garrick's Lear appears in the *London Daily Advertiser and Literary Gazette*, 4 November 1751.

56. The mark in question is a cross-hatch symbol, often used to cue entrances. See Edward A. Langhans, *Restoration Promptbooks* (Carbondale: Southern Illinois University Press, 1981), p. xxvii.

57. *London Daily Advertiser and Literary Gazette*, 2 November 1751.

58. See James Harriman-Smith, '*Comédien*-Actor-*Paradoxe*: The Anglo-French Sources of Diderot's *Paradoxe sur le comédien*', *Theatre Journal*, 67.1 (2015), 83–96.

59. John Hill, *The Actor: A Treatise on the Art of Playing* (London: Griffiths, 1750), pp. 290–91. Further references to this publication in this section will be given in the text.

60. Pierre Rémond de Sainte-Albine, *Le Comédien* (Paris: Desaint & Saillant, 1747), p. 293.

61. Davies, *Miscellanies*, II, p. 263.

62. Davies, *Miscellanies*, II, pp. 264–65.

63. Gentleman, *Censor*, I, pp. 361–62.

64. Hill follows Sainte-Albine in making this distinction. See Sainte-Albine, *Comédien*, p. 34.

65. Kames, *Elements*, I, p. 68.

66. Kames, *Elements*, I, p. 68.

67. Kames, *Elements*, II, p. 678.

68. Kames, *Elements*, II, p. 678.

69. Kames, *Elements*, II, p. 679.

70. Natalie Phillips notes Johnson's 'rhetorical strategy' of 'leveraging distraction [...] to economize focus': Natalie M. Phillips, *Distraction: Problems of Attention in Eighteenth-Century Literature* (Baltimore: Johns Hopkins University Press, 2016), p. 60. Andrew Ashfield and Peter de Bolla remark on the significance of 'repose' to Smith's work on the sublime: *The Sublime: A Reader in British Eighteenth-Century Aesthetic Theory*, ed. by Andrew Ashfield and Peter De Bolla (Cambridge: Cambridge University Press, 1996), p. 198.

71. Davies, *Miscellanies*, II, p. 320.

72. Dryden's play appeared in 1681, the same year that Tate published his *King Lear*.

73. Blair Hoxby, 'What Was Tragedy? The World We Have Lost, 1550–1795', *Comparative Literature*, 64.1 (2012), 1–32 (pp. 9–10). See my discussion of Hoxby's work in the Introduction.

74. See the discussion of the circle symbol in Langhans, *Restoration Promptbooks*, p. xxvii.

75. *Gazetteer and New Daily Advertiser*, 14 December 1765; Garrick was well-known for his skill at performing such awakenings. Hogarth's painting of Richard III is the most famous example. See William Hogarth, *David Garrick as Richard III*, c. 1745, oil on canvas, 190.5 × 250.8 cm, Walker Art Gallery, Liverpool.

76. The same symbol also appears next to the 'Be your tears wet?' dialogue (p. 56), in the midst of Gloucester's speech describing the noise of the battle (p. 59), and during Edmund and Edgar's conversation before their duel (p. 63).

77. John Dryden, *The Indian Emperour, or, The Conquest of Mexico by the Spaniards Being the Sequel of The Indian Queen* (London: Herringman, 1667), p. 68.

78. *London Daily Advertiser and Literary Gazette*, 4 November 1751.

79. Cibber, 'The Second Dissertation', p. 41.

80. Gentleman, *Censor*, I, p. 366.

81. *The Plays of William Shakespeare in Eight Volumes*, VI, p. 159; for further discussion of this comment, see Freya Johnston, 'Samuel Johnson', in *Dryden – Pope – Johnson – Malone*, ed. by Claude Julien Rawson (London: Continuum, 2010), pp. 115–59 (pp. 143, 149, and 152).

82. Gentleman, *Censor*, I, p. 357.

5 Dramatic Character

1. Elizabeth Montagu, *An Essay on the Writings and Genius of Shakespear, Compared with the Greek and French Dramatic Poets. With Some Remarks upon the Misrepresentations of Mons. de Voltaire* (London: Dodsley, 1769), pp. 183–84. Further references to this publication in this section will be given in the text.

2. Montagu is quoting Hamlet's reflections on what the Player King might do, 'Had he the motive and the cue for passion | That I have?'. See William Shakespeare, 'Hamlet', in *The Arden Shakespeare Complete Works*, ed. by G. R. Proudfoot, Ann Thompson, and David Scott Kastan, revised ed. (London: Thomson Learning, 2007), pp. 291–332, (p. 308; ll. 2. 560–61).

3. Voltaire, *Letters Concerning the English Nation* (London: Tonson, 1728), p. 142.

4. See Jonathan Bate, *Shakespearean Constitutions: Politics, Theatre, Criticism 1730–1830* (Oxford: Oxford University Press, 1989), p. 26.

5. See Vanessa Cunningham, *Shakespeare and Garrick* (Cambridge: Cambridge University Press, 2008), pp. 4–5.

6. Antonia Forster, 'Shakespeare in the Reviews', in *Shakespeare in the Eighteenth Century*, ed. by Fiona Ritchie and Peter Sabor (Cambridge: Cambridge University Press, 2012), pp. 60–77 (p. 63).

7. For an insightful account of just how combative Montagu's essay was, particularly against Samuel Johnson, see Elizabeth Eger, '"Out Rushed a Female to Protect the Bard": The Bluestocking Defense of Shakespeare', *The Huntington Library Quarterly*, 65.1 (2002), 127–51.

8. John Dennis, *The Advancement and Reformation of Modern Poetry* (London: Parker, 1701), p. 36; Aaron Hill, *The Prompter*, 27 June 1735.

9. Maurice Morgann, *An Essay on the Dramatic Character of Sir John Falstaff* (London: Davies, 1777), p. 4. Further references to this publication in this section will be given in the text.

10. Philip Fisher, *The Vehement Passions* (Princeton: Princeton University Press, 2002), p. 4.

11. Text from a private letter between Montagu and her father, quoted in Eger, 'Out Rushed a Female to Protect the Bard', p. 134.

12. Samuel Johnson, 'Preface to the Edition of Shakespeare's Plays (1765)', in *Samuel Johnson on Shakespeare*, ed. by Henry Woudhuysen (Harmondsworth: Penguin, 1989), pp. 120–65 (pp. 134–36). Seeking to defend Shakespeare from the neoclassical charge of having 'shewn no regard' to the unities of time and place, Johnson had proposed 'a nearer view of the principles on which [these unities] stand' in order to 'diminish their value' (p. 133). The central principle supporting the 'necessity of observing the unities' is meant to be the 'necessity of making the drama credible' (p. 133), but Johnson considers this an error, either because any audience's 'Delusion, if delusion be admitted, has no certain limitation' (p. 134) or because no play is ever found credible, since 'the spectators are always in their senses' (p. 135). For further discussion of this matter, see G. F. Parker, *Johnson's Shakespeare* (Oxford: Clarendon, 1989).

13. Johnson, 'Preface', p. 136.

14. Johnson, 'Preface', p. 134.

15. On the significance of Garrick's Lear, see Chapter 4; on the performance history of *King John*, see Eugene M. Waith, 'King John and the Drama of History', *Shakespeare Quarterly*, 29.2 (1978), 192–211.

16. Eger, 'Out Rushed a Female to Protect the Bard', p. 139.

17. Voltaire, *Letters Concerning the English Nation*, p. 150.

18. William Richardson, *A Philosophical Analysis and Illustration of Some of Shakespeare's Remarkable Characters* (London: Murray, 1774), p. 1. Further references to this publication in this section will be given in the text.

19. For more on Shakespeare and eighteenth-century Newtonianism, see Gefen Bar-On Santor, 'The Culture of Newtonianism and Shakespeare's Editors: From Pope to Johnson', *Eighteenth Century Fiction*, 21.4 (2009), 593–614.

20. For further discussion of this trope, see Jonathan Bate, *Shakespeare and the English Romantic Imagination* (Oxford: Oxford University Press, 1986), p. 164.

21. Lisa A. Freeman, *Character's Theater: Genre and Identity on the Eighteenth-Century English Stage* (Philadelphia: University of Pennsylvania Press, 2002), p. 27.

22. William Shakespeare, *Bell's Edition of Shakespeare's Plays*, ed. by Francis Gentleman, 9 vols (London: Bell and Etherington, 1773–74), III, p. 55.

23. William Richardson, *Essays on Shakespeare's Dramatic Characters of Richard the Third, King Lear, and Timon of Athens, To Which Are Added, an Essay on the Faults of Shakespeare, and Additional Observations on the Character of Hamlet* (London: Murray, 1784), p. 12; William Richardson, *Essays on Shakespeare's Dramatic Character of Sir John Falstaff, and on His Imitation of Female Characters* (London: Murray, 1789), p. 90.

24. Richardson, *Sir John Falstaff*, p. 90.

25. Richardson's formulation here nicely echoes Macbeth's own thought on when 'We'd jump the life to come'. William Shakespeare, 'Macbeth', in *The Arden Shakespeare Complete Works*, ed. by G. R. Proudfoot, Ann Thompson, and David Scott Kastan, revised ed. (London: Thomson Learning, 2007), pp. 773–800 (p. 779; 1. 7. 7).

26. Richardson's explanatory work might also be compared to that undertaken by those who adapted Shakespeare's plays for eighteenth-century audiences, often clarifying them in the process. Take, for example, the addition of an on-stage death for Macbeth, during which the thane describes how he has suffered in the grip of 'Ambition's vain, delusive dreams'. David Garrick, *The Plays of David Garrick*, ed. by Harry William Pedicord and Frederick Louis Bergmann, 6 vols (Carbondale: Southern Illinois University Press, 1982), III, p. 72.

27. 'Le temps dramatique, le seul dont le dramaturge s'inquiète, est transformé en temps historique' (my translation) – Michèle Willems, *La Genèse du mythe shakespearien* (Rouen: Presses universitaires de France, 1979), p. 282.

28. William Shakespeare, 'King Henry IV, Part 1', in *The Arden Shakespeare Complete Works*, ed. by G. R. Proudfoot, Ann Thompson, and David Scott Kastan, revised ed. (London: Thomson Learning, 2007), pp. 361–92 (p. 364; 1. 2. 1).

29. Morgann returns here to the same controversy that Montagu and Johnson clashed over. Rymer's argument can be found in his *A Short View of Tragedy* (1693).

30. See Dennis, *Advancement*, p. 26.

31. Hume's chapter constitutes section 1.4.6 of his *Treatise*. Further references to this publication in this section will be given in the text.

32. Donald C. Ainslie, 'Hume's Reflections on the Identity and Simplicity of Mind', *Philosophy and Phenomenological Research*, 62.3 (2001), 557–78 (p. 573).

33. See, for example, A. E. Pitson, *Hume's Philosophy of the Self* (London: Routledge, 2006); Alessandra Stradella, 'The Dramatic Nature of Our Selves: David Hume and the Theatre Metaphor', *Literature & Aesthetics*, 20 (2010), 154–67; David Cole, *Words for the Theatre* (London: Milton, 2019); Daniel E. Flage, *David Hume's Theory of Mind* (London: Routledge, 2019).

34. Hume's discussion contains the caveat: 'And here 'tis evident we must confine ourselves to resemblance and causation, and must drop contiguity, which has little or no influence in the present case' (p. 260).

Coda

1. Charles Lamb, 'ART. IX.–THEATRALIA. No. 1.–On Garrick, and Acting; and the Plays of Shakspeare, Considered with Reference to Their Fitness for Stage Representation', *The Reflector*, June 1811, 298–313 (p. 298). Further references to this publication in this section will be given in the text.

2. Richard Steele, *The Tatler*, 2 May 1710. Further references to this publication in this section will be given in the text.

3. David Hume, *A Treatise of Human Nature*, ed. by L. A. Selby-Bigge and P. H. Nidditch (Oxford: Oxford University Press, 1978), p. 208.

4. Thomas Davies, *Dramatic Miscellanies*, 3 vols (London: Davies, 1783), II, p. 320.

5. Ben Jonson, 'To the Memory of My Beloved, the Author Mr. William Shakespeare: And What He Hath Left Us', in *Mr William Shakespeares Comedies, Histories, & Tragedies. Published According to the True Originall Copies* (London: Blount and Jaggard, 1623), sigs A4r–A4v (sig. A4v); 'David & Eva Garrick', *Westminster Abbey*, www.westminster-abbey.org/abbey-commemor ations/commemorations/david-eva-garrick#i13816 [accessed 2 June 2020].

6. Roy Park, 'Lamb, Shakespeare, and the Stage', *Shakespeare Quarterly*, 33.2 (1982), 164–77 (p. 170).

7. Garrick's transitions were even compared to a conjuring 'Trick' during his lifetime. See Samuel Foote, *A Treatise on the Passions so Far as They Regard the Stage; with a Critical Enquiry into the Theatrical Merit of Mr. G-k, Mr. Q-n, and Mr. B-y* (London: Corbet, 1747), p. 18.

8. Simon Hull, 'The Ideology of the Unspectacular: Theatricality and Charles Lamb's Essayistic Figure', *Romanticism on the Net*, 46, 2007; William Hazlitt, 'Theatrical Examiner No. 193: Mr Kean's Richard II', *The Examiner*, 19 March 1815, 190–92 (p. 191); on Kean and pantomime, see Jane Moody, *Illegitimate Theatre in London, 1770–1840* (Cambridge: Cambridge University Press, 2000).

9. Aaron Hill, *The Prompter*, 27 June 1735.

10. Hogarth, *David Garrick as Richard III*; Shearer West, *The Image of the Actor: Verbal and Visual Representation in the Age of Garrick and Kemble* (New York: St Martin's, 1991), pp. 2–3.

11. Arthur Murphy, *The Life of David Garrick, Esq.*, 2 vols (London: Wright, 1801), I, p. 23.

12. Murphy, *Life of David Garrick*, I, p. 24; Stuart Sillars, *Painting Shakespeare: The Artist as Critic, 1720–1820* (Cambridge: Cambridge University Press, 2006), p. 46.

13. Sillars, *Painting Shakespeare*, p. 51.

14. Sillars, *Painting Shakespeare*, pp. 48–52.

15. Sillars, *Painting Shakespeare*, p. 52.

16. William Hogarth, *The Analysis of Beauty* (London: Reeves, 1753), p. 16.

17. Wye J. Allanbrook, *The Secular Commedia: Comic Mimesis in Late Eighteenth-Century Music*, ed. by Richard Taruskin and Mary Ann Smart (Oakland: University of California Press, 2014), p. 38; Hogarth, *Analysis*, p. 25.

Bibliography

Primary Texts

Aristotle's Ars Poetica, ed. by Rudolph Kassel (Oxford: Clarendon, 1966).

Austin, Gilbert, *Chironomia, or A Treatise on Rhetorical Delivery* (London: Cadell and Davies, 1806).

Avison, Charles, 'An Essay on Musical Expression (1752)', in *Musical Aesthetics: A Historical Reader*, ed. by Edward Lippman, 4 vols (New York: Pendragon, 1986), I, pp. 185–99.

Batteux, Charles, *Les Beaux Arts réduits à un même principe*, revised ed. (Paris: Durand, 1747).

Beattie, James, *Essays: On Poetry and Music, as They Affect the Mind*, 3rd ed. (Edinburgh: Dilly and Creech, 1779).

Bell's British Theatre, Consisting of the Most Esteemed English Plays, ed. by Francis Gentleman, 20 vols (London: Bell and Etherington, 1776).

Boswell, James, 'To the Printer of the Public Advertiser', *The Public Advertiser*, 16 September 1769, 1–2.

— 'On the Profession of a Player – Essay I', in *The London Magazine, or Gentleman's Monthly Intelligencer for the Year 1770* (London: Baldwin, 1770), XXXIX, 397–98.

— 'On the Profession of a Player – Essay II', in *The London Magazine, or Gentleman's Monthly Intelligencer for the Year 1770* (London: Baldwin, 1770), XXXIX, 468–71.

— 'On the Profession of a Player – Essay III', in *The London Magazine, or Gentleman's Monthly Intelligencer for the Year 1770* (London: Baldwin, 1770), XXXIX, 513–17.

Brown, John, *A Dissertation on the Rise, Union, and Power, the Progressions, Separations, and Corruptions, of Poetry and Music* (London: Davis and Reymers, 1763).

Burgh, James, *The Art of Speaking* (London: Longman, 1761).

Burgoyne, John, *The Lord of the Manor* (London: Evans, 1781).

Burke, Edmund, *A Philosophical Enquiry into the Origin of Our Ideas of the Sublime and Beautiful* (London: Dodsley, 1757).

Cibber, Theophilus, 'The First Dissertation', in *Cibber's Two Dissertations on the Theatres: With an Appendix, in Three Parts. The Whole Containing a General*

View of the Stage, With Many Curious Anecdotes and Remarks on the Laws Concerning the Theatres (London: Griffiths, 1756), pp. 1–76.

'The Second Dissertation', in *Cibber's Two Dissertations on the Theatres: With an Appendix, in Three Parts. The Whole Containing a General View of the Stage, With Many Curious Anecdotes and Remarks on the Laws Concerning the Theatres* (London: Griffiths, 1756), pp. 1–47.

The Lives and Characters of the Most Eminent Actors and Actresses of Great-Britain and Ireland: From Shakespear to the Present Time. Interspersed with a General History of the Stage (London: Griffiths, 1753).

Collins, William, 'The Passions. An Ode for Music', in *Odes on Several Descriptive and Allegoric Subjects* (London: Millar, 1746), pp. 46–52.

Condillac, Etienne Bonnot de, *Essai sur l'origine des connaissances humaines*, 2 vols (Amsterdam: Mortier, 1746).

Cooke, William, *The Elements of Dramatic Criticism* (London: Kearsly and Robinson, 1775).

Memoirs of Richard Cumberland, Written by Himself, Containing An Account of His Life and Writings, Interspersed with Characters of Several of the Most Distinguished Persons of His Time with Whom He Has Had Intercourse and Connection (Philadelphia: Bradford, 1806).

Daniel, George, ed., *A Collection of Illustrations, Portraits, Newspaper Cuttings, Extracts from Books and Sale Catalogues, Advertisements, Manuscripts and Playbills, Relating Principally to the Shakespeare Jubilee of 1769, and in Particular to David Garrick's Part Therein*, British Library General Reference Collection, C.61.e.2.

Davies, Thomas, *Dramatic Miscellanies, Consisting of Critical Observations on Several Plays of Shakespeare, with a Review of His Principal Characters, and Those of Various Eminent Writers, as Represented by Mr Garrick and Other Celebrated Comedians*, 3 vols (London: Davies, 1783).

Memoirs of the Life of David Garrick, 2 vols (London: Davies, 1780).

Dennis, John, *The Advancement and Reformation of Modern Poetry* (London: Parker, 1701).

The Grounds of Criticism in Poetry (London: Strahan and Lintot, 1704).

Descartes, René, 'Les Passions de l'âme', in *Œuvres de Descartes*, 12 vols (Paris: Léopold Cerf, 1909), IX, pp. 288–498.

Dibdin, Charles, *Queen Mab, or the Fairies' Jubilee* (London: Johnston, 1769).

Dickens, Charles, *Great Expectations*, ed. by Angus Calder (London: Penguin, 1985).

Dryden, John, 'Alexander's Feast', in *John Dryden: The Major Works*, ed. by Keith Walker (Oxford: Oxford University Press, 2003), pp. 545–50.

The Indian Emperour, or, The Conquest of Mexico by the Spaniards Being the Sequel of The Indian Queen (London: Herringman, 1667).

The Major Works, ed. by Keith Walker (Oxford: Oxford University Press, 2003).

The Spanish Fryar, or The Double Discovery (London: Tonson and Tonson, 1681).

The Spanish Fryar, or The Double Discovery (London: Tonson and Tonson, 1686).

The Spanish Fryar, or The Double Discovery (London: Tonson and Tonson, 1690).

The Spanish Fryar, or The Double Discovery (London: Tonson and Tonson, 1695).

The Spanish Fryar; or, The Double Discovery (London: Tonson, 1733).

Dubos, Jean-Baptiste, 'Réflexions critiques sur la poësie et sur la peinture (1719)', in *Music and Aesthetics in the Eighteenth and Early-Nineteenth Centuries*, ed. by Peter le Huray and James Day, Cambridge Readings in the Literature of Music (Cambridge: Cambridge University Press, 1981), pp. 17–22.

An Exact Description of the Two Fam'd Entertainments of Harlequin Doctor Faustus (London: Payne, 1724).

Fitzpatrick, Thaddeus, *An Enquiry into the Real Merit of a Certain Popular Performer in a Series of Letters, First Published in the Craftsman or Gray's-Inn Journal; with an Introduction to D–D G—K, Esq.* (London: Thrush, 1760).

Foote, Samuel, *A Treatise on the Passions so Far as They Regard the Stage; with a Critical Enquiry into the Theatrical Merit of Mr. G-k, Mr. Q-n, and Mr. B-y* (London: Corbet, 1747).

Garrick, David, 'Aaron Hill, Zara, A Tragedy, 1754', in *The Plays of David Garrick*, ed. by Harry William Pedicord and Fredrick Louis Bergmann, 6 vols (Carbondale: Southern Illinois University Press, 1982), VI, pp. 135–200.

'Epilogue to the Clandestine Marriage', in *The Poetical Works of David Garrick, Esq.*, 2 vols (London: Kearsley, 1785), I, pp. 205–12.

The Letters of David Garrick, ed. by David M. Little and George M. Kahrl, 3 vols (London: Oxford University Press, 1963).

An Ode upon Dedicating a Building, and Erecting a Statue, to Shakespeare (London: Becket and de Hondt, 1769).

The Plays of David Garrick, ed. by Harry William Pedicord and Fredrick Louis Bergmann, 6 vols (Carbondale: Southern Illinois University Press, 1982).

The Poetical Works of David Garrick, Esq. Now First Collected into Two Volumes. With Explanatory Notes, 2 vols (London: George Kearsley, 1785).

Garrick, David and Thomas Arne, *Ode upon Dedicating a Building to Shakespeare* (London: Johnston, 1769).

Gentleman, Francis, ed., *Bell's British Theatre, Consisting of the Most Esteemed English Plays*, 20 vols (London: Bell and Etherington, 1776).

The Dramatic Censor; or, Critical Companion, 2 vols (London: Bell and Etherington, 1770).

Gildon, Charles, *The Life of Mr. Thomas Betterton, the Late Eminent Tragedian* (London: Gosling, 1710).

Goethe, Johann Wolfgang von, 'Noten und Abhandlungen zu besserem Verstandnis des West-Ostichen Diwans', in *Goethes Werke*, 15 vols (Munich: Beck, 1981), II, pp. 187–89.

Harris, James, 'Three Treatises Concerning Art (1744)', in *Musical Aesthetics: A Historical Reader*, ed. by Edward Lippman, 4 vols (New York: Pendragon, 1986), 1, pp. 177–84.

Havard, William, 'Ode to the Memory of Shakespeare', in *William Shakespeare: The Critical Heritage 1753–1765*, ed. by Brian Vickers (London: Routledge, 2000), pp. 289–91.

Hazlitt, William, 'Theatrical Examiner No. 193: Mr Kean's Richard II', *The Examiner*, 19 March 1815, 190–92.

Hill, Aaron, *The Fatal Vision: Or, The Fall of Siam. A Tragedy: As It Is Acted at the New Theatre in Lincoln's-Inn-Fields* (London: Nutt, 1716).

The Plain Dealer, 14 December 1724.

The Plain Dealer, 18 January 1725.

The Prompter, 12 November 1734.

The Prompter, 19 November 1734.

The Prompter, 13 December 1734.

The Prompter, 6 June 1735.

The Prompter, 13 June 1735.

The Prompter, 27 June 1735.

The Prompter, 4 November 1735.

The Prompter, 26 December 1735.

The Prompter, 3 February 1736.

The Prompter, 14 May 1736.

The Tragedy of Zara, As It Is Acted at the Theatre Royal in Drury-Lane (London: Watts, 1736).

The Works of the Late Aaron Hill, Esq.; In Four Volumes, Consisting of Letters on Various Subjects, and of Original Poems, Moral and Facetious, with an Essay on the Art of Acting, 4 vols (London: 1753).

Hill, Aaron and David Garrick, *The Tragedy of Zara*, ed. by Richard Cumberland (London: Cooke, 1817).

Hill, John, *The Actor: A Treatise on the Art of Playing* (London: Griffiths, 1750).

The Actor; or, a Treatise on the Art of Playing (London: Griffiths, 1755).

Hogarth, William, *The Analysis of Beauty* (London: Reeves, 1753).

Home, Henry, Lord Kames, *Elements of Criticism*, ed. by Peter Jones, 2 vols (Indianapolis: Liberty Fund, 2005).

Hume, David, 'Of Tragedy', in *Essays, Moral, Political and Literary*, ed. by Eugene F. Miller (Indianapolis: Liberty Fund, 1987), pp. 216–25.

A Treatise of Human Nature, ed. by L. A. Selby-Bigge and P. H. Nidditch (Oxford: Oxford University Press, 1978).

Johnson, Samuel, *A Dictionary of the English Language*, 2 vols (London: Knapton; Longman; Hitch and Hawes; Millar; and Dodsley, 1775).

'Preface to the Edition of Shakespeare's Plays (1765)', in *Samuel Johnson on Shakespeare*, ed. by Henry Woudhuysen (Harmondsworth: Penguin, 1989), pp. 120–65.

Jonson, Ben, 'To the Memory of My Beloved, the Author Mr. William Shakespeare: And What He Hath Left Us', in *Mr William Shakespeares*

Comedies, Histories, & Tragedies. Published According to the True Originall Copies (London: Blount and Jaggard, 1623), sigs A4r–A4v.

Knox, George, 'Remarks on Collins's Ode on the Passions', *The Edinburgh Magazine; or Literary Miscellany*, March 1801, 206–10.

Lamb, Charles, 'ART. IX.–THEATRALIA. No. 1.–On Garrick, and Acting; and the Plays of Shakspeare, Considered with Reference to Their Fitness for Stage Representation', *The Reflector*, June 1811, 298–313.

Lessing, Gotthold Ephraim, *Laokoon, oder über die Grenzen der Mahlerei und Poesie* (Berlin: Voss, 1766).

Lichtenberg, Georg Christoph, 'Briefe aus England', in *Vermischte Schriften*, 9 vols (Goettigen: Dieterich, 1801), III, pp. 239–372.

Locke, John, *An Essay Concerning Human Understanding in Four Books* (London: Dring and Manship, 1694).

Milton, John, 'On Shakespeare', in *John Milton: The Major Works*, ed. by Stephen Orgel and Jonathan Goldberg, revised ed. (Oxford: Oxford University Press, 2003), p. 20.

Paradise Lost, ed. by Stephen Orgel and Jonathan Goldberg (Oxford: Oxford University Press, 2004).

Montagu, Elizabeth, *An Essay on the Writings and Genius of Shakespear, Compared with the Greek and French Dramatic Poets. With Some Remarks upon the Misrepresentations of Mons. de Voltaire* (London: Dodsley, 1769).

Morgann, Maurice, *An Essay on the Dramatic Character of Sir John Falstaff* (London: Davies, 1777).

Murphy, Arthur, *The Life of David Garrick, Esq.*, 2 vols (London: Wright, 1801).

Newton, Charles, *Studies in the Science and Practice of Public Speaking, Reading, and Recitation* (Norwich: Burke and Kinnebrook, 1800).

Newton, Isaac, *Opticks: Or, A Treatise of the Reflections, Refractions, Inflexions and Colours of Light*, 3 vols (London: Innys, 1718).

Otway, Thomas, 'Venice Preserv'd', in *The Works of Thomas Otway*, ed. by J. C. Ghosh, 2 vols (Oxford: Oxford University Press, 1968), ii, pp. 197–290.

A Poetical Epistle from Shakespear in Elysium to David Garrick at Drury Lane, to Which Is Added a View from Heymon Hill near Shrewsbury, A Solitudinarian Ode (London: Newberry and Owen, 1752).

Popple, William, *The Prompter*, 27 December 1734.

Pursuit after Happiness: A Poem. To Which is Added, An Ode to Mr Garrick, On his Quitting the Stage. Also an Elegy on the Death of Mr Barry (London: Kearsley, 1777).

Quintilian with an English Translation, trans. by Harold Edgeworth Butler (London: Heinemann, 1922).

Richardson, William, *Essays on Shakespeare's Dramatic Characters of Richard the Third, King Lear, and Timon of Athens, To Which Are Added, an Essay on the Faults of Shakespeare, and Additional Observations on the Character of Hamlet* (London: Murray, 1784).

Essays on Shakespeare's Dramatic Character of Sir John Falstaff, and on His Imitation of Female Characters (London: Murray, 1789).

A Philosophical Analysis and Illustration of Some of Shakespeare's Remarkable Characters (London: Murray, 1774).

Rousseau, Jean-Jacques, *Dictionnaire de Musique* (Paris: Duchesne, 1768).

Rowe, Nicholas, *The Plays and Poems of Nicholas Rowe: The Late Plays.*, ed. by Stephen Bernard and Claudine van Hensbergen, 5 vols (London: Routledge, 2016).

'Some Account of the Life, &c. of Mr William Shakespear', in *The Works of Mr. William Shakespear*, ed. by Nicholas Rowe, 6 vols (London: Tonson, 1709), I, pp. i–xl.

The Tragedy of Jane Shore (London: Lintot, 1714).

The Critical Works of Thomas Rymer, ed. by Curt Zimansky (New Haven: Yale University Press, 1956).

Sainte-Albine, Pierre Rémond de, *Le Comédien* (Paris: Desaint & Saillant, 1747).

Shakespeare, William, *The Arden Shakespeare Complete Works*, ed. by G. R. Proudfoot, Ann Thompson, and David Scott Kastan, revised ed. (London: Thomson Learning, 2007).

Bell's Edition of Shakespeare's Plays, ed. by Francis Gentleman, 9 vols (London: Bell and Etherington, 1773–74).

Mr William Shakespeares Comedies, Histories, & Tragedies. Published According to the True Originall Copies (London: Blount and Jaggard, 1623).

The Plays of William Shakespeare in Eight Volumes, ed. by Samuel Johnson, 8 vols (London: Tonson, 1765).

True Chronicle History of the Life and Death of King Lear and His Three Daughters (London: Butter, 1608).

The Works of Mr. William Shakespear, ed. by Nicholas Rowe, 6 vols (London: Tonson, 1709).

Sheridan, Thomas, *A Course of Lectures on Elocution: Together with Two Dissertations on Language and Some Other Tracts Relative to Those Subjects* (London: Strahan, 1762).

Smith, Adam, *Essays on Philosophical Subjects* (London: Cadell and Davies, 1795).

Steele, Joshua, *An Essay towards Establishing the Melody and Measure of Speech to Be Expressed and Perpetuated by Peculiar Symbols* (London: Almon, 1775).

'The Stratford Jubilee', *The Scots Magazine*, September 1769.

Steele, Richard, *The Tatler*, 2 May 1710.

Steevens, George, 'Shakespeare's Feast', *The Public Advertiser*, 5 August 1769, 2.

Talma, François-Joseph, *Réflexions sur Lekain et sur l'art dramatique* (Paris: Tenré, 1825).

Tate, Nahum and David Garrick, *The History of King Lear, A Tragedy; As It Is Now Acted at the King's Theatres* (London: Hitch, Hawes, Brindley, Hodges, Longman, Corbett, King, Reeve, Cooper, Noble, 1756), British Library General Reference Collection C.119.dd.22.

Theobald, Lewis and John Rich, *The Vocal Parts of an Entertainment Call'd The Necromancer: Or, Harlequin Doctor Faustus* (London: Dodd, 1723).

Thurmond, John, *Harlequin Doctor Faustus: With the Masque of the Deities* (London: Chetwood, 1724).

Voltaire, *Letters Concerning the English Nation* (London: Tonson, 1728).

'Zaïre', in *Zaïre – Le Fanatisme ou Mahomet le Prophète – Nanine ou l'Homme sans préjugé – Le Café ou l'Ecossaise*, ed. by Jean Goldzink (Paris: G. F. Flammarion, 2004), pp. 47–132.

Ward, Ned, *The Dancing Devils, or the Roaring Dragon* (London: Bettesworth, Bately, and Brotherton, 1724).

Warton, Joseph, *An Essay on the Writings and Genius of Pope*, 2 vols (London: Cooper, 1756).

Weaver, John, *The Loves of Mars and Venus* (London: Mears and Browne, 1717).

Webb, Daniel, *Observations on the Correspondence Between Poetry and Music* (London: Dodsley, 1769).

Remarks on the Beauties of Poetry (London: Dodsley, 1753).

Periodicals

Diary or Woodfall's Register, 13 January 1792.

The Edinburgh Magazine; or Literary Miscellany, March 1801.

Entertainer, 12 November 1754.

The Examiner, 19 March 1815.

Gazetteer and New Daily Advertiser, 26 November 1765.

Gazetteer and New Daily Advertiser, 14 December 1765.

Gazetteer and New Daily Advertiser, 25 August 1787.

General Advertiser, 13 October 1786.

General Evening Post, 16 January 1777.

London Daily Advertiser and Literary Gazette, 2 November 1751.

London Daily Advertiser and Literary Gazette, 4 November 1751.

London Daily Post and General Advertiser, 15 January 1743.

London Daily Post and General Advertiser, 27 December 1743.

London Evening Post, 19 January 1762.

Morning Chronicle, 15 May 1773.

Morning Chronicle, 23 July 1774.

Morning Chronicle, 26 November 1774.

Morning Chronicle and London Advertiser, 5 August 1774.

Morning Post and Daily Advertiser, 2 October 1778.

Morning Post and Daily Advertiser, 31 July 1786.

The Plain Dealer, 14 December 1724.

The Plain Dealer, 18 January 1725.

The Prompter, 12 November 1734.

The Prompter, 19 November 1734.

The Prompter, 13 December 1734.

The Prompter, 27 December 1734.

The Prompter, 6 June 1735.

The Prompter, 13 June 1735.
The Prompter, 27 June 1735.
The Prompter, 4 November 1735.
The Prompter, 26 December 1735.
The Prompter, 3 February 1736.
The Prompter, 14 May 1736.
Public Advertiser, 5 July 1763.
Public Advertiser, 5 August 1769.
Public Advertiser, 16 September 1769.
Public Advertiser, 25 September 1776.
Public Advertiser, 17 September 1778.
Public Advertiser, 16 October 1783.
The Reflector, June 1811.
The Scots Magazine, September 1769.
St James's Chronicle, 15 September 1761.
St James's Chronicle, 15 May 1764.
St James's Chronicle or the British Evening Post, 22 January 1788.
St James's Chronicle or the British Evening Post, 20 September 1800.
The Tatler, 2 May 1710.
World and Fashionable Advertiser, 25 January 1788.

Works of Art

Hogarth, William, *David Garrick as Richard III*, *c.* 1745, oil on canvas, 190.5 × 250.8 cm, Walker Art Gallery, Liverpool.
Reynolds, Joshua, *Garrick Between Tragedy and Comedy*, 1761, oil on canvas, 148 × 183 cm, Waddesdon Manor, Buckinghamshire.
Sly, Evan, Garrick and Hogarth or the Artist Puzzled, 1845, lithograph print, 25 × 26.7 cm, Victoria and Albert Museum, London.
Zoffany, Johan, *David Garrick as Jaffeir and Susannah Cibber as Belvidera in 'Venice Preserv'd' by Thomas Otway*, c. 1763, oil on canvas, 101.5 × 127 cm, Holburne Museum, Bath.

Secondary Sources

Ainslie, Donald C., 'Hume's Reflections on the Identity and Simplicity of Mind', *Philosophy and Phenomenological Research*, 62.3 (2001), 557–78.
Alexander, Catherine, 'Province of Pirates: The Editing and Publication of Shakespeare's Poems in the Eighteenth Century', in *Reading Readings: Essays on Shakespeare Editing in the Eighteenth Century*, ed. by Joanna Gondris (London: Associated University Presses, 1998), pp. 345–65.
Allanbrook, Wye J., *The Secular Commedia: Comic Mimesis in Late Eighteenth-Century Music*, ed. by Richard Taruskin and Mary Ann Smart (Oakland: University of California Press, 2014).

Ashfield, Andrew and Peter De Bolla, eds, *The Sublime: A Reader in British Eighteenth-Century Aesthetic Theory* (Cambridge: Cambridge University Press, 1996).

Barnett, Dene and Jeanette Massy-Westropp, *The Art of Gesture: The Practices and Principles of 18th Century Acting* (Heidelberg: Carl Winter, 1987).

Bate, Jonathan, *Shakespeare and the English Romantic Imagination* (Oxford: Oxford University Press, 1986).

  Shakespearean Constitutions: Politics, Theatre, Criticism 1730–1830 (Oxford: Oxford University Press, 1989).

Bergmann, Fredrick Louis, 'Garrick's Zara', *PMLA*, 74.3 (1959), 225–32.

Bradley, Lynne, *Adapting King Lear for the Stage* (London: Routledge, 2016).

Brooks, Helen E. M., *Actresses, Gender, and the Eighteenth-Century Stage: Playing Women* (Basingstoke: Palgrave Macmillan, 2015).

Burnim, Kalman A., *David Garrick, Director* (Pittsburgh: University of Pittsburgh, 1961).

Caines, Michael, *Shakespeare and the Eighteenth Century*, Oxford Shakespeare Topics (Oxford: Oxford University Press, 2013).

Cole, David, *Words for the Theatre* (Milton: Routledge, 2019).

Cordner, Michael and Peter Holland, eds, *Players, Playwrights, Playhouses: Investigating Performance, 1660–1800* (Basingstoke: Palgrave Macmillan, 2007).

Culler, Jonathan, *Theory of the Lyric* (Cambridge: Harvard University Press, 2015).

Cunningham, Vanessa, *Shakespeare and Garrick* (Cambridge: Cambridge University Press, 2008).

'David & Eva Garrick', *Westminster Abbey*, 2020, www.westminster-abbey.org/abbey-commemorations/commemorations/david-eva-garrick#i13816 [accessed 2 June 2020].

Del Balzo, Angelina, 'The Sultan's Tears in *Zara, an Oriental Tragedy*', *Studies in English Literature, 1500–1900*, 55.3 (2015), 501–21.

Delehanty, Anne T., 'Mapping the Aesthetic Mind: John Dennis and Nicolas Boileau', *Journal of the History of Ideas*, 68.2 (2007), 233–53.

Dobson, Michael, *The Making of the National Poet: Shakespeare, Adaptation and Authorship, 1660–1769* (Oxford: Oxford University Press, 1992).

Domingo, Darryl P., *The Rhetoric of Diversion in English Literature and Culture, 1690–1760* (Cambridge: Cambridge University Press, 2016).

Donnelly, Phillip J., 'Enthusiastic Poetry and Rationalized Christianity: The Poetic Theory of John Dennis', *Christianity and Literature*, 54.2 (2005), 235–64.

Eger, Elizabeth, '"Out Rushed a Female to Protect the Bard": The Bluestocking Defense of Shakespeare', *The Huntington Library Quarterly*, 65.1 (2002), 127–51.

Eron, Sarah, *Inspiration in the Age of Enlightenment* (Newark: University of Delaware Press, 2014).

Fairer, David, '"Love Was in the Next Degree": Lyric, Satire, and Inventive Modulation', *Journal for Eighteenth-Century Studies*, 34.2 (2011), 147–66.

Fisher, Philip, *The Vehement Passions* (Princeton: Princeton University Press, 2002).

Flage, Daniel E., *David Hume's Theory of Mind* (London: Routledge, 2019).

Forster, Antonia, 'Shakespeare in the Reviews', in *Shakespeare in the Eighteenth Century*, ed. by Fiona Ritchie and Peter Sabor (Cambridge: Cambridge University Press, 2012), pp. 60–77.

Franklin, Colin, *Shakespeare Domesticated: The Eighteenth-Century Editions* (Aldershot: Scholar Press, 1991).

Freeman, Lisa A., *Character's Theater: Genre and Identity on the Eighteenth-Century English Stage* (Philadelphia: University of Pennsylvania Press, 2002).

Gavin, Paul, J., *Shakespeare and the Imprints of Performance*, History of Text Technologies (New York: Palgrave Macmillan, 2014).

Genette, Gérard, 'The Architext (1979; Trans. 1992)', in *The Lyric Theory Reader: A Critical Anthology*, ed. by Virginia Jackson and Yopie Prins (Baltimore: Johns Hopkins University Press, 2014), pp. 17–29.

Gerrard, Christine, *Aaron Hill: The Muses' Projector 1685–1750* (Oxford: Oxford University Press, 2003).

Gilman, Todd, *The Theatre Career of Thomas Arne* (Newark: University of Delaware Press, 2013).

Google, *Google Trends*, https://trends.google.com/trends/explore?geo=GB&q=transition [accessed 28 February 2020].

Griffiths, Eric and Freya Johnston, *If Not Critical* (Oxford: Oxford University Press, 2018).

Hammond, Brean S., *Professional Imaginative Writing in England, 1670–1740: Hackney for Bread* (Oxford: Clarendon, 1997).

Harriman-Smith, James, '*Comédien*-Actor-*Paradoxe*: The Anglo-French Sources of Diderot's *Paradoxe sur le comédien*', *Theatre Journal*, 67.1 (2015), 83–96.

Hensbergen, Claudine van, 'Publication History and Textual Note to *The Tragedy of Jane Shore* and *The Tragedy of the Lady Jane Gray*', in *The Plays and Poems of Nicholas Rowe: The Late Plays.*, ed. by Stephen Bernard and Claudine van Hensbergen, 5 vols (London: Routledge, 2016), III, pp. 25–31.

Holland, Peter, 'David Garrick', in *Garrick – Kemble – Siddons – Kean*, ed. by Peter Holland, Great Shakespeareans, 18 vols (London: Pickering & Chatto, 2010), II, pp. 8–54.

'Hearing the Dead: The Sound of David Garrick', in *Players, Playwrights, Playhouses: Investigating Performance, 1660–1800* (Basingstoke: Palgrave Macmillan, 2007), pp. 248–70.

Hopkins, David and Paul Hammond, eds., *John Dryden: Tercentenary Essays* (Oxford: Oxford University Press, 2000).

Hoxby, Blair, *What Was Tragedy? Theory and the Early Modern Canon* (Oxford: Oxford University Press, 2015).

'What Was Tragedy? The World We Have Lost, 1550–1795', *Comparative Literature*, 64.1 (2012), 1–32.

Hull, Simon, 'The Ideology of the Unspectacular: Theatricality and Charles Lamb's Essayistic Figure', *Romanticism on the Net*, 46, 2007.

le Huray, Peter and James Day, eds, *Music and Aesthetics in the Eighteenth and Early-Nineteenth Centuries*, Cambridge Readings in the Literature of Music (Cambridge: Cambridge University Press, 1981).

Irlam, Shaun, *Elations: The Poetics of Enthusiasm in Eighteenth-Century Britain* (Stanford: Stanford University Press, 1999).

Jackson, Virginia and Yopie Prins, 'General Introduction', in *The Lyric Theory Reader: A Critical Anthology*, ed. by Virginia Jackson and Yopie Prins (Baltimore: Johns Hopkins University Press, 2014), pp. 1–10.

Jajdelska, Elspeth, '"The Very Defective and Erroneous Method": Reading Instruction and Social Identity in Elite Eighteenth-Century Learners', *Oxford Review of Education*, 36.2 (2010), 141–56.

Jarvis, Simon, *Scholars and Gentlemen: Shakespearean Textual Criticism and Representations of Scholarly Labour, 1725–1765* (Oxford: Clarendon, 1995).

Johnston, Freya, 'Samuel Johnson', in *Dryden – Pope – Johnson – Malone*, ed. by Claude Julien Rawson, Great Shakespeareans (London: Continuum, 2010), pp. 115–59.

Joseph, Bertram, *The Tragic Actor* (London: Routledge, 1959).

Kareem, Sarah Tindal, *Eighteenth-Century Fiction and the Reinvention of Wonder* (Oxford: Oxford University Press, 2014).

Kennaway, James, 'Stimulating Music: The Pleasures and Dangers of "Electric Music," 1750–1900', *Configurations*, 19.2 (2011), 191–211.

Koehler, Margaret, 'Odes of Absorption in the Restoration and Early Eighteenth Century', *SEL: Studies in English Literature, 1500–1900*, 47.3 (2007), 659–78.

Poetry of Attention in the Eighteenth Century (New York: Palgrave Macmillan, 2012).

Landreth, Sara, '"Set His Image in Motion": John Dennis and Early Eighteenth-Century Motion Imagery', *Eighteenth-Century Life*, 40.1 (2016), 59–83.

Langhans, Edward A., *Eighteenth Century British and Irish Promptbooks: A Descriptive Bibliography* (New York: Greenwood, 1987).

Restoration Promptbooks (Carbondale: Southern Illinois University Press, 1981).

Lippman, Edward, ed., *Musical Aesthetics: A Historical Reader*, 4 vols (New York: Pendragon, 1986).

London Stage Database, https://londonstagedatabase.usu.edu/ [accessed 16 January 2020].

Lupton, Christina, *Reading and the Making of Time in the Eighteenth Century* (Baltimore: Johns Hopkins University Press, 2018).

Malek, James, 'Physiology and Art: Daniel Webb's Aesthetics', *Neuphilologische Mitteilungen*, 71.4 (1970), 691–99.

Marker, Lise-Lone and Frederick J. Marker, 'Aaron Hill and Eighteenth-Century Acting Theory', *Quarterly Journal of Speech*, 61.4 (1975), 416–27.

Marsden, Jean I., *Theatres of Feeling: Affect, Performance, and the Eighteenth-Century Stage* (Cambridge: Cambridge University Press, 2019).

Mason, Tom and Adam Rounce, '*Alexander's Feast; or The Power of Musique*: The Poem and Its Readers', in *John Dryden: Tercentenary Essays*, ed. by

David Hopkins and Paul Hammond (Oxford: Oxford University Press, 2000), pp. 140–73.

McGillivray, Glen, 'Rant, Cant and Tone: The Voice of the Eighteenth-Century Actor and Sarah Siddons', *Theatre Notebook*, 71.1 (2017), 2–20.

McIntyre, Ian, *Garrick*, 2nd ed. (Harmondsworth: Penguin, 2000).

Monson, Dale E., Jack Westrup, and Julian Budden, 'Recitative', in *Grove Music Online* (Oxford: Oxford University Press, 2001), www.oxfordmusiconline.com/grovemusic/view/10.1093/gmo/9781561592630.001.0001/omo-9781561592630-e-0000023019 [accessed 14 February 2019].

Moody, Jane, *Illegitimate Theatre in London, 1770–1840* (Cambridge: Cambridge University Press, 2000).

Moody, Jane and Daniel O'Quinn, eds., *The Cambridge Companion to British Theatre, 1730–1830* (Cambridge: Cambridge University Press, 2007).

Morillo, John, 'John Dennis: Enthusiastic Passions, Cultural Memory and Literary Theory', *Eighteenth-Century Studies*, 34.1 (2000), 21–41.

Moseley, Nick, *Actioning and How to Do It* (London: Nick Hern, 2016).

Nussbaum, Felicity, *Rival Queens: Actresses, Performance, and the Eighteenth-Century British Theater* (Philadelphia: University of Pennsylvania Press, 2011).

O'Brien, John, *Harlequin Britain: Pantomime and Entertainment, 1690–1760* (Baltimore: Johns Hopkins University Press, 2004).

'Pantomime', in *The Cambridge Companion to British Theatre, 1730–1830*, ed. by Jane Moody and Daniel O'Quinn (Cambridge: Cambridge University Press, 2007), pp. 103–15.

Orr, Bridget, *British Enlightenment Theatre: Dramatizing Difference* (Cambridge: Cambridge University Press, 2019).

Palfrey, Simon and Tiffany Stern, *Shakespeare in Parts* (Oxford: Oxford University Press, 2007).

Park, Roy, 'Lamb, Shakespeare, and the Stage', *Shakespeare Quarterly*, 33.2 (1982), 164–77.

Parker, G. F., *Johnson's Shakespeare* (Oxford: Clarendon, 1989).

Perrin, Noel, *Dr. Bowdler's Legacy: A History of Expurgated Books in England and America* (London: MacMillan, 1970).

Phillips, Natalie M., *Distraction: Problems of Attention in Eighteenth-Century Literature* (Baltimore: Johns Hopkins University Press, 2016).

Pisani, Michael V., *Music for the Melodramatic Theatre in Nineteenth-Century London & New York*, Studies in Theatre History and Culture (Iowa City: University of Iowa Press, 2014).

Pitson, A. E., *Hume's Philosophy of the Self* (London: Routledge, 2006).

Porter, Roy, *Flesh in the Age of Reason* (Harmondsworth: Penguin, 2004).

Poser, Norman S., *The Birth of Modern Theatre: Rivalry, Riots, and Romance in the Age of Garrick* (New York: Routledge, 2019).

Rawson, Claude Julien, ed., *Dryden – Pope – Johnson – Malone*, Great Shakespeareans (London: Continuum, 2010).

Ritchie, Fiona and Peter Sabor, eds, *Shakespeare in the Eighteenth Century* (Cambridge: Cambridge University Press, 2012).

Ritchie, Leslie, *David Garrick and the Mediation of Celebrity* (Cambridge: Cambridge University Press, 2019).

Roach, Joseph, *The Player's Passion: Studies in the Science of Acting* (Ann Arbor: University of Michigan Press, 1993).

Rumbold, Kate, 'Shakespeare and the Stratford Jubilee', in *Shakespeare in the Eighteenth Century*, ed. by Fiona Ritchie and Peter Sabor (Cambridge: Cambridge University Press, 2012), pp. 254–76.

Santor, Gefen Bar-On, 'The Culture of Newtonianism and Shakespeare's Editors: From Pope to Johnson', *Eighteenth Century Fiction*, 21.4 (2009), 593–614.

Semmens, Richard, *Studies in the English Pantomime, 1712–1733* (Hillsdale: Pendragon, 2016).

Shuster, George, *The English Ode from Milton to Keats* (New York: Columbia University Press, 1940).

Sillars, Stuart, *Painting Shakespeare: The Artist as Critic, 1720–1820* (Cambridge: Cambridge University Press, 2006).

Stern, Tiffany, *Rehearsal from Shakespeare to Sheridan* (Oxford: Oxford University Press, 2000).

Stonewall, *Glossary of Terms*, www.stonewall.org.uk/help-advice/faqs-and-gloss ary/glossary-terms [accessed 2 June 2020].

Stradella, Alessandra, 'The Dramatic Nature of Our Selves: David Hume and the Theatre Metaphor', *Literature & Aesthetics*, 20 (2010), 154–67.

Sutton, Ray, 'Re-Playing Macbeth: A View of Eighteenth-Century Acting', *Studies in Theatre and Performance*, 30.2 (2010), 145–56.

Swindells, Julia and David Francis Taylor, eds, *The Oxford Handbook of the Georgian Theatre 1737–1832* (Oxford: Oxford University Press, 2014).

Toner, Anne, *Ellipsis in English Literature: Signs of Omission* (Cambridge: Cambridge University Press, 2015).

Vickers, Brian, ed., *William Shakespeare: The Critical Heritage 1753–1765* (London: Routledge, 2000).

Waith, Eugene M., 'King John and the Drama of History', *Shakespeare Quarterly*, 29.2 (1978), 192–211.

West, Shearer, *The Image of the Actor: Verbal and Visual Representation in the Age of Garrick and Kemble* (New York: St Martin's, 1991).

Willems, Michèle, *La Genèse du mythe shakespearien* (Rouen: Presses universitaires de France, 1979).

Williams, Abigail, *The Social Life of Books: Reading Together in the Eighteenth-Century Home* (New Haven: Yale University Press, 2017).

Worthen, William B., *The Idea of the Actor: Drama and the Ethics of Performance* (Princeton: Princeton University Press, 1984).

Index

Page numbers in *italics* indicate a figure or illustration.

Lightning Source UK Ltd.
Milton Keynes UK
UKHW022113100321
380145UK00003B/53